As the nineteenth century was the age of the railway, so the twentieth century is the age of the automobile, and Harold Perkin, Professor of Social History and Head of the History Department at the University of Lancaster, follows the success of his fascinating book *The Age of the Railway* with this new history. Both grew out of series written for Granada Television.

This is not simply the story of developments in the motor car and its sinister cousins the tank and the warplane, but also of their impact on society in war and peace from Edwardian times to the present. The author shows how the invention of the tank broke the deadlock of the First World War and how the bomber in the Second brought home to civilian populations the meaning of 'total war', and he parallels the proliferation of the motor car with the levelling of classes and the growth of the welfare state.

But the motor car has produced quite new problems, unforeseen seventy years ago. Fuel and pollution crises, assembly-line mass production, the changed face of our roads and cities – these will mean still greater changes in society, and Harold Perkin's final chapters look into the future at the options open to us to ensure that the 'well-intentioned' automobile does not continue careering towards its – and our – destruction.

THE AGE OF THE AUTOMOBILE

HAROLD PERKIN

QUARTET BOOKS   LONDON

First published by Quartet Books Limited 1976
A member of the Namara Group
27 Goodge Street, London W1P 1FD

Copyright © 1976 by Harold Perkin

ISBN 0 704 32112 2

Typesetting by Bedford Typesetters Ltd

Printed in Great Britain by litho by
The Anchor Press Ltd Tiptree, Essex

for Julian
who likes motor cars

List of illustrations   viii
Preface   xi
Introduction   1
  1. Between Two Worlds   7
  2. The Coming of the Motor Car   31
  3. Engines of War   57
  4. Peace Without Prosperity   81
  5. The Automobile and Mass Production   105
  6. The Car and the Community:
       I. Between the Wars   129
  7. The Road to the Sun   153
  8. Mechanized War   171
  9. The Car and the Community:
       II. Since the War   199
 10. The End of the Automobile Age?   225
Index   243

LIST OF ILLUSTRATIONS

1   A Precursor: Walter Hancock's Steam Omnibus, 1833

2a   Royal Christening: the Prince of Wales in Mr Montagu's Daimler, 1899

2b   Women's Liberation: the first woman chauffeur, 1910

3a and b   Mixed Traffic, 1912

4a   The Automobile Airborne: the Hon. Charles Rolls, 1910

4b   Riding the Step: B-type omnibus, 1914

5a and b   Engines of War:
              1. German biplane and British tank
              2. British tanks and American troops, St Quentin, September 1918

6a   The Home Front: women car mechanics, 1916

6b   The Deadlock-breaker: a British tank and German prisoners on the Amiens – Royce Road, August 1918

7   The People's Car: charabancs at Plymouth on an outing to Dartmoor, 1922

8a	The Baby Car: 'Bright Young Things', 1923
8b	The Rival: trams between the Wars
9a	Suburban Sprawl: council estate at Southall, Middlesex, 1931
9b	The Age of the By-pass: Mickleham By-pass, 1939
10a	Peace in Our Time: Neville Chamberlain returns from Munich, September 1938
10b	War in Our Time: German tanks in Poland, September 1939
11a and b	Mechanized Warfare:
	1. American troops practising for D-Day
	2. a German 'Royal Tiger' Panzer squadron being briefed for the attack
12a and b	The Automobile and Mass Production:
	1. a Morris assembly line in the 1930s
	2. a British Leyland assembly line in the 1970s
13a and b	Planning for the Automobile:
	1. pedestrian shopping centre at Coventry, 1956
	2. pedestrian university campus at Leicester, 1975
14a and b	Planning for the Automobile:
	1. pedestrian way and motor road at Cumbernauld New Town
	2. a 'spaghetti junction' on the M4 motorway
15a	The Road to the Sun: the first turbojet service, 1950
15b	Beyond the Automobile: the 'Cabtrack' system of urban transport
16	The End of an Age?: traffic jam near the Elephant and Castle, London, 1966

ix

ACKNOWLEDGEMENTS

Acknowledgement and thanks are due to the following for supplying photographs for reproduction: the British Leyland Motor Corporation for plates 12a and 12b; Dr Denis Chapman of the University of Liverpool for plate 2b; Cumbernauld Development Corporation for plate 14a; the Imperial War Museum, London, for plates 5b, 6b, 11a and 11b; P. W. Joslin, 18 Dalton Square, Lancaster, for plate 13b; London Transport for plates 8b and 16; the Radio Times Hulton Picture Library for plates 2a, 3a, 3b, 4a, 4b, 5a, 6a, 7, 8a, 9a, 9b, 10a, 10b, 13a and 15a; the Science Museum, London for plate 1; and the Transport and Road Research Laboratory, Crowthorne, Berks, for plates 14b and 15b.

PREFACE

      This book is a sequel to *The Age of the Railway*.
Like its predecessor it is not just a history of a form of transport;
it is an attempt to provide a general social history of Britain in
the twentieth century by exploring the impact of the automobile,
in all its many shapes from the motor car and motor bus to the
tank and aeroplane, upon the lives of ordinary people in peace
and war. In particular it is concerned with the evolution of
society through three distinct phases, separated by the two World
Wars: from the wealthy plutocracy of Edwardian Britain,
symbolized by the motor car as a rich man's toy and marred by
the harsh and grinding poverty of the bottom third of the
nation, through the transitional society of the inter-war period,
symbolized by the motor car as a middle-class privilege and
marred by the mass unemployment of the Depression, to the
welfare state of the post-war period, symbolized by the motor
car as the vehicle of a mass democracy and marred by the
survival of greater inequality than is generally believed and by
Britain's continuing difficulty in paying her way in the world.
In the process it deals with the effect of motorized transport
on how and where we live, in sprawling suburbs, satellite towns

and villages which have grown into conurbations around all our great cities; on how and where we work, especially in the mass production industries of which motor manufacture is the most striking example; and on how and where we spend our leisure and holidays, from weekend car trips to the countryside to cheap air trips to foreign sunshine. It also deals with the decisive role of those sinister developments of the automobile, the tank and the warplane, in the two World Wars. Alongside all this it traces the twofold, paradoxical experience of Britain in the twentieth century, her political and economic decline as a world power and the leading industrial nation, and her moral rise as the leading pioneer of the welfare state. Finally it speculates on the future of the motor car and its possible alternatives. Are we coming to the end of the automobile age? Will the oil crisis or the sheer self-frustration of this lovable, prolific, congestive monster bring it to a halt and force us to live huddled together within walking distance of work, school and other amenities? If it survives, will it merely intensify the concentration of population in great cities and conurbations which has been the trend of civilization ever since it began? Or will it reverse the trend, turning away from the *civis* and evolving a new kind of dispersed, neo-rural life in which everyone lives and works and plays in scattered places accessible only by road? Either way, the automobile or its successors will have a profound effect upon society.

The book, like its predecessor, grew out of a series of television programmes which I wrote and presented some years ago for Granada Television. As before, I should like to express my gratitude for their help and inspiration to the producer, Jack Smith, and the director, Eric Harrison. I should also like to thank Professor Theo Barker and my wife, Joan, for reading the manuscript and saving me from many minor errors, and my secretary, Pauline Holmes, for her patience in typing more than one draft.

To my great regret, in order to keep the price within the reach of the reader's pocket in these days of rising printing costs, I have had to dispense with the footnotes and table of dates which graced *The Age of the Railway*. I hope the reader who wishes to follow up a point or theme will find sufficient help in the Further Reading at the end of each chapter.

Borwicks   HAROLD PERKIN
Caton
Lancaster

INTRODUCTION

All civilization depends on communication. Just as the world until the Industrial Revolution depended on the horse and the Victorian age on the steam engine, so the twentieth century has come to depend on the internal combustion engine in its manifold forms and applications, from the motor car to the aeroplane. Although the modern world has a remarkable range of prime movers at its command, from the steam turbine to the solid-fuelled rocket, it is the internal combustion engine which has so far proved to be the most versatile and ubiquitous. On the one hand it has replaced most other forms of power, especially animal and human, in the humblest tasks: carrying people either individually or in 'packets' of up to seventy-odd in the coach or bus, pulling loads from a few hundredweight to forty tons or more, ploughing the earth, digging ditches, shovelling minerals, making roads, driving ships, and a host of other humdrum tasks. On the other hand, in its increasingly sophisticated forms from the conventional piston engine through the turbo-jet to the liquid-fuelled rocket (unlike the solid-fuelled, essentially a development of the i.c.e.), it has enabled men to travel on land at over 600 m.p.h., in the

1

air at over 4,000 m.p.h. and in space at over 25,000 m.p.h., and even to make controlled landings and take-offs on the moon.

Yet for the ordinary man its most important conquest has been much nearer home: the triumph of personal mobility, the freedom to go where he wants when he wants to, without having to rely on his own weak legs or on public transport. This book is chiefly about the impact of the private car, which has become the most universally desired of all the desirable consumer goods of twentieth-century society. The motor vehicle, public and private, has come to dominate our lives, to determine where we live, where we work, where we spend our leisure time and take our holidays, the shape and size of our cities and towns, indeed, a large part of our whole physical environment. It has added a whole new dimension to living. Yet living with the motor vehicle, and with the danger, pollution, congestion and chaos it causes, has become one of the greatest problems of our time. In the title used by Sir Colin Buchanan for one of the best books on planning for the motor vehicle, it is a mixed blessing.

More than that, it has helped to shape, for better or worse, the very structure of our society. Just as in the pre-industrial world the horse, an expensive beast which ate as much as two men and needed much cheap labour for its maintenance, helped to create an unequal society in which the man on horseback, rich and powerful, ruled a large mass of the labouring poor; just as the steam horse on its iron road, joining the great cities in a grand bourgeois alliance, helped to create the middle-class civilization of Victorian Britain; so the motor vehicle has helped to create the distinctive shape of modern industrial society, at one and the same time more democratic and, in terms of the power of the giant corporation and the bureaucratic state, more oligarchical than any previous society. On the one hand the private car gives so much choice and freedom to the citizen that he becomes more difficult for governments to control: according to one American commentator, W. W. Rostow, the Soviet system of political control could not survive mass ownership of the private car

2

(which is perhaps why Krushchev opposed it and preferred the idea of State taxis instead). On the other hand the motor vehicle itself, in the form of the police car, the 'Black Maria', the riot-control vehicle, the water-cannon, the troop-carrier and the tank, has become one of the main instruments of political control. In a more sinister sense than ever Buchanan intended, it is a mixed blessing indeed.

Yet in this it in no way differs from other technological innovations. All technology, like all knowledge, is power, and it is power to be used or abused, for good or for evil. The motor vehicle is exceptional only in the scale of its impact on society and in the fact that the good and evil it produces are so inextricably mixed, so much of the evil so obviously unintended by its makers and users. None of the inventors who strove in the decades around the beginning of this century to produce a horseless carriage wanted, no one who buys a motor car today wants, to kill thousands and maim hundreds of thousands of people in Britain alone every year, to assault the senses of the public with noise and fumes and vibrations, to scar the peaceful countryside with ribbons of roaring traffic, to cut small towns and villages into inaccessible halves, to suffocate the cities with congestion, to make a chaos of environmental planning, to call forth whole canons of restrictive laws, to create vast international bureaucratic corporations for the production of vehicles, accessories and fuels as rich and powerful as many nation states, or to squander the raw materials and pollute the atmosphere, soil and waters of the earth to the point of exhaustion and possible destruction of the planet. The road to hell is paved with good intentions, and down it roars the well-intentioned motor car.

This book is a social history of Britain hung on the peg of modern transport. It is as much concerned with society as with the automobile. In particular, it is concerned with the changes in British society brought about not only by the motor vehicle but by the double helix which has characterized Britain in the twentieth century. First, there has been the downward spiral by which Britain declined from its Victorian summit as the workshop, carrier, banker, insurance underwriter and purveyor of parliamentary institutions and democratic ideas to the world, the head of the greatest empire the world had ever seen, the richest and most influential country in the world, to become just one advanced industrial country amongst many and by no means the most powerful. In this decline the motor vehicle was both an instrument and a symbol: an instrument of war in the two world-wide conflicts in which Britain won but at enormous cost to her economic strength and political standing; and a symbol of modern industry and economic organization in which other countries overtook and forged ahead of her.

Secondly, there has been an upward spiral by which Britain led the way in creating a more just and equitable society in which the young, healthy and active, employed and wealthier members care for and maintain their old, sick, disabled, unemployed and poorer neighbours. This rise we associate with the growth of the welfare state, but it is more than an increase in state intervention and administration. It is the moral aspect – moral in that it extends to every citizen the concept of 'who is my neighbour?' – of the democratic revolution of twentieth-century Britain. If the ideal society is not one which is rich and powerful in terms of international politics and military might at the expense of appalling poverty, squalor, sickness, unemployment and ignorance for a large part of the population such as existed in Britain at the beginning of this century, but one in which wealth is more equitably distributed and the poorest member has a right to maintenance, education and a chance in life, then Britain in the last quarter of the twentieth century is slightly nearer that ideal than she was at the beginning. How near, of course, is a matter for debate, as we shall see. But in so far as Britain consciously pioneered the welfare state and made, belatedly perhaps but earlier than most, a declaration of intent to work towards a more equitable society, this upward spiral was perhaps a more significant movement in the sum of human history than the downward one of Britain's decline from great power status.

It would be casuistry to claim any direct part in that upward spiral for the motor vehicle. If it played any part at all, it was as a symbol of the democratic revolution, a democratic vehicle for a democratic age. Beginning around the start of the century as a rich man's toy, a selfish vehicle for the idle rich which covered the ordinary man with dust and endangered his life and limb, it has increasingly become the personal transport of an ever-widening circle of the general public. Today there are two motor cars for every three families in Britain. Allowing for business cars and two-car families, a majority of families, 54% in 1973, have the use of at least one car. By the 1980s, despite the oil crisis, there will be nearly as many cars as families, and only the relatively poor will be without the use of personal transport.

The motor vehicle is the symbol, too, of the mass consumer goods whose widespread if not yet universal distribution is one aspect of economic equity. When every family which wants one can own a motor car – whatever the cost in congestion and amenity – at least the direct aspects of inequality will have been mitigated. Meanwhile, many non-owners benefit from public transport, dispersion of homes in better suburbs, door-to-door deliveries, neighbourhood shops and supermarkets with a remarkable variety of freshly-delivered goods, cheap coach trips and air holidays, and a share in the general economic benefits, in employment, sustained demand and the balance of payments, of a major sector of production and the export trade. Whether such gains outweigh the loss in 'relative deprivation' which the non-owner may feel towards the car driver is impossible to say, since psychological attitudes may or may not be as real as consumer durables. But the material benefits, at least, can be measured. They illustrate the extent to which we have all, car owners and non-owners alike, become dependent on the motor vehicle. If oil became so scarce or expensive as to

5

make motoring impossible for the majority, the very structure of our way of life would collapse.

Whether the people of Britain are worse or better off as a result of the double spiral of rise and decline is a question as difficult to answer as whether we are worse or better off for the automobile. It depends, one might say, on which side of the steering wheel you are, and on where you want to go. If you are more interested in international power and national glory you will mourn the loss of empire, economic hegemony and political leadership. If you are more interested in human liberty, welfare and social equity you will celebrate the emancipation of subject peoples and our own submerged masses, and the triumph of a more just society unburdened by overseas responsibilities morally and politically too heavy to bear. The credits and debits, moral as well as political and economic, are very finely balanced.

The answer, if there is one, lies in the history of British society in the twentieth century. That history is like a journey by motor car, a long and tortuous journey on good roads and bad, through landscapes bright with promise and glowering with imminent catastrophe, around dangerous bends overhanging vertiginous precipices but with breathtaking views of possible futures. It is a journey which, unless we break down, blow up or run out of petrol – all too frightening possibilities – never ends. But it is salutary now and then to stop and look back at where we have come from, partly for its own sake and interest, partly so as to make a better guess at where we are going and the nature and direction of the road ahead. For those who would like such a break in the journey, looking before and after, this book is intended.

1. BETWEEN TWO WORLDS

In December 1894 a Mr Henry Hewetson imported the first motor car into England. It was a Benz three horse-power two-seater, and it cost about £80 at the works in Mannheim, Germany. He collected it at the docks and drove it across London to Charing Cross railway station. He was stopped by the police for the offence, under the 1865 'Red Flag' Act, of not being preceded by a man on foot, and warned not to do it again. But he had begun for Britain, although on the smallest possible scale, the age of the automobile.

Every detail of this story is significant, not merely for the history of the motor car but for the whole position of Britain in the development of modern technology, and therefore in the modern world. Until the internal combustion engine, almost every major technological innovation since the beginning of the eighteenth century – the steam engine, coke smelting and the mass production of wrought iron, textile machinery, the heavy chemical industry, paper-making machinery, steam printing, machine tools, rotary calico printing, the electric telegraph, dynamo and motor, the mass production of steel – had been invented in Britain (not in every case by British inventors).

7

The Industrial Revolution itself, and thus in a sense the modern world, had begun in Britain. The steam railway, which changed the face of the landscape and the pace of life not only in Britain but throughout every continent, was a wholly British invention, and British engineers and navvies, locomotives and rails had carried it to the rest of the world. The railway age, too, had begun with a bang not a whimper, with acts of Parliament backed by massive capital investment, with compulsory purchase of great swathes of land between almost every city and town in the country, the construction of huge earthworks, cuttings, embankments, bridges and tunnels, and a visible revolution in transport, from the ten or twelve miles an hour of the fastest coach and the three or four miles an hour of the waggon or canal barge to the twenty and later fifty miles an hour of the railway train.

By contrast, the motor car was imported, a foreign invention rooted in French, German and American experiments with the gas engine and brought to fruition in the four-wheeled car in Germany in 1886. It was symbolic of a new phase in the history of technology and the modern world, in which other countries coming belatedly to industrialism were able to leapfrog Britain by starting where she left off, with the latest and most efficient processes such as mass-produced steel or fine chemicals, and building on them not the same industries to compete in established fields but new ones in which Britain had no special advantage. Britain's lack of interest in the automobile was epitomized in the 'Red Flag' Act of 1865 (and an Act of 1878 which dispensed with the red flag but not the man), designed to keep the steam locomotive off the public roads. Britain had more railway line per square mile and per head of population than any other country, every town and most villages were connected to the railway system, and there were no wide open spaces requiring a cheaper and more flexible vehicle for their exploitation. And the railway companies were enormously wealthy and powerful corporations, with enough representatives in Parliament and influence with the government to hobble any competitor which they saw as a threat to their monopoly.

The motor car, too, was symbolic of a still more fundamental threat to Britain's technological leadership. Its inventors were products of new systems of technical education which promised a more systematic application of science to industry. The Industrial Revolution in Britain had been the creation of a host of self-taught inventors and entrepreneurs and of craftsmen trained by the traditional method of apprenticeship. Some attempt was made by the literary and scientific societies of the eighteenth century and the mechanics' institutes of the early nineteenth to disseminate interest in applied science, but this was very informal and constantly tended to peter out. A more systematic attempt to encourage the teaching of science and industrial design in schools and evening classes was made by the Science and Art Department of the Privy Council from 1859, expanded after a Royal Commission on Technical Instruction in 1881 and aided by the so-called 'whisky money' (diverted from the compensation for discontinued public house licences) in 1890. But all this was too little and too late to improve Britain's competitive position. How could a few supplementary classes in elementary science and design compare with the great French *école polytechnique*, the American land-grant colleges or the German *technisches-hochschulen*? There was all the difference here between the part-time training of craftsmen and technicians and the university education of professional scientists and engineers.

This difference of approach to education for industry sprang from deep down in the nature of the different societies. It was not simply that Britain spurned science and technology because her society was too aristocratic and traditional. Germany and to a lesser extent France were more aristocratic, but in the latter the aristocracy had been by-passed and in the former it had managed to harness the power of the State and the army to the drive for industrialism. In Britain the landed aristocracy and gentry had welcomed industrial development and played a key role in agricultural improvements to supply food for the towns, in mining, in the building of roads and canals, and in the planning of towns. But they had left industrial innovation itself and the requisite training for it to the spontaneous initiative of the industrialists and skilled workers, with (until 1870) only minimal help from the State in the shape of small grants in aid of elementary education and even tinier ones to technical instruction. This arrangement suited the industrial middle class, whose ideal of self-help and hard work as the road to individual fortune came to dominate the whole of Victorian society since self-education and learning on the job had given them world leadership in industry and commerce. It also came to infect the landed class itself, whose non-technical education in the classics and innate 'effortless superiority' had given them world leadership in war, diplomacy and empire. There seemed to be no need for a change in the system of education for either business or politics since both had worked so well.

Yet spontaneous self-education and effortless superiority were doubly vulnerable. In the first place, foreign nations jealous of Britain's wealth and power and ambitious to surpass her could not afford to adopt the same methods and were forced to use more professional and efficient means of technological education. Secondly, the two British educational traditions cross-infected each other to their mutual detriment. The reform of the aristocratic public schools and the ancient universities was undoubtedly influenced by the strenuous middle-class ideal of self-help and hard work, which replaced the more casual and cultivated ideal of the leisured gentleman, but its very amateurism enabled the reformers to neglect science and ignore technology as unnecessary to those whose native intelligence and powers of leadership would enable them to manage men and learn whatever technical knowledge they needed on the job. From the other side, the enormous prestige of a refurbished aristocratic culture based in the dead civilizations of Greece

10

and Rome set the pattern for the middle-class boarding and grammar schools, so that technical and vocational education was automatically branded as narrow, mercenary and inferior. In both the public boarding and the private day schools, that is throughout almost the whole of British secondary education, the classical scholar versed in the history, literature and philosophy of the ancient world and disdainful of the aims and achievement of modern industrial civilization became the ideal.

Nothing is more revealing of the dominance of these anti-industrial values within the educational system and British society than the post-school careers of the increasing numbers of boys from business families who went to the reformed public schools. As W. J. Reader has shown, the vast majority went into the professions, the clergy, the law, medicine, teaching in the public schools and universities, the armed forces, and the civil service at home, in India or the colonies. Only a small minority went into business, and most of those into banking and commerce rather than 'dirty-handed' industry. They did not thereby reject the ideals of hard work and service to the community: on the contrary, in their own view they raised them to a higher power. But it is significant that in the public school system of values hard work and unselfish service should inhere in professional careers rather than in the self-interested pursuit of business.

This is not to say that there were to be no more self-made men in British industry. On the contrary, there were to be many of them, not least in the motor and aircraft industries. But with few exceptions they were not to be public schoolboys or the sons of business men wealthy enough to be infected by the anti-industrial mores of the aristocratic-cum-high-professional class which came to dominate late Victorian education. The new men, like F. W. Lanchester, William Morris, Herbert Austin and F. H. Royce, were to be self-made men in the old mould, men of technical education if any at all, insulated by their humble origins from the public-school tradition, though they might be helped by aristocratic 'salesmen' like the Hon. Charles Rolls or the Earl of Shrewsbury. The alternative tradition of self-education and training on the job was still powerful enough to salvage some share in the automobile and other growth industries of the twentieth century, or Britain would have been left out of the race altogether. But in a century when industry would come to be based more and more on the discoveries and systematic application of science the amateur tradition was not enough, and goes far to explain why Britain was leapfrogged and took so long to get back into the race.

The experience of technological leadership lost and to some extent regained was both painful and therapeutic. In the thirty years before the First World War, under the threat of foreign and especially German economic competition, strenuous efforts were made to encourage technical education and to establish polytechnics and technical colleges like the Manchester Technical School (formed out of the Mechanics' Institute in 1883) and the Regent Street Poly (day classes, 1886). A number of provincial universities in Manchester, Leeds, Liverpool, Birmingham, Bristol and other industrial cities evolved out of medical schools and civic colleges which were more relevant than Oxford and Cambridge to the practical needs of their regions. Oxford and Cambridge themselves became more aware of the existence of the needs and problems of industrial society, and tried to meet them with such modern developments as the Cavendish laboratories at Cambridge, the extension lectures by travelling tutors from the same university, and the school of social concern and industrial study radiating from the Balliol of A. L. Smith and his patronage of the Workers' Educational Association (1903).

Such attempts to adapt British education and society illustrate the transitional state of Britain at the beginning of the age of the automobile. Britain then stood between two worlds, one dying but by no means dead, the other struggling to be born. On one side stood Imperial Britain, the centre of an empire on which the

12

sun never set. Twelve million square miles, nearly a quarter of the earth's land surface, were painted red on the map, containing 400 million inhabitants, a quarter of the earth's population. That empire and the still larger informal economic empire dependent on Britain for capital, credit, the chief market for food and raw materials and the main source of manufactured goods, were a product of Britain's leadership in the Industrial Revolution. This had given Britain the economic surpluses on her trade with the rest of the world to build up overseas balances which amounted to £2,400 million in 1900 and to £4,000 million in 1914. Trade had led, almost casually, to the acquiring of territory, partly to safeguard British merchants and investments in 'unstable' areas where only British bayonets could keep law and order, partly to safeguard the shipping lanes with a chain of island and coastal bases girdling the earth. Leadership in technology had clinched the imperial process, by providing massive fire-power to back up trade and diplomacy, notably in the shape of the Royal Navy's huge fleet of iron, big-gunned, steam-driven ships. Other countries might boast larger armies, but Britain was the only truly world-wide military power, able to strike with overwhelming strength in almost any quarter of the globe.

Yet on the other side a new world was awakening, more dangerous and challenging than the old. The economic challenge of newly industrializing countries brought them into the race for empire, especially in areas like Africa and the South Pacific where land free from European domination still remained. The scramble for Africa in the 1880s and 1890s brought Britain into competition with France and Germany which occasionally, as at Fashoda in 1898, nearly flared up into war between the European powers. Competition from Germany, rapidly becoming the strongest European economic and military power, was potentially more dangerous, and the German naval law of 1898, which began the attempt to outbuild the Royal Navy's battle fleet, was the start of the arms race which was to lead, amongst other causes, to the First World War.

Another awakening was that of the subject peoples of the Empire. In India the first stirrings of Hindu nationalism gained Indian representation on the provincial Councils in 1909. In Egypt a 'Young Egyptian' movement and in the Sudan an Arab rising had to be suppressed in 1906 by British troops from Malta. But these, like the troubles in Ireland to which we shall return, looked little different from the usual incidents of colonial rule. A more obvious threat to the hitherto unchallenged supremacy of British imperialism came in South Africa, and from a tiny people of European stock, the Boers. Though technically a war between sovereign states, the Boer War of 1899–1902 was the first modern anti-colonial war with lightly armed and widely scattered guerrillas taking on the whole might of a great imperial power. The guerrillas had the moral support of most of the onlooking world, and the physical support in the shape of modern armaments and ammunition of some of the imperial power's enemies, notably Germany. They invented the hit-and-run tactics, striking out of the blue and melting back into the subject population, of the classical anti-colonial kind later to be preached by Mao Tse-Tung and Che Guevara. The imperial power by reaction was forced to use more and more Draconian methods to defeat these tactics, including the use of mass imprisonment of men, women and children in the newly invented concentration camps. In the end the imperial power won, but only at enormous expense in men, money, armaments and moral obloquy. The peace was even more portentous. After the briefest interval for political self-respect, the imperial power granted self-government on the most generous terms (much too generous from the point of view of the subject people's own subject people, the black majority) and the Boers, albeit under a federation with their English-speaking neighbours, won by diplomacy what they had failed to win by force. Either way, by guerrilla warfare or by playing on the conscience and 'rule-weariness' of the imperial power, the Boers anticipated the whole process of twentieth-century decolonization.

At home the transition was epitomized by the state of transport. This was still to all appearances the world of the steam railways, now at their zenith. The motor vehicle was not yet a competitor but rather an auxiliary, providing feeder services in much the same way as the horse bus, carriage and waggon had done. The Great Western used two Milnes-Daimlers in 1903 to save themselves extending the branch line from Helston to the Lizard, and built up a fleet of eighty touring coaches in Devon and Cornwall, while the North Eastern started a bus service in the East Riding, the Great North of Scotland one to serve Balmoral, the Great Eastern built its own buses and the LNWR based bus fleets at Watford and in North Wales. Far more effective as a competitor, at least for urban and inner suburban traffic, was the electric tram, whose route mileage grew from 1,000 miles in 1900 to 2,500 in 1914, but still scarcely touched the bulk of the traffic.

The railway companies dominated the economy and their troubles dominated politics. Their arrogance towards their customers and employees alike had brought a nemesis which threatened to humble their pride in the last two decades before the First World War. The abuse of their monopoly, particularly in charging arbitrary and discriminatory freight rates on different traffic and to different customers, had brought down on them the wrath of the united Chambers of Commerce and of Parliament, in the shape of two Acts in 1888 and 1894 which in effect pegged freight rates at a level which squeezed railway profits in the ensuing price rise from 1896 to 1914. This in turn forced them to resist the demands of their workers for wage increases, particularly during the inflation of the last few years before the War, and to refuse recognition of the railway unions.

The result was a series of strikes with grave national political implications which came to evoke the intervention of the law courts, of Parliament and of the government itself. The first was the Taff Vale strike in August 1900, after which the railway company sued the Amalgamated Society of Railway Servants

15

for restraint of trade and won their appeal to the House of Lords with damages and costs against the union amounting to £42,000. By making strike action suicidal the Taff Vale judgment destroyed the basis of trade unionism and did more than anything to ensure trade-union support for the infant Labour Party (formed as the Labour Representation Committee in 1899). It helped to produce the Conservative defeat and Liberal landslide of 1906, and the reversal of the judgment by the immunity of non-criminal trade union activities from the civil law under the Trade Disputes Act of 1906.

This Act cleared the way for the 'all grades movement' by which the ASRS and the General Railway Workers' Union sought to improve the wages, hours and conditions of all categories of railway workers, culminating in a threatened national strike in November 1907. For the first time in history the government intervened directly in an industrial dispute, when David Lloyd George, President of the Board of Trade, met both sides and negotiated a conciliation scheme which stopped short of full trade-union recognition. The scheme worked with increasing friction until August 1911, when it broke down completely in the first national railway strike. Two hundred thousand railwaymen stopped work and the jobs of millions of other workers were threatened by the shortage of coal. The government deployed 58,000 troops, and some strikers at Liverpool and Llanelly were shot. Public opinion swung round behind the strikers, and the government was forced to intervene again. Lloyd George, now Chancellor of the Exchequer, organized a round-table meeting of company spokesmen and trade union leaders – itself the first recognition of the unions – and the strike was called off in exchange for a Commission of Inquiry and a reformed conciliation machinery which negotiated modest improvements in wages and hours. Finally, in 1913 the root cause of the trouble, the statutory limitation on fares and freight rates, was lifted by Parliament.

The railway companies and the unions thus failed to make the most of their monopoly in the last days of the railway age. After the War the monopoly would be broken, and neither the companies nor the unions would be able again to hold the country to ransom. The food lorries and armoured cars of the General Strike of 1926 were to signify the end of the might of the railways.

In social terms the railways symbolized the world of Victorian class society which they had helped to create. Their three classes of passenger accommodation, first, second and third, reflected its tripartite divisions, with a converging plutocracy of rich capitalists and landowners at the top, a substantial and comfortable middle class of professional and lesser business men in the centre, and the great mass of manual workers, graded from the prosperous and self-respecting artisans of the so-called aristocracy of labour down to the poor labourers of the urban slums and rural hovels, at the bottom.

In that society inequality was considered a law of nature. The belief in the self-made man and the gospel of work was still very powerful. It was enshrined in the popular music hall songs of the age:

> Work, boys, work and be contented,
> As long as you've enough to buy a meal.
> A man, you may rely,
> Will be wealthy by and by
> If he'll only put his shoulder to the wheel.

There was just enough truth in it to enable the rich to claim with some plausibility that anyone with sufficient talent and diligence could make his fortune and join their ranks. They could point to self-made men like Alfred Harmsworth, the free-lance journalist who became a millionaire newspaper proprietor and Lord Northcliffe in 1905, Sir Thomas Lipton, the millionaire tea retailer who began life in a Glasgow tenement, W. H. Lever, the Wigan grocer who founded an international soap and fats empire and became a baronet in 1911 and Lord Leverhulme in 1917, and many more.

17

Most of the rich, however, were from old-established families. Some of them were older than others. The great landowners may not have been as ancient as they thought themselves, but they were still amongst the wealthiest in the land. In the later Victorian age they were increasingly joined by a rising class of large capitalists, bankers, brewers, railway directors and industrialists much richer and more influential than the millowners and merchants of the Industrial Revolution, though less interested in technological progress and more in financial control and manipulation. In the days of the Anti-Corn Law League this new group of immensely rich businessmen – many of them, like the railway chairmen Richard Potter, Beatrice Webb's father, of the Great Western and Sir Edwin Watkin of the Great Central, Metropolitan and South-Eastern Railways, sons of Anti-Corn-Law Leaguers – might have formed a separate class in opposition to the landed aristocracy. But in the late Victorian and Edwardian age they were embraced by the landed aristocracy, who in turn rushed to gain a foothold in business. By 1896 a quarter of the peers held directorships of companies. The great landowners and the millionaire capitalists increasingly amalgamated in a plutocracy of wealth which transcended their origins. They united in the same life style in the dining-rooms and ball-rooms of great London and country houses, international hotels and ocean liners, and even in the courts of princes. The Kaiser's sneer on Edward VII's visit to Sir Thomas Lipton's steam yacht, 'The King of England has gone boating with his grocer', celebrated the marriage of the plutocrats.

In that society income was very unequally divided. In 1904, when the national income was about £40 per head or £200 per family, Sir Leo Chiozza Money divided the UK population of 43 millions into those living in 'riches', about a quarter of a million families with over £700 p.a. who received over a third of the national income; those living in 'comfort', with £160–£700 p.a., about three quarters of a million families who received about a ninth of the national income; and the rest, those living

18

in 'poverty', 38 million people who received just over half the national income. The rich averaged £2,340 p.a. per family, though some great landlords and millionaires rose to over £50,000 p.a., the comfortable £327 p.a., and the poor £105 p.a. Since income tax was then only a shilling in the pound and there was no surtax, income after tax was far more unequal than today.

Only a rich Fabian, however, would have described the whole non-taxpaying class as in poverty. More accurate statistics of poverty were produced by two famous social surveys, of London in the 1880s by Charles Booth, and of York in 1899 by B. Seebohm Rowntree. They proved that poverty was too large a problem and too deeply rooted in the social and economic system for it to be solved by individual effort, whether in response to the deterrent stick of the Poor Law or the cajoling carrot of charity. Their studies of the extent and causes of poverty were the most important example of the new knowledge about society which set government social policy on a new track which was to take it far from the moralizing individualism of the Victorian middle-class idea in the direction of mutual interdependence of the welfare state.

Booth invented and Rowntree defined the concept of the poverty line, below which families, after paying house rent, did not receive enough income to keep themselves alive, healthy and fit for work. Booth, working through 'mass interviewing' of the new school attendance officers in London in the 1880s, was the more impressionistic, and divided the families in the streets known to them into the 'lowest class of criminals and loafers' (0·9%), the 'very poor' (7·5%), the 'poor' (22·3%), the comfortable working class (51·5%), and the middle class and above (17·8%). Thus nearly a third of the population, 31% (about 40% of the working class), was categorized as below the poverty line, and therefore without enough to eat. In some slum areas of the East End and Southwark the proportion in poverty rose as high as two thirds.

Rowntree arrived at his poverty line more scientifically, by

19

estimating from the data of medical research the minimum dietary needs of men and women in moderate work and their children, together with minimal allowances for clothing and fuel, and conducted his research more systematically, by means of a house-to-house survey of the working-class streets of York in 1899 by a paid investigator. He found that 28% of the population (over 43% of the working class) were living below the poverty line. Of these about 10% (over 15% of the working class) were in 'primary' poverty, and did not have enough income after paying rent for food, clothing and fuel, and the rest in 'secondary' poverty, which meant they had barely enough but misspent part of their income on the wrong foods or other useful goods or on wasteful expenditure such as drink or gambling.

More important was their analysis of the causes of poverty. Booth showed that the vast majority of his 'poor' and 'very poor' were in poverty because of low earnings from irregular or casual work, large family commitments, or illness or infirmity of the main breadwinner. Only a small fraction, 13–14%, were there because of drink or thriftlessness. Rowntree admitted that the 18% in 'secondary' poverty in York were there because of drink, gambling or improvidence, but showed that the 10% in 'primary' poverty were so because of low wages, large families, irregular work or the death, illness or unemployment of the chief breadwinner. The poverty line for a man, wife and three children in York in 1899 was 21s. 8d. The average wage for unskilled labourers was 18s. As Rowntree put it, 'the wages paid for unskilled labour in York are insufficient to provide food, shelter and clothing adequate to maintain a family of moderate size in a state of bare physical efficiency'.

Booth and Rowntree also discovered the poverty cycle, by which a much larger fraction of the working class than was in poverty at any one time spent a considerable part of their lives below the poverty line. Most working-class children were born into poverty, since their coming reduced or abolished the mother's earnings and increased the family's commitments;

20

they rose out of poverty in their teens and early adulthood when they started work and had few commitments; they sank into poverty again when they married and had children of their own; rose out of it again when their children began to earn; and declined into permanent poverty in old age when they could no longer earn. With only two periods of 'affluence', not allowing for sickness or unemployment, to balance three periods of poverty, the middle-class notion that the poor could provide by saving for the contingencies of life was shown to be false.

The new facts about poverty were an indictment of the traditional nineteenth-century view that it was chiefly a moral problem, due to the individual's personal inadequacy, idleness, improvidence or vice. They gave support to a new view, held until then only by a small minority of radicals and socialists, that poverty was largely a product of the social and economic system, and mostly caused by contingencies of life, sickness, death or lack of work of the breadwinner, and by defects of the labour market, low wages, casual work and seasonal and cyclical unemployment, which were utterly beyond the control of the individual. The old remedies, individual self-help aided in deserving cases by the charity of the rich and backed up only as a last resort by a harsh, deterrent Poor Law, were inept and irrelevant. New remedies would have to be found which treated the causes of the disease rather than its symptom, poverty, and set out to prevent sickness, unemployment, irregularity of work and low wages, and to bring the support of the community to the aid of those who fell victim to them. This implied a profound change in social values, from the moral individualism of Victorian class society to the mutual aid which came to characterize the twentieth-century welfare state.

The new knowledge was confirmed by a succession of social observers from Andrew Mearns's *The Bitter Cry of Outcast London* (1883) and Salvation Army General William Booth's *In Darkest England* (1890) to C. F. G. Masterman's *The Condi-*

tion of England (1909); by the discovery, by school teachers and charitable workers, of large numbers of schoolchildren sitting numb and chill on the benches, unable to learn for want of food; by the complaints of dock employers that dockers could not work beyond 4 o'clock in the afternoon because their famished strength gave out; and, to the alarm of General Sir Frederick Maurice and the War Office, by the reports that a large percentage of recruits in the Boer War had to be rejected on grounds of physical unfitness. Maurice swelled the cry which had been growing since the 1880s, that the poverty, squalor and overcrowding of the urban slums were causing the working class to degenerate in health, physique, energy and even intelligence, as enfeebled parents, it was claimed, passed on their increasing defects to their progressively more enfeebled children. The implications of this process of degeneracy, if true, were alarming both for the continued progress of British industry and for the defence of the country against the sturdy armies of the continental powers.

After the Boer War, the government set up a Select Committee on Physical Deterioration. Its report in 1904 completely rejected the concept of physical degeneration, but gathered together a great deal of the new knowledge concerning the effects on the working class, and especially on their children, of poverty, overcrowding and insanitary conditions. It made an immense number of specific recommendations, including improved provision of medical officers of health, control of overcrowding, smoke pollution and food adulteration, the sterilization of milk, greater provision of open spaces in towns, the medical inspection of schoolchildren, school meals for under-fed children, physical exercise and domestic science training in schools, and much else. It was one of the most influential public documents ever published, and to it can be traced many of the social reforms of the Edwardian age, including school meals and medical inspection and the first town-planning act in 1909.

Another breakthrough in social knowledge was in the systematic study of unemployment. This began when the temporary measures taken to meet the distress of 1905 in the shape of public works and a system of voluntary labour exchanges in London provided a young social worker at Toynbee Hall, William Beveridge, with the necessary statistics to analyse the problem. With the aid of these and the trade union returns of unemployment collected by the Board of Trade since 1892, he was able to publish a book in 1909, significantly entitled *Unemployment: A Problem of Industry*. In it he analysed the nature and causes of the different types of unemployment, and was able to show that very little of it was voluntary idleness on the part of the individual, but that the industrial system required and created a reserve army of unemployed workers, or rather a large number of distinct pools of reservists, which were necessary to meet the fluctuations of demand for labour at different seasons of the year and different phases of the trade cycle. The remedies, he argued, were twofold: a system of labour exchanges to create a single market for labour and smooth the flow of men into vacancies; and a system of mutual insurance to support the inevitable but continually rotating residuum of the unemployed. Once again this new knowledge was to lead to specific remedies with large implications for the future.

Meanwhile the debate on the causes of poverty came to a head in the Royal Commission on the Poor Laws and the Relief of Distress which sat from 1905 to 1909. It became a battlefield between the traditionalist majority of the commissioners, led by Charles Loch, Helen Bosanquet and Octavia Hill of the Charity Organization Society, and the reforming minority, led by the Fabian Beatrice Webb and George Lansbury, a Labour councillor and poor law guardian from Poplar. The traditionalists still insisted that poverty was principally a moral problem, to be cured by helping the more independent to stand on their own feet through voluntary bodies like the Charity Organization Society, leaving the incorrigibly idle and vicious and the deserving but 'helpless' cases to the deterrent Poor

23

Law. The reforming minority rejected Public Assistance as but old Poor Law writ large. A 'destitution authority' was a misnomer, treating poverty as a moral disease instead of a symptom of distinct social defects which should be dealt with at the root by distinct authorities. They therefore recommended the 'break-up of the Poor Law', and its replacement by a range of separate services for the non-able-bodied managed by different committees of the county and county borough councils, and for the able-bodied, a Ministry of Labour to organize the labour market through labour exchanges and to provide full maintenance for the unemployed.

Neither the majority nor the minority report had much effect on Edwardian social policy. In the longer term, the Guardians were replaced by Public Assistance Committees in 1929 and the Poor Law was gradually broken up, as central government agencies for pensions, national insurance, unemployment assistance, the old Poor Law infirmaries, and the like, took over from the Guardians and the Public Assistance Committees, culminating in the establishment of the Ministry of National Insurance and the National Assistance Board in 1946–8. The Commission was simply a focus for the argument between the old social philosophy of individual self-dependence and the new one of collective inter-dependence. To that extent it marks the point of balance between the old world and the new.

The turning point was marked more practically by the actual social reforms of the Edwardian age. They were not a concerted programme but a series of piecemeal remedies for specific problems in the light of the new knowledge about poverty. Yet if the welfare state consists of four walls, social security, a health service, an egalitarian education system and some deliberate redistribution of income in favour of the poor, the Liberal Government of 1906–14 laid the foundations of them all. The first bricks of social security were laid by the provision of old-age pensions – tiny non-contributory pensions on a means test for the over-seventies – in 1908, and the National Insurance

24

Act of 1911, which provided health insurance for all manual and other low-paid workers and a pilot scheme of unemployment insurance for two million workers in vulnerable industries. The same act laid the first footings of a national health service, by the provision of a panel doctor scheme for insured workers and the State support of tuberculosis sanatoria for the whole population. A more egalitarian education system began in a small way with the establishment of scholarships from the elementary to the grammar schools in 1907, with school meals for poor children in 1906 and school medical inspection in 1907, to be followed in 1913 by state support for school clinics. Children were also benefited by the encouragement of local authority provision of midwives, health visitors, and milk depots and child welfare clinics, and by the Children Act of 1908 which protected them from cruelty, negligence, smoking and drink, and set up the juvenile courts and the probation service.

The first important step towards a fairer distribution of income came in Lloyd George's 'People's Budget' of 1909, ostensibly more concerned with the building of Dreadnoughts. The ensuing uproar and constitutional crisis left no doubt, however, that the rich saw the budget as an attack upon themselves by socialists and levellers. The main provisions were a graduated income tax rising from 9d. to 1s. 2d., plus a supertax of 6d. on incomes over £5,000 p.a. and 9d. over £6,000; more steeply graduated death duties, rising to 15% on estates over £1,500,000; a group of taxes on land which included a 20% charge on unearned increment every time an estate changed hands and a charge on undeveloped land and minerals; additional taxes on alcohol, tobacco, and new taxes on motor cars and petrol. It is true that the motor taxes were earmarked for expenditure on the roads, under Lloyd George's famous pledge which was to create so much complaint and resentment by the motoring interests between the Wars, but they were one more example of 'soaking the rich' which caused the Conservative majority in the House of Lords to throw out the budget.

25

The constitutional crisis marked another turning point from the old world to the new, from the old political system in which property was entrenched in the constitution to a new one in which it was forced to maintain itself by persuasion of the non-propertied electors. After two elections in 1910 and a royal promise to create a majority of Liberal peers, the elective House asserted its supreme sovereignty and reduced the hereditary House's rights over legislation to a delaying power of two sessions for most bills and of one month only for money bills. Though wealth might still persuade its way to power it could no longer exercise a veto over legislation.

The twentieth century was to be a far more violent age than its predecessor, and the last few years before the First World War were marked by violence and the threat of violence on a scale scarcely seen in Britain since the days of the Chartists. It came from three directions. Like the railwaymen the miners, dockers and other transport workers, shipbuilders and many more were caught in the familiar squeeze between rising prices and lagging wages which, the inter-war years apart, has become such a feature of the twentieth-century economy. The result was a record outbreak of strikes in 1910–14, with more man-days' work lost in 1912 than in any year before or since except for 1926, the year of the General Strike. Feelings were bitter, with passions inflamed by propaganda of revolutionary syndicalism amongst the strikers, and by the troops called out by the government and the shootings at Liverpool, Llanelly and elsewhere. Although all the major strikes were settled peacefully, on the eve of the War the triple alliance of miners, railwaymen and transport workers still seemed, though misleadingly as it turned out, to threaten something approaching a general strike.

The second threat of violence came from the suffragettes, the militant women's liberation group which demanded the parliamentary vote on the same terms as men. In Edwardian terms this meant a vote for women householders and property owners which by then would mainly have added to the conservative electorate, and the Liberal Government refused to grant it until there was universal suffrage for men. The response of the suffragettes was to commit violence against public property, by burning or bombing public buildings and Post Office pillar boxes, and against politicians: one militant stoned Lloyd George's windows, another horse-whipped Winston Churchill, while a third committed suicide by throwing herself under the king's horse at the Derby in 1913. On the eve of the War the metaphorical battle between the sexes seemed about to become a real one.

The third threat of violence was far more serious. It came, as so often in the twentieth century, from Ireland, and specifically from Ulster. The elections of 1910 and the taming of the House of Lords by the Parliament Act of 1913 brought the Irish question to boiling point, by giving the Irish nationalists the casting vote in the House of Commons and removing the block to Home Rule of the Lord's veto. The consequent Home Rule Bill was due to become law despite the Lords' opposition in 1914, but as the time approached it became clear that the Ulster Protestants, led by Sir Edward Carson and encouraged by the Conservative leader, Bonar Law, would fight rather than accept the rule of the Catholic majority. Gun running by both sides threatened to lead to civil war, and all-party discussions to avert the catastrophe were in progress when the European war broke out.

The threatened violence of the trade unions, the suffragettes and the Irish may have been one factor in persuading the Kaiser that Britain would not fight when he invaded Belgium in August 1914. If so, he was wrong. On the outbreak of international war all three abandoned their threat for the duration (though a separate group of Irish republicans were to make their bid for an independent Ireland in Easter Week, 1916, with immense repercussions in the post-war crisis). Nevertheless, the threat of violence is a reminder that the world before the First World War was not the sunlit afternoon of garden parties, Derby Days

27

and harmonious class relations which it appears in some memoirs. Rather was it the twilight between the two worlds of Victorian self-confident achievement and of twentieth-century self-questioning doubt. It was in this twilight that the motor car made its modest but portentous debut.

Like the railway, it came when it was needed. As F. M. L. Thompson has shown, the horse, on which the Victorians depended for private and public local transport and goods distribution from and between the railway stations, was an expensive beast with a voracious appetite. It ate six tons or more of food a year, the product of four or five acres of land, and a private carriage required two servants, a coachman and groom, plus off-street stabling as large as a house. A horse bus or tram needed 10–12 horses to keep it on the road for sixteen hours a day, and the horses lasted only about four years. The expense plus the demand for land to house and feed the horse had given a sharp check to the growth of the carriage trade from 1870 and by the Edwardian age with the price of fodder rising horse bus and tram proprietors were looking for some cheaper way of conveying people. The electric tram and the electrified tube railway were two effective solutions, but limited to heavily trafficked lines. Steam buses and electric-battery buses were tried with little success. The ultimate solution, both for personal and public transport, lay with the petrol-driven motor vehicle.

FURTHER READING

E. Halevy, *A History of the English People in the Nineteenth Century*, vol. V, *Imperialism and the Rise of Labour (1895–1905)*, and vol. VI, *The Rule of Democracy (1905–1914)* (Benn, 1961)

S. Nowell-Smith, ed., *Edwardian England, 1901–1914* (Oxford University Press, 1964)

O. M. V. Argles, *South Kensington to Robbins: English technical and scientific education since 1851* (Longmans, 1964)

M. Sanderson, *The Universities and British Industry, 1850–1970* (Routledge, 1972)

W. J. Reader, *Professional Men: The Rise of the Professional Classes in Nineteenth-century England* (Weidenfeld, 1966)

P. S. Bagwell, *The Railwaymen: The History of the National Union of Railwaymen* (Allen & Unwin, 1963)

E. H. Phelps Brown, *The Growth of British Industrial Relations: A Study from the Standpoint of 1906–14* (Macmillan, 1959)

G. Stedman Jones, *Outcast London: A Study in the Relationship between Classes in Victorian Society* (Clarendon Press, 1971)

Robert Roberts, *The Classic Slum: Salford Life in the First Quarter of the Century* (Manchester University Press, 1971)

L. G. Chiozza Money, *Riches and Poverty* (Methuen, 1905)

Charles Booth, *Life and Labour of the People in London* (Macmillan, 17 vols, 1902–3), esp. vol. II

B. S. Rowntree, *Poverty: A Study of Town Life* (Macmillan, 1901)

T. S. and M. B. Simey, *Charles Booth, Social Scientist* (Oxford University Press, 1960)

Asa Briggs, *Social Thought and Social Action: A Study of the Work of Seebohm Rowntree, 1871–1954* (Longmans, 1961)

Lord Beveridge, *Power and Influence* (Hodder & Stoughton, 1953)

Maurice Bruce, *The Coming of the Welfare State* (Batsford, 1961), ch. 5

Derek Fraser, *The Evolution of the British Welfare State* (Macmillan, 1973)

J. R. Hay, *The Origins of the Liberal Welfare Reforms, 1906–14* (Macmillan, 1975)

Roy Jenkins, *Mr Balfour's Poodle: An Account of the Struggle Between the House of Lords and the Government of Mr Asquith* (Collins, 1968)

George Dangerfield, *The Strange Death of Liberal England* (MacGibbon, 1966)

Roger Fulford, *Votes for Women: The Story of a Struggle* (Faber, 1957)

F. M. L. Thompson, *Victorian England: The Horse-drawn Society* (Inaugural lecture, Bedford College, London, 1970)

T. C. Barker and Michael Robbins, *A History of London Transport*, Vol. II, *The Twentieth Century to 1970* (Allen & Unwin, 1974)

29

2. THE COMING OF THE MOTOR CAR

The motor car has a long pre-history which goes back to the seventeenth century. In 1686 Ferdinand Verbiest, a Flemish Jesuit missionary to China, described how he had moved a model carriage by applying jets of steam to vanes on the wheel – a sort of external steam turbine. In 1698 Denis Papin in France made another model worked by steam through a piston, cylinder and ratchet drive to the rear wheel. In 1769 Nicholas Cugnot, a French military engineer, built the first full-sized steam road vehicle, which could run for 15 minutes at over 2 m.p.h. About 1786 William Murdock, Boulton and Watt's ingenious foreman at their Soho foundry in Birmingham, experimented with a model steam carriage. These and many other experiments, however, came to nothing, and the first successful self-propelled road vehicle was that of Richard Trevithick, the father of the railway locomotive. In the last years of the eighteenth century this Cornish mining engineer invented a high-pressure engine which was as great an advance on James Watt's cumbersome low-pressure engine as Watt's was on Newcomen's atmospheric engine. Its great virtue was its high power-to-weight ratio, which meant that, unlike its predecessors, it could carry itself about. At Camborne in Cornwall he applied it to a road carriage which on Christmas Eve, 1801, went faster than walking pace. Two years later another model made several journeys around London at speeds from 4 to 9 m.p.h. But the roads at that time were too rough for such an unsprung carriage, and the project was abandoned. Trevithick turned his attention to the smoother colliery plateways and railways, where horses already pulled much larger loads than they could on the roads. He married his engine to the plateway, with flanged rails taking ordinary flat-tyred wheels, at Merthyr Tydfil in 1804, and to the railway itself, with flanged wheels, at Gateshead in 1805. Unfortunately, both locomotives were too heavy for the contemporary track and were converted to stationary engines. Trevithick died in poverty, but his pioneering work was followed up by Blenkinsop and Murray, Blackett and Hedley and, finally, George and Robert Stephenson, who developed the swift, economical steam locomotives of the railway age.

After 1815 the roads were greatly improved by McAdam, Telford and their imitators, so that the flying coaches of the 1820s and 1830s increased in speed, averaging 10 m.p.h. or more. The demand for high-speed travel, the needs of the new factory system of the Industrial Revolution for rapid transit of heavy goods, the high cost and short life of coach horses and the expense of fodder, all turned men's minds to the idea of mechanical transport. Leaving aside the colliery railroads, steam road vehicles seemed the easiest solution since they did not require a special road. In 1819 G. Medhurst built a steam carriage and staged a demonstration run between Paddington and Islington, and other experimental vehicles were made in the 1820s, notably by Sir Goldsworthy Gurney in 1827–31. He sold his coaches to Sir Charles Dance who in 1831 started a regular service between Gloucester and Cheltenham. It was soon stopped, however, by the opposition of the horse coach proprietors and innkeepers.

The most successful of the early steam carriages were those of

Walter Hancock, who started regular services in London which ran on and off from 1831 to 1840. Like John Scott Russell who ran a service between Glasgow and Paisley, and Colonel Maceroni and John Squire who ran one for some weeks in 1833 between Paddington and Edgware, he was defeated partly by the opposition of the parish road authorities and the turnpike trusts, who charged enormous tolls on mechanically propelled vehicles, but mostly by frequent breakdowns and boiler explosions and the general unsuitability of steam to small-scale vehicles.

The fundamental reason for their defeat was the success of the competing railway, which began in its modern form with the Liverpool and Manchester Railway in 1830 and spread to most of the major cities of Britain in the next twenty years. The steam engine was a cumbersome beast, needing large quantities of water and solid fuel, and weighing in its optimally efficient form several tons. It was therefore better adapted as a locomotive drawing a fuel-and-water tender and a train of carriages on a railway than as a road carriage combining engine, fuel and passenger accommodation in the same vehicle. The steam carriage inventors knew what the problem was, and made many ingenious attempts to increase the speed and efficiency of the boiler so as to reduce both its weight and the fuel required for steam-raising. Jacob Perkins in 1823 experimented with pumping hot water through red-hot tubes to produce superheated steam at very high pressure, anticipating the 'flash-boiler' with which Léon Serpollet was to power a steam-car in 1902 at the world speed record of over 75 m.p.h. But the materials and engineering techniques of the early nineteenth century were not up to such solutions, and by 1840 there were no more steam carriages on the road. No doubt if the railways had not come when they did, both the steam carriages and the roads would have been improved to provide the rapid transport which industry and society now demanded.

As it was, there remained some need for mechanically

propelled vehicles not tied to the railways, most obviously in agriculture, both for work in the fields and for haulage of threshing machines between farms. In 1842 Ransomes and May, agricultural machinery engineers of Ipswich, built a traction engine designed by W. Worby, and exhibited it at the Royal Agricultural Show at Bristol. It ran at 4–6 m.p.h. and could drive a threshing machine in the farmyard, but it was not a commercial success. R. W. Thomson, inventor of the first, unsuccessful, pneumatic tyre in 1845, collaborated in the manufacture of several traction engines, and was followed by Thomas Aveling, Richard Tangye, Edwin Foden and other famous makers. John Fowler's showman's locomotive of 1895, which hauled fair and circus vans and powered the funfairs, coloured lights and organs of the fairground, made traction engines a well-loved sight to generations of children down to recent times. Agricultural tractors, however, were generally too heavy for the ground. J. Boydell in 1846 patented a tractor each wheel of which had five thick flat shoes – a primitive track-laying vehicle which looked forward to the caterpillar traction of the Edwardian age – and many of his designs were tried on the large arable fields of Lincolnshire and East Anglia. But such devices were unsuitable for roads and not much better off them. Although a great deal of agricultural machinery, drills, rakes, mowing and reaping machines and combine harvesters came into use in the Victorian age it was generally horse-drawn. Experiments with stationary engines and cable-drawn ploughs and other tools failed to solve the problem, and agriculture, like road transport, waited for a lighter power unit.

Around mid-century when the railways had begun to connect most of the towns and it became obvious that branch lines could never economically serve the remoter areas, there was a revival of interest in the light steam passenger carriage. Amongst the enthusiasts were the Marquess of Stafford and the Earl of Caithness, with vast estates in the north of Scotland. In 1858 and 1860 Thomas Rickett built steam carriages for them, the second of

1. A Precursor Walter Hancock's 'Enterprise' steam omnibus between the City and Paddington, 23 April 1833. *Photo: Science Museum, London*

2a. Royal Christening The Prince of Wales with Mr Montagu (later Lord Montagu of Beaulieu) in the latter's 12-h.p. Daimler at Highcliffe Castle, July 1899. *Photo: Radio Times Hulton Picture Library*

2b. Women's Liberation The first woman chauffeur, Miss Dorothy Levitt (from *The Girls' Realm Annual*, 1910). *Photo: kindly supplied by Dr Denis Chapman, University of Liverpool*

3a and b. Mixed Traffic in the Days of Transition London street scenes in 1912. *Photos: Radio Times Hulton Picture Library*

4a. The Automobile Airborne   The Hon. Charles Rolls, co-founder of Rolls-Royce, in his machine at the Aero Club's flying field at Eastchurch, January 1910. *Photo: Radio Times Hulton Picture Library*

4b. Riding the Step   A B-type omnibus, March 1914. Over a thousand of these were to carry the British Expeditionary Force to the front line in August. *Photo: Imperial War Museum*

which carried the Earl and Countess over the thousand-foot-high Ord of Caithness. By this time the power of the turnpike trusts was withering under railway competition, and in 1861 a Locomotive Act made the same charge for road locomotives as for horse-drawn vehicles with the same loads (agricultural vehicles of both kinds being exempt). Although steam carriages were regulated by size and weight, limited to 10 m.p.h. in the countryside and 5 m.p.h. in the towns, and had to have two attendants, the competition between road and rail now promised to become fairer. New steam passenger carriages were built by Garrett, Tangye and others – not so roomy as Hancock's and Gurney's coaches, but small-scale personal vehicles looking forward to the motor car.

They were vociferously opposed by the carriage-owning classes and the many railway directors in Parliament, however, and in 1865 the famous 'Red Flag' Act was passed, which restricted speeds to 4 m.p.h. in the country and 2 m.p.h. in towns, and required every road locomotive to have three attendants, one to walk not less than sixty yards in front bearing a red flag. Blowing off steam and sounding a whistle were prohibited, and any person on horseback or in a horse-drawn vehicle could demand that the locomotive be stopped while he passed. Local authorities could regulate the hours during which locomotives could pass through towns and villages, and the Home Secretary could, and did, make an order prohibiting them from passing along turnpike roads except between midnight and 6 a.m. Under such restrictions the development of mechanically propelled road vehicles (other than electric tramcars, from 1879) almost came to a stop in Britain. Only the mainly agricultural traction engine continued in use. Britain was effectively excluded from the subsequent development of the steam passenger carriage, which the French, notably Joseph Ravel, Amédée Bollée, Count de Dion and Léon Serpollet were to develop into splendid vehicles which for a time outpaced the new petrol-engined cars of the 1890s.

35

One alternative was the bicycle, important for the motor car since so many British cycle makers were to turn their attention to car manufacture and recover the ground which the Act had lost. Man-propelled machines had long been known in Britain, chiefly in the form of the primitive two-wheeled hobby horse. The Rev. Edmund Cartwright of the power loom had invented a quadricycle in 1819 and Macmillan, a Scottish blacksmith, a treadle bicycle twenty years later, but there was little serious interest until Turner imported a 'boneshaker' from France around 1869. He thus began a new industry in Coventry, then suffering from the collapse, due to French competition after the 1860 treaty, of its silk-ribbon trade. The 'ordinary' bicycle, really the extraordinary penny-farthing, was introduced in 1870, and became the rage for young bloods like Oxford and Cambridge undergraduates. For the less athletic, tricycles became popular between 1878 and 1885, until they were replaced by Harry J. Lawson's chain-driven 'safety' bicycle, essentially the modern two-wheeler, from about 1884. The 'bicycle boom' of the mid-nineties cheapened and brought it within reach of a much wider public. From then until the First World War was the golden age of cycling, when increasing numbers of young men and women from widening strata of society came to be liberated from cramping houses, confining streets and the prying eyes of their elders. The 'new woman' with her cigarettes and cycling breeches was emancipated more by the bicycle than by the Married Women's Property Acts. Cycling clubs sprang up under the auspices of the Cyclists' Touring Club of 1878, the National Cyclists' Union of 1883 and Robert Blatchford's *Clarion* clubs in which many future Labour politicians served their apprenticeship to socialism and fresh air.

The future lay, however, not with steam or man-propulsion but with the internal combustion engine. Its pre-history, too, goes back to the seventeenth century. In 1680 Christian Huygens, Dutch physicist and inventor of the pendulum clock, made a piston engine powered by gunpowder. Edmund Cartwright, inventor of the power loom and the quadricycle, designed an alcohol engine (1797) and Samuel Brown an ingenious gas-vacuum engine (1826). The idea of gas as an alternative to steam was sufficiently accepted for the Parliamentary Committee of 1831 to 'enquire generally into the state and future prospects of steam or gas propelled vehicles'. In 1838–9 three Americans, Barnett, Wright and Johnston, invented separate gas engines, and in 1855 Alfred Drake of Philadelphia exhibited one at the Crystal Palace Exhibition in New York. The first commercially successful gas engine was that of Étienne Lenoir, patented in 1860, which he used to power machinery in his Paris workshop. Two years later he fitted one to a vehicle which made a successful trip of six miles. But Lenoir could not overcome the difficulty of vaporizing a liquid fuel, and he abandoned the project to concentrate on stationary engines. The idea was taken up by other inventors. In Austria, Siegfried Markus invented an internal combustion engine for use in airships and displayed a motor car at the Vienna Exhibition of 1873. In Germany Nicholas Otto and Eugen Langen of Cologne produced a rough and noisy gas engine in 1867 which they developed into the famous Otto 'silent' gas engine of 1878, using the four-stroke cycle propounded by the Frenchman Beau de Rochas.

Gottlieb Daimler of Cannstatt, Dr Otto's ex-assistant, made the essential breakthrough to liquid fuel. The problems were carburation, the turning of a light oil into vapour, and its ignition in the cylinder. Daimler solved these problems in 1883–4 by means of a surface carburettor and a hot tube of heated platinum. (In 1893 his assistant Wilhelm Maybach immensely improved on the first with his spray carburettor.) The engine was much lighter and faster than earlier models, developing 1 horse-power for each 90 lb. weight, and running at 800 revolutions per minute. With this high power-to-weight ratio and liberated by the use of liquid fuel, it was ideally suited to marriage with a road vehicle. Daimler fitted it to a bicycle in 1885 and to a clumsy four-wheeled vehicle the following year. Meanwhile his rival, Karl Benz of Mannheim, had also solved the same problems, and produced a motor tricycle in 1885, followed by a four-wheeled car in 1886, the same year as Daimler's. Benz was the first to commence commercial production of motor cars, in 1890, Daimler being more interested in selling engines for stationary use or under licence for the manufacture of motor vehicles.

The most important of Daimler's licensees were the French firms of Panhard and Levassor and Peugeot, who introduced the motor car to France where it rapidly developed its modern lay-out and fundamental characteristics. Panhard and Levassor originated in 1891 the basic formula on which most modern designs are based: front-mounted engine under a bonnet, connected by a flywheel cone clutch, three- or four-speed lay-shaft gearbox, and transmission by propellor shaft and differential cross-shaft to the rear wheels. The Peugeot model was not so mechanically advanced but was joint winner with the Panhard-Levassor of the first ever road race, from Paris to Rouen, in 1894, after the de Dion-Bouton steam 'Victoria', which finished first, had been disqualified. After this Count de Dion and his partner, who had already made many improvements in springing and transmission, including their famous differential-drive rear axle, transferred their abilities to the petrol-driven car, and developed, amongst other items, the high-speed, light-weight engine (1,500 r.p.m. and 1 h.p. for each 25 lb. weight) and the modern coil-and-battery ignition system. Louis Renault later completed 'le système Panhard' by the addition of the direct drive by a differential and bevel gear to a 'live' rear axle. The important French contribution to the early development of the motor car is enshrined in much of its terminology, from 'chassis', 'carburettor' and 'chauffeur', derived from the stoker of the steam locomotive, to the word 'automobile' itself.

In the United States there was little interest in the motor car, despite the early patent for a petrol-driven four-wheeled vehicle by G. B. Selden in 1879 – an impracticable piece of guesswork by a non-engineer who merely intended to cash in on the efforts of genuine inventors – until Charles Duryea built the first car there in 1891–92 and Henry Ford his 'quadricycle' at Detroit in 1896. Even then many American automobile engineers, like the Stanley and the White brothers, preferred to develop the steam-driven car. A Stanley steamer broke the world record in 1906 at 121.5 m.p.h. They also experimented with electric cars, already tried out since 1881 by Jeantaud and de Parrodil in France and Park and others in England. In 1891 the Electric Road Carriage Company of Boston began to manufacture them for sale, and they became very popular after the Chicago World Exhibition of 1893. Camille Jenatzy's electric 'Jamais Contente' held the world speed record at over 65 m.p.h. in 1899, but was soon surpassed in speed and range by the internal combustion engine.

The British were left behind in all three fields, handicapped by their restrictive traffic laws. With considerable experience in cycle and general engineering, British inventors did not lack the necessary skill, and Edward Butler patented a petrol-engined motor bicycle in 1885, the same year as Daimler's, and built one in 1888, but he abandoned it because of the restrictions. Roots, Knight and Bremer all produced petrol-driven three-wheelers with imported parts in the early 1890s, and the Knight was converted in 1895 to what was claimed to be the first four-wheeled car manufactured in Britain. Nevertheless, the first motor car to be seen in Britain was the Benz imported in 1894 by Henry Hewetson, who became the English agent for the Benz company. His agency did invaluable service to the infant British motor industry, since it helped to break the attempted monopoly by the British Motor Syndicate set up in 1895 by the notorious Harry J. Lawson, pantentee of the safety bicycle, and his accomplices, Martin Rucker and Terence Hooley, who acquired the Daimler manufacturing rights in Britain and tried to claim royalties on every motor car manufactured or imported. Most of the early cars sold by its subsidiaries were really foreign vehicles, Canstatt-Daimlers and de Dion-Boutons, with English name plates. The first wholly British four-wheeler was Frederick Lanchester's, which made its trial run in February 1896.

These developments were in anticipation of a change in the traffic laws, the result of an agitation led by two aristocratic motoring enthusiasts, the Hon. Evelyn Ellis and Sir David Salomons, and their Self-Propelled Traffic Association. In 1896 the 1865 and 1878 Acts were repealed and the speed limit for road locomotives raised from 4 m.p.h. to '14 m.p.h. or less than this as the Local Government Board may decide'. As finally determined by the Board, the maximum speeds for vehicles of varying weights were: under $1\frac{1}{2}$ tons, 12 m.p.h.; $1\frac{1}{2}$–2 tons, 8 m.p.h.; over 2 tons, 5 m.p.h. With his usual showmanship Harry J. Lawson organized the first London to Brighton run, ostensibly to celebrate the liberation of the motor car but really to advertise his companies' automobiles. Lawson tried to do for the motor car what George Hudson did for the railway, become king of the new transport revolution. Fortunately for the British motor industry, he did not succeed. Although the English Daimler Company went on under other management to earn its reputation for quality cars, the Lawson empire, after his patents were defeated in the courts in 1903, declined and broke up.

The collapse of his monopoly, and the further raising of the speed limit to 20 m.p.h. in 1904, brought a flood of British car manufacturers into the field. Many of them were cycle manufacturers, with names which became famous automobile marques: Ariel, Humber, Morgan, Riley, Rover, Sunbeam, Swift, Triumph, and so on. Most of their products were tricars and quadricycles, lightly built on tubular frames, leading to the so-called 'cyclecars' of the 1910s. Britain's lead in cycle manufacture had also benefitted accessory makers who were to become vital to the motor industry, notably the Lucas Company, pioneers of cycle lamps, who were to achieve a near-monopoly of automobile electrical equipment, and J. B. Dunlop, re-inventor in

1888 of the pneumatic tyre, though he resisted its application to motor cars until it had been proved by the Michelin brothers in France.

Other motor cars were built by general machine makers and foundries, and tended to be large and more imposing vehicles called voiturettes. Herbert Austin produced the first Wolseley car for the Wolseley Sheep-Shearing Machine Co. of Birmingham in 1901, and built up a thriving business for them before starting up on his own with the Austin 10 in 1911, the herald of motoring for the masses. The Vauxhall voiturette of 1901 was made by the iron foundry of that name. At the larger end of this group were the high-performance luxury cars stemming from the perfectionist tradition of Frederick Lanchester: the Clement-Talbot, later the Talbot, built to French designs by a company financed by the Earl of Shrewsbury and Talbot; the Crossley, based on the Mercedes developed by Daimler's assistant Maybach (named after the daughter of the Daimler representative on the French Riviera, Mercédès Jellinek); the Napier, developed from the Panhard-Levassor by Montagu Napier for S. F. Edge, Dunlop's London manager; and the Lanchester itself, brought to a high standard in the first production model of 1900.

There were in fact two separate lines of evolution of the motor car, for two distinct social markets, although some manufacturers like Austin and Rover might cross over from one to the other. One was the luxury car for the rich, a superb hand-made vehicle built for high performance and comfort. The other was the light car built for economy rather than convenience and, potentially at least, for the mass market. On the Continent, where only the rich could afford automobiles, luxury makes like the Mercedes, the Panhard-Levassor and the Hispano-Suiza predominated. In America until about 1908 the luxury car predominated, but a vast and scattered public was increasingly able and willing to pay for their own personal transport and the mass-produced car soon won the day – the Oldsmobile, the

Chevrolet, above all the Model-T Ford, over fifteen million of which sold between 1910 and 1926 – though with their wide open spaces the Americans always preferred a large, big-engined cheap car to the baby car of the European mass market. In Britain, socially half-way between Europe and America, with a rich and pleasure-loving plutocracy led in the early years of this century by a motoring enthusiast king and two motoring prime ministers, Salisbury and Balfour, and with a wide and solid middle class of prosperous business and professional men, there was room for both markets. Hilaire Belloc satirized them in 'The Garden Party':

> The rich arrived in pairs
>   And also in Rolls-Royces;
> They talked of their affairs
>   In loud and strident voices.

> The poor arrived in Fords,
>   Whose features they resembled;
> They laughed to see so many Lords
>   And Ladies all assembled.

Two famous British pioneers of the motor industry epitomized these two markets, F. H. Royce and William Morris.

Both Royce and Morris were self-taught engineers of humble origin who rose in the traditional way by their native ability to great wealth. Frederick Henry Royce was the son of an unsuccessful miller and began life as a newspaper boy and telegraph messenger before his uncompleted apprenticeship at the Great Northern Railway works at Peterborough and jobs at the Electric Light and Power Company in London and Liverpool. Out of work at the age of twenty-one in 1884, he set up a partnership in a back-street workshop in Manchester, making lamp-holders and filaments, an electric bell of his own design and, eventually, high-quality dynamos and electric cranes. During a slump in the electrical engineering market due to foreign competition, he amused himself by improving a second-hand

Decauville and finally built a two-cylinder car of his own, which made its first trial run in 1904, and then two more for his partners. The new third partner, Henry Edmunds, a motoring enthusiast and member of the Automobile Club committee, showed his car to his London friends, Claude Johnson and the Hon. Charles Rolls, son of Lord Llangattock and winner of the AA Thousand Miles Trial in 1900. They were so impressed by its quietness, smoothness and pulling power that they went into partnership with Royce to produce and sell it commercially.

Rolls-Royce cars were an immediate success, making the fastest non-stop run at the 1905 Manx Touring Trophy race and winning outright in 1906, and making a record time from Monte Carlo to London in 1905 at over 27 m.p.h. More important, they soon established themselves as the quietest, smoothest and most reliable cars on the market. By 1907 the company had evolved the ultimate car for silence and reliability, the Silver Ghost. The company settled down to produce this one model, which sold substantially unchanged for nineteen years – longer than the Model-T Ford – and claimed it as the best car in the world. It sold to monarchs and millionaires, sheiks and maharajahs, as well as to lesser mortals with money to spare for perfection in personal travel or for keeping up with the Joneses. Meanwhile, both Rolls and Royce took up the new cult of flying. Rolls was the first man to fly both ways across the Channel, before meeting his death in a competition at Bournemouth in 1910 at the age of thirty-three. Royce designed aero-engines for the war-planes of the First World War, from which a new Rolls-Royce Company was born, ultimately to outgrow the car manufacturing business.

The eldest son of a farm bailiff near Oxford, William Morris in 1893 at the age of fifteen was forced by his father's illness to go out to work to help support a family of five. He began work as an assistant to a bicycle repairer, but set up on his own at the age of sixteen on a capital of £5, repairing and soon making custom-built bicycles. He graduated via motor cycles to selling, repairing and hiring out motor cars. In 1910 he began to work on the designs for a car. His aim was to manufacture a cheap, mass-produced, popular, all-British car to compete with the Model-T Fords which from 1910 began to be assembled at Ford's subsidiary at Old Trafford, Manchester. As far as possible, he emulated Ford's methods: until the latter revolutionized production all motor cars had been made as individual machines, one at a time. Ford first of all introduced batch production, the production of cars in groups on a large factory floor, with specialized mechanics moving from one to the next. When Morris began, Ford had not yet invented the assembly line, which was to become the main basis of twentieth-century mass production. The advantage of batch production was the cheapness with which large numbers of constituent parts could be made if manufactured by specialist workers doing nothing else. Morris's genius was for persuading sub-contractors that they could make a handsome profit by volume production at what seemed impossibly low prices. Thus the engine might be halved in price (from £50 to £25) if it could be made in quantities of fifty or more a week. This system became responsible for the subdivision of the motor industry into hundreds of component manufacturers.

His first model, the Morris Oxford (8·9 horse-power, weighing 12½ cwt, and capable of 55 m.p.h. and petrol consumption of 50 miles to the gallon) appeared at the Motor Show in 1912. Hitherto most cars of this size and performance had cost £250 to £400. The two-seater Oxford retailed at £165. Though not the cheapest car on the market, it was so successful that Morris obtained orders for 400, and immediately leased the old Military Academy at Cowley near Oxford and planned to produce 1,500 cars a year. He did not achieve this, quite, in 1914, mainly because of the war when he switched to the mass production of howitzer bomb-cases, but he had laid the foundations of British mass production of motor cars.

Morris was not the only manufacturer of cars for the mass or, strictly, the middle-class market. In 1914 there were no less than seventy different light cars on the British market, plus a large number of cyclecars. When registration of cars began in 1904 there were 17,810 vehicles on the road, under half of them cars. By 1914 there were 354,232, including 122,035 cars and 118,045 motor cycles. This was fewer relative to population than in the United States, where Ford, General Motors, Willys-Overland and other producers were turning cars out by the thousand, but it was more than on the Continent where the large touring car still predominated. In the space of twenty years Britain had regained the lost ground over its Continental rivals.

Typical of the new middle-class market was the country doctor who wanted a means of transport faster and more reliable than the pony and trap. Hugh Tracey's father in *Father's First Car* was a West Country doctor whose wife brought him a modest fortune which enabled him to buy a 10–12 horse power Peugeot as early as 1907. It was the first car in the district and caused a sensation. He wrote to his wife: 'I am just wild with delight. This car is an event in our life and I am sure we will enjoy it amazingly.' The salesman had told him it would do 20 miles to the gallon of petrol at 1s. 4d. a gallon, the tyres would last 8,000 miles, the driver's licences for himself and Gunner, his erstwhile groom turned chauffeur, cost 5s. each, the car licence £2 10s. and insurance £10. Ignoring depreciation, he calculated that the savings on horses, dog-cart, harness and fodder would leave him a handsome profit. With great delight he and various members of his large family of eleven children rushed around the deep lanes of Devon at speeds up to 40 m.p.h. (the speed limit was 20 m.p.h.), and he christened it Bird because it flew like one.

Then his troubles, so typical of early motoring, began. The tyres burst with alarming regularity. The fuel system sprang secret leaks, and consumption deteriorated to 6 miles per gallon. The sprockets taking the chain drive to the rear axle broke, gear cogs broke off, the magneto refused to spark, the brakes bound, tappets burnt clean off and, last indignity, the car occasionally had to be towed home by flesh-and-blood horse power. Worst of all, the groom-chauffeur's subconscious seems to have taken against mechanical contraptions: he forgot to grease vital parts, backed into gate posts and even forgot to put water in the engine so that the cylinder block got red-hot and cracked. So often was it off the road that the doctor bought a second car, stoically another Peugeot, a 'baby' 8 horse-power two-seater Victoria called Puffy, which also gave trouble. But he never despaired. After enormous expenses on 'mechanicians' from London and Bristol, and a great deal of crude patchwork by the local blacksmith and carpenter, he got Bird back to 20 miles per gallon and 40 m.p.h. and Puffy to climb the steep Devon hills, at least when his wife got out and walked.

The less well-off were not neglected altogether. Their share in the motor vehicle took the form of the motor bus and charabanc. Around the turn of the century there was a general movement to replace the horse bus and tram because of expense, which developed into a considerable rivalry between the electric tram and the electric-battery bus, the steambus and the motor bus. The electric tram won hands down where the traffic warranted investment in lines and overhead wires, and its competition forced the London Underground railways to speed up their electrification programme. Power-driven buses were to offer even stiffer competition, and when they came into general use no more tube railways were built for half a century. The North West London tube, authorized in 1899, was never built. Each bus had it devotees and for a long time it was by no means certain which of them would win. The electric-battery bus was the first in the field, with experiments in London in 1889 and Liverpool in 1894, but its short range was against its general introduction. Steam buses were tried in London from 1899, and the Thornycroft steamer introduced in 1902 met with some short-lived success. The first motor buses, which began in Edinburgh, Llandudno, Torquay and elsewhere in 1898, were really minibuses, open 'wagonettes' or converted motor cars, chiefly Daimlers, which carried too few passengers to pay their way. The first purpose-built motor bus was a Straker-Squire which Lawson's Motor Traction Company ran between Kennington Park and Victoria from October 1899 to December 1900. But at the beginning of 1905 there were still only twenty motor buses in London. What emancipated the motor bus was an Order of 1904 under the 1903 Act, which raised the maximum unladen weight of heavy vehicles to 5 tons and their maximum speed, if rubber-tyred, to 12 m.p.h. The 'bus boom' of 1905 marked the turning point. In London new motor bus companies were floated, and the horse-bus companies *en bloc* began to turn over to motor traction. By September 124 London motor buses were in operation. By 1908 there were 1,066 mechanical buses in London, 1,015 driven by petrol, thirty-five by steam, fifteen battery-electric and one petrol-electric. It was the B-type bus introduced in 1910 which finally decided the issue. A reliable, hard-wearing, open-topped double decker, it soon surpassed all its rivals and drove the horse bus out of service. In the First World War over a thousand of them were used in France to carry troops up to the front line.

Heavy goods vehicles were also liberated by the 1896 and 1903 Acts. At first steam, with the long tradition of traction engines behind it, took the lead, and well-known firms like Thornycroft, Foden and Lifu (the Liquid Fuel Company) built steam lorries for the new market. The Thornycrofts were praised by Lord Kitchener for their work in South Africa in the Boer War, and later developed into the famous 'Sentinel' of the 1930s which could cruise at 50 m.p.h. But the internal combustion engine soon won in this field as it had done in private motoring and bus transport. Thornycroft began to make petrol-engined lorries and private cars in 1903, and in the following year the Lancashire Steam Co., which had developed out of a small agricultural engineering firm at Leyland bought by the enterprising James Sumner in 1892, began to make the petrol lorries and bus

47

chassis which were to make the name Leyland famous through-out the world. Over 5,000 Leyland three-tonners were supplied to the forces during the First World War. By then the motor lorry was a reliable and moderately economical vehicle which would emerge from the War ready to challenge the railways for the cream of the goods traffic. Its final triumph was due to another German invention, as brilliant as Daimler's and Benz's, the sparkless, high-compression, heavy-oil engine of Rudolf Diesel, developed in association with Krupps of Essen in 1897, which increased the pulling power and reduced the fuel costs of the heavy transport engine.

The diesel engine was to play its part in the replacement of steam on the railways, mostly after the Second World War. It was also to play a part in marine transport: the first large ship to be powered by it, the *Selandia*, was launched at Copenhagen in 1912. But before the War motor ships were a rarity, and even oil-burning steam-ships uncommon. Britain still built 60% of the world's shipping, and the vast majority were still tradi-tional coal-burning, steam piston-engined ships. Things were changing, however, even in this conservative field. The steam turbine, patented in 1884 by Sir Charles Parsons, the last of the great Victorian engineering geniuses, for electricity generation, was fitted to a small ship, the *Turbinia*, which displayed its marvellous turn of speed and manoeuvrability at the Diamond Jubilee naval review at Spithead in 1897. Combined with oil-fired boilers it was the answer to the Navy's need for high-speed battleships independent of the grimy, labour- and time-consum-ing process of coaling. The *Dreadnought*, the first of the new class of giant, turbine-driven capital ships, was launched in 1906, and instantly rendered all previous warships obsolete. In its oil-burning form, in the five *Queen Elizabeths* of the Fast Division of the 1912–14 programme, its also gave the Admiralty an interest in acquiring its own source of oil, which it did when the British government became the major shareholder in the Anglo-Persian Oil Company in 1913.

Oil, the universal fuel of the automobile age as coal was of the railway age, was by then becoming big business. The industry only began in 1850 when James Young, a Glasgow chemist, extracted crude paraffin from oil seepages from the Derbyshire coal measures. The first well was sunk by the self-styled 'Colonel' Drake amongst the oil springs at Oil Creek, Pennsylvania in 1859. Although mainly used for lighting and heating, it was so convenient and portable a fuel that it led to a scramble by prospectors and by large capitalists to control its production and transport. John D. Rockefeller's building of the first great oil trust, Standard Oil, in the 1880s, the creation of Mexican-Eagle and Anglo-Mexican Petroleum by Weetman Pearson, first Viscount Cowdray, and the machinations of the Paris house of Rothschild, Royal Dutch and Shell in Rumania and the Caucasus are classic sagas of modern finance capitalism. By 1914 the big international oil companies were already a new and powerful force in the world economy and international politics.

One vast potential market for the oil industry was to be aviation. The internal combustion engine, with its compact size, high speed of rotation and high power-to-weight ratio, was even more vital to heavier-than-air flight than it was to mechanical road transport. Men's dreams of flying go back to Icarus and the mythical pre-history of the Greeks, the ancient Chinese man-lifting kite, and the fourteenth-century European windmill toy or string-pull helicopter. Leonardo da Vinci designed cumbersome ornithopters, machines imitating birds, but incapable of flight. But the origins of modern flight go back to Sir George Cayley, a scientifically minded Yorkshire landowner who between 1799 and 1809 worked out the aerodynamics and flight control of fixed wing aircraft and designed and built the first working model aeroplanes. Like all his nineteenth-century successors, du Temple (c. 1857), Mozhaiski (1884), Phillips (1884 and 1891), Ader (1890) and others who built full-sized machines mostly driven by steam, he was defeated by lack of a sufficiently light and powerful engine. Cayley experimented with hot-air and gunpowder engines, and correctly forecast that internal combustion, in the form then of the gas engine, would be the solution to the problem.

F. W. Lanchester, who designed and built the first all-British car in 1896, also made an important contribution to the theory of flight. In 1892 he began to experiment with model gliders, one of them powered by an elastic motor, and within two years announced his vortex or circulation theory of sustaining a fixed wing in flight. His papers, however, were couched in obscure language, and although the Royal Aeronautical Society in 1909 was to claim that 'his two books form the foundation of flight as we know it', his work had no effect on the first aeroplane flights.

It was the American brothers, Orville and Wilbur Wright, who applied the new internal combustion engine to their already successful gliders. On 17 December 1903 at Kill Devil Hills near Dayton, Ohio, they made two flights of twelve and fifty-nine seconds respectively, and in 1904 more than eighty brief flights, including one of over five minutes. In 1905, in Flyer III, the world's first practical powered aircraft, they finally mastered the art of controlled flying, with flights of over half an hour, including banking, turning, circles and figures of eight. Their success stimulated emulators, notably Farman, Voisin, Delagrange, Santos-Dumont and Blériot in France, to make the first flights in Europe in 1908. Henri Farman, son of an English father, made the first true flight of over one minute, but Britain was well behind in the race, and the first flight here was made in October 1908 by an expatriate American, S. F. Cody, working for the British Army. The first Briton to make a powered flight was J. T. C. Moore-Brabazon, later Lord Brabazon, who flew a Voisin a distance of 200 metres at Issy in France in December 1908. Soon other British pioneers came on the scene: A. V. Roe, whose triplanes made short hops in 1909; the Hon. Charles Rolls, Royce's partner, who in October 1909 flew a Wright biplane built under licence by Short Brothers before becoming the first English pilot to be killed, at Bournemouth in 1910; Frederick Handley Page, who built his first, successful, *Blue Bird* in 1909; Geoffrey de Havilland, who migrated from motor cars to become the first aircraft designer to the government factory at Farnborough in 1910; and T. O. M. Sopwith, the future designer with Harry Hawker of fighter planes.

A. V. Roe, Short Brothers, Rolls-Royce, Handley Page, de Havilland and Hawker were all to become famous names in aircraft production, but before the War Britain was conscious of lagging behind in a race which it would be not merely humiliating but dangerous to lose. Blériot's flight across the Channel in July 1909 had the same impact on the British that the first Russian Sputnik in 1957 had on the Americans. According to H. G. Wells, writing in the *Daily Mail*, it had two meanings. The first, 'unpalatable enough to our national pride', was that like the motor car it had been made abroad, and that 'the world cannot wait for the English . . . Either we are a people essentially and incurably inferior, or there is something wrong with our training, something benumbing in our atmosphere and circumstances . . . The second is that, in spite of our fleet, this is no longer, from the military point of view, an inaccessible island.' Unfortunately the armed forces, impressed by the success since 1900 of Count von Zeppelin's airships, were obsessed with lighter-than-air flight, and the Committee on Imperial Defence reported in 1909 in favour of allocating £45,000 to airship building and of cutting off the meagre £2,000 spent at Farnborough on aeroplane development. In the Cabinet, however, Lloyd George and Churchill were more realistic; the technical success of heavier-than-air craft at the first air show at Rheims later in 1909 impressed the military men, and the government in 1911 began to invest seriously in aircraft research and development. The Royal Flying Corps was founded in 1912, and stimulated the production of the Avro, Sopwith and other prototypes of the First World War scout and fighter planes. Early in 1914 a Sopwith Tabloid won the second Schneider trophy speed contest, and Britain was back in the race, just in time. But before the War aviation, with the possible exception of the German Zeppelins which between 1910 and 1914 carried 35,000 passengers 170,000 miles, was of no commercial importance and its effect on society still lay in the future.

Another technological triumph of immediate importance to war and aviation was wireless telegraphy. Derived from Clerk-Maxwell's discovery at Cambridge of electro-magnetic radiation in the 1870s, it was successfully developed in Italy in 1895 by Guglielmo Marconi who, transferring his main activity to Britain, established for the Post Office a link from the Kent mainland to the South Goodwin lightship in 1900 and from Cornwall to Newfoundland in 1903. The Royal Navy and many shipping companies equipped their bigger ships with wireless, and the government entered into a contract in 1912 with the Marconi Company to set up a chain of wireless telegraph stations throughout the Empire. By 1914 the Navy was equipped and the Royal Flying Corps was experimenting with the wireless telegraph, which was to play a vital part in the War. Although the American, Reginald Fessenden, had broadcast speech as early as 1900, however, and Sir Ambrose Fleming and another American, Lee de Forest, had developed the electronic valves which made modern radio possible, public broadcasting was to wait until after the War.

Meanwhile, the motor car itself in the last years before the War became aggressive and importunate enough to make itself an important political issue. The growth in the number of vehicles to more than a third of a million, and the rise in fatal accidents from 373 in 1909 to 1,329 in 1914, made it a problem for everybody, but a benefit only to a selfish minority. As Masterman put it in 1909:

Wandering machines, travelling with an incredible rate of speed, scramble and smash and shriek along all the rural ways. You can see them on a Sunday afternoon, piled 20 or 30 deep outside the new popular inns, while their occupants regale themselves within. You can see evidence of their activity in the dust-laden hedges of the south country roads, a grey mud colour, with no evidence of green; in the ruined cottage gardens of the south country villages.

A handbill distributed in Fulham the year before told the 'Men of England':

> Your birthright is being taken from you by reckless motor drivers . . . Reckless motorists drive over and kill your children . . . Men of England . . . rise up, join together, and bring pressure on your representatives in Parliament, and otherwise make it unpleasant and costly to the tyrants who endanger your lives and the lives of your dear ones.

The motorists for their part demanded road improvements, tar spraying to lay the dust, and the abolition of the speed limit of 20 m.p.h. imposed by the 1903 Act as unnecessary and impossible to enforce without 'unfair' police methods. On the first the *Economist* commented in 1908: 'Here public expenditure is calmly suggested in order to please the richest class of pleasure seekers.' The country was coming to be divided into two nations – not simply Disraeli's rich and poor, since many of the carriage classes and especially the rural magistrates were against the motor car, but into motorists and anti-motorists.

The more intelligent motorists like Charles Rolls, Claude Johnson and the leading figures of the (Royal) Automobile Club, founded in 1897, argued that cars had come to stay, and that the proper course was to make them safe for the roads and the roads safe for traffic. But the RAC was a small, select group, and there was a much more impatient and aggressive motoring lobby in its much larger offshoot, the Motor Union, established in 1907, which parted company with the parent body in 1907 and merged in 1910 with the equally aggressive Automobile Association of 1905. Both the MU and the AA flatly opposed all legislative restrictions on the motorist, the latter especially frustrating the law by means of such malpractices as employing scouts on bicycles to warn motorists of police speed-traps. The speed-traps and the harsh penalties meted out to motorists by magistrates in some counties such as Surrey and Sussex led to a feud between the AA and the Home Office, in which the 'association of burglars' complained of 'mean persecution' of their scouts by the police. The anti-motoring lobby in Parliament, led by J. F. R. Remnant, asked why the AA scouts were allowed to use the roads 'for the purpose of interfering with the police and preventing them from carrying out the law with regard to motor traffic and so safeguarding the lives and liberties of the poor members of our population?'

The difficulty was that not only Parliament and the public but the government and the Home Office itself were divided in their attitude to the motorist. F. L. D. Elliott, an influential Home Office official and motoring enthusiast, himself an AA member, pointed out in 1909 that the Lord Chancellor, the Lord Chief Justice, both Law Officers, five members of the government, the leader of the opposition, and many bishops and chief constables were members of the AA, which was not 'a mere selfish conspiracy of law-breakers'. The *Economist* on the other hand complained in 1913 that: 'The vehicles of the rich kill and maim far more people than the vehicles of the poor . . . But then nearly all politicians and officials constantly drive at an excessive speed themselves.'

Despite a Select Committee on Motor Traffic in 1913 to amend the 1903 Act, nothing further was done before the War either to restrict or to liberate the motor car. The only exception to this was the motor taxation clauses of the 1909 Budget already noticed, which despite the anti-motoring speeches of Lloyd George and the protests of the motoring lobby represented a compromise between the conflicting interests. Indeed, they constituted a bargain between government and a particular section of taxpayers of doubtful constitutional propriety, which subsequent governments came to regret. In return for acceptance of the new motor taxes – a tax on imported oil of 3d. a gallon (with a 50% rebate for commercial vehicles) and a tax on horsepower rising from £3 a year on 6½–12 h.p. to £42 on over 60 h.p. – the net proceeds, deducting the old vehicle tax and the cost of collection, were to be spent on the roads. As a guarantee, the money would be paid into a Road Fund adminis- tered by the Road Board, set up under the chairmanship of Sir George Gibb, a former railway director, in 1910. Lloyd George's so-called 'pledge', misinterpreted to mean that not only the 1909 taxes but all future motor taxation should be spent on roads, was seized on by the motoring organizations to embarrass later chancellors of the exchequer.

The Road Fund temporarily solved the road problem. Most of the money was spent via grants to local authorities in replacing the old water-bound macadam surfaces of the existing roads, dusty in summer and muddy in winter, by tar macadam. With the dust and mud the complaints of pedestrians, cyclists, farmers and local authorities subsided. But the motor car was a prolific animal and was multiplying apace. It could only be a matter of time before it outgrew the existing road system and demanded living space commensurate with its numbers.

FURTHER READING

St J. C. Nixon, *The Invention of the Automobile* (Country Life, 1936)

D. St J. Thomas, *The Motor Revolution* (Longmans, 1969)

Anthony Bird, *The Motor Car, 1765–1914* (Batsford, 1960); and *Roads and Vehicles* (Longmans, 1969)

L. T. C. Rolt, *Horseless Carriage* (Constable, 1950); and *A Picture History of Motoring* (Hulton, 1956)

C. F. Caunter, *The Light Car: a technical history; Motor Cycles: a technical history;* and *The History and Development of Cycles* (Science Museum, 1970, 1970 and 1955)

C. St C. B. Davison, *History of Steam Road Vehicles* (Science Museum, 1970)

Allan Nevins, *Ford: The Times, the Man and the Company* (Scribner's, New York, 1954)

Harold Nockolds, *The Magic of a Name* (Rolls-Royce) (Foulis, 1961)

P. W. S. Andrews and Elizabeth Brunner, *Life of Lord Nuffield* (Blackwell, 1955)

D. J. Trussler, *Early Buses and Trams* (Evelyn, 1964)

John Hibbs, *A History of British Bus Services* (David & Charles, 1968)

E. L. Cornwell, *Commercial Vehicles* (Batsford, 1960)

C. H. Gibbs-Smith, *Aviation: an historical survey from its origins to the end of World War II* (Science Museum, 1970)

William Plowden, *The Motor Car and Politics, 1896–1970* (Bodley Head, 1971)

H. J. Dyos and D. H. Aldcroft, *British Transport: An Economic Survey from the Seventeenth to the Twentieth Century* (Leicester University Press, 1971)

Hugh Tracey, *Father's First Car* (Routledge, 1966)

T. C. Barker and Michael Robbins, *A History of London Transport* Vol. II, *The Twentieth Century to 1970* (Allen & Unwin, 1974)

3. ENGINES OF WAR

In the first week of August 1914, when most British people were enjoying the glorious summer weather, the second most destructive war in history suddenly broke out. The immediate cause was casual, even trivial. The Archduke Franz Ferdinand, Habsburg heir to the Austro-Hungarian Empire, and his morganatic wife – prevented by her low breeding as a mere countess from appearing at most public occasions – were inspecting the Imperial army at Sarajevo, the capital of the province of Bosnia on the borders of Serbia, on 28 June when a Serbian schoolboy, full of southern Slav nationalism, stepped on to the running board of their motor car and shot them both. By a kind of mad logic which nobody wanted but nobody could stop this gratuitous murder led, through a series of threats, ultimatums, interlocking alliances, formal treaties and tacit understandings, to the first general European war for a century.

The polyglot Austro-Hungarian Empire, threatened by the dissident nationalisms of its subject peoples and their independent relatives outside, had been humiliated time and again for more than half a century by the rival great powers, by France in the cause of Italian unity in 1859, by Prussia in the loss of

Venezia and Holstein in 1866, and by Russia in innumerable incidents in the Balkans, where the latter claimed to be the protector of all the Slav peoples against Austria and Turkey, from the 1870s to the eve of 1914. The Austro-Hungarians were not going to be humiliated again, and certainly not by an upstart Serbia, swollen by gains in the Balkan Wars of 1912 and 1913 at the expense of Turkey and Bulgaria, and apparently now threatening by assassination and revolution to unite all the southern Slavs at the expense of the Habsburg Empire. Armed with the promise of German backing, the Habsburg government issued an ultimatum to Serbia, demanding the rounding up and punishment of the revolutionaries on Serbian soil under Austrian supervision. The Serbian government, thoroughly frightened, accepted all the demands, only substituting international supervision for Austrian, but to show their determination to defend themselves, injudiciously mobilized their troops. The Habsburg government replied on 28 July by declaring war.

Perhaps the declaration was no more than a threat, meant to frighten the Serbs into demobilizing, and then to be withdrawn. But before it could be, it brought Russia into the conflict as defender of the Serbs. Germany, which until now had not taken the crisis seriously – the Kaiser had gone cruising off Norway and General von Moltke, his Chief of Staff, remained on holiday – could not stand aside while the Tsar's troops invaded Austria-Hungary, and on 1 August declared war on Russia. But neither could she deal with Russia while Russia's ally and Germany's arch-enemy France threatened her rear. Moreover, the famous Schlieffen Plan required the German armies to destroy France first, by outflanking the hilly and heavily fortified Lorraine frontier and invading the much more vulnerable northern plain through Belgium. On the same night, therefore, the German armies seized Luxembourg and its vital rail junctions, and the following day demanded free passage through Belgium. The Belgian government refused, in courageous terms. The Germans invaded, and only then, on 3 August, declared war on France.

The invasion of Belgium brought Britain into the war. Sir Edward Grey, the Foreign Secretary, had tried valiantly to avert open conflict by diplomatic appeals and by a scheme for a general conference of the great powers. Half the cabinet were against Britain taking part, in spite of her tacit commitments to France, including the naval defence of the latter's Atlantic and Channel ports in case of a German attack. Germany, over-impressed by Britain's internal troubles, with the trade unions, the militant suffragettes and the seeming threat of civil war in Ireland, may have hoped that she would stand aside, and even offered a guarantee not to attack the French coast from the sea – though this was probably due more to over-confidence in a swift victory on land – but at bottom the German generals were contemptuous of Britain's capacity to intervene effectively on the Continent. 'Gallant little Belgium' tipped the scales, both in the cabinet and in Britain at large. Heedless of the consequences, the German government ignored Britain's ultimatum to quit Belgium, and at midnight on 4 August Britain was at war.

Other countries were drawn in by the same mixture of accident and supposed vital interest or windfall opportunity: Japan (August 1914) by the chance of seizing German holdings in China; Turkey (November 1914) by her enmity and fear of Russia; Italy (May 1915) by hatred of Austria and the desire to free the last remnants of Italian soil still under Habsburg domination; Bulgaria (October 1915) by revenge on Serbia for the losses of the Second Balkan War; Egypt (from the entry of Turkey) and Greece (June 1916) by the uninvited presence of Allied forces; the United States (April 1917) by the intensification of the German submarine campaign; and Rumania (August 1917) by the, as it transpired, abortive hope of gains from Austria-Hungary and Bulgaria. The inexorable logic of alliance, self-interest and fear of loss pulled into the hostilities all the great powers and a great many smaller ones, together with all their many colonies, and touched at every point the life and welfare of the neutral states.

In many ways it was a more shocking war than the Second, and a greater turning point in world history: more unexpected after four generations of peace or small-scale conflict, more blood-stirring in its enthusiasms and hopes, more mind-numbing in the magnitude and senselessness of its slaughter in the field, more disenchanting as the machine guns and howitzers took the glamour out of merely human courage, more wearying as the warfare of blockade and attrition brought hunger and disease, sometimes near the point of starvation and epidemic, to the civilian populations far from the battle fronts, and above all more obliterative of the old political entities and landmarks of an earlier age. The war utterly destroyed four of the most powerful empires and most ancient monarchies, Tsarist Russia, Habsburg Austria-Hungary, Hohenzollern Germany and (by 1922) Ottoman Turkey, and left in their place a hotch-potch of unstable successor states whose ideological and territorial rivalries could not be settled without further war and revolution. And it was all the more shocking because, unlike the Second World War, it was so accidental and unnecessary.

There were, of course, deeper causes which historians, rational men in search of rationality, have preferred to the accidental and impulsive: the French *revanchissement* for Alsace-Lorraine and the German fear of that revenge; the nationalisms of south-eastern Europe and the Austrian and Turkish repression of them, aggravated by fear of Russian opportunism; the Anglo-German naval arms race in ever larger, faster, bigger-gunned battleships, the deadly symbols of Germany's demand for a place in the sun and Britain's fear of domestic starvation and the threat to the British Empire. But these were insufficient causes which, but for the accident of Sarajevo, would not have come into operation. It was a useless, unnecessary war, and in that strict sense irrational.

It was also the first mechanized war. The American Civil

War had shown the destructive power of the machine gun and the explosive shell. The Boer War had introduced the armoured train and even an armoured road vehicle (a Fowler steam tractor hauling armoured waggons). The First World War was the first to pit self-propelled fighting machines of vast power and size against the flesh and blood of men and horses, the first in which the issue was decided by factory-made engines of war. Amongst these pride of place must go to the monster of the pre-war arms race, the largest engine of war – though by no means the most destructive – ever built by man, the super-dreadnought battleship. In its final form in the last British battleships launched for the War the super-dreadnought displaced over 27,000 tons, wore armour-plate up to thirteen inches thick, could steam with its oil-burning turbines at twenty-five knots, and carried eight fifteen-inch guns each of which could sling a shell weighing nearly a ton a distance of more than twenty miles. With five of these monsters outgunning anything on the German side and a British superiority of sixty-five to thirty-eight in battleships and battlecruisers, it is small wonder that, with the exception of a day at the Dogger Bank, 15–16 December 1914, and another at the Battle of Jutland, 31 May 1916, the German High Seas Fleet preferred to stay at home behind its minefields in the Heligoland Bight. Apart from a few German commerce raiders, all but one sunk, captured or interned by Christmas 1914 (the cruiser *Dresden* escaped from the battle of the Falkland Islands, 7 December 1914, to be sunk three months later), the only way that Germany could challenge the British blockade and attack the Allied merchant ships on which the survival of Britain and the prosecution of the War depended was by the hidden weapon of the submarine.

There were many other naval engines of war, some 4,000 of them on the British side, from light cruisers through destroyers and torpedo boats to the little trawlers and drifters which swept mines and manned the anti-submarine nets of the Dover patrol. The only one which came near to being decisive was the submarine, invented by the Americans Holland and Lake about 1900. Though it had a longer prehistory than the motor car, going back to the Dutchman Drebbel in 1620, the submarine was just as dependent for its practical success on the internal combustion engine, to drive the submarine on the surface and to charge the electric batteries for underwater propulsion.

At first the submarine was a mere auxiliary weapon, a short-range, submerged torpedo boat for coastal defence and fleet harrying in the narrow seas. Here, as in other naval vessels, Britain had at the start of the war a superiority of seventy-four, plus thirty-one building, to thirty-three plus twenty-eight. The U-boat was rightly feared by the Royal Navy as the invisible trap into which the German Fleet would inevitably try to lure the Grand Fleet in any pursuit. This was the fear which dogged Admiral Jellicoe throughout his command, and which robbed him of his opportunity of destroying the High Seas Fleet on the one occasion when he had it within arm's length, at Jutland. But in this it was only a somewhat more insidious extension of normal naval tactics, like the screen of destroyers, surface torpedo boats and other craft with which all battle squadrons operated, and probably less effective than mines, which were an equally important factor to be taken into account in any fleet action.

It was the Royal Navy's supremacy which forced Germany to turn the submarine into a major weapon of war. If Britain ruled the waves, then the German Navy could challenge her only beneath the waves. Germany set about building a massive fleet of ocean-going submarines, over 200 of them by 1917, able to survive for a month away from base, including the long passage round the north of Scotland, more if replenished from a disguised 'mother ship' or a neutral port. They enabled the German Navy to harry Allied commerce in the Atlantic approaches and to dream of ending the war by a counter-blockade which would starve Britain of food and war materials and bring the Allies to their knees. This in 1917 it very nearly did. In the second quarter of 1917 Allied shipping losses were running at half a million tons a month, about three times the rate of replacement, and at that rate would have driven Britain out of the war within twelve months. But the U-boat was less unanswerable than the Germans thought. The convoy system, introduced at Prime Minister Lloyd George's insistence against the wishes of the admirals, reduced the losses within tolerable limits, and mines, depth charges, anti-submarine nets and gunfire from armed merchant ships and 'Q-ships' (gunboats disguised as unarmed merchantmen) turned the hunter into the hunted. Moreover, the U-boat was a double-edged weapon, which hurt the attacker more than his prey, and helped to lose him the war. Since its main strategem was surprise, and it could not follow the traditional seafaring code of capturing ships and rescuing their inmates, it could only be used indiscriminately against enemies and neutrals alike and without quarter to civilian crews and passengers. This inevitably brought the one remaining great power, the United States, into the balance against Germany, just in time to counter the loss to the Allied cause of Tsarist Russia. Whether the United States contributed decisively to the Allied victory in a material sense may be debated, since the American army did not appear in the field as an organized force until within twelve weeks of the end of the War, but the moral effect on the Allies in 1917 at the nadir of their fortunes and on the Germans in 1918 at the end of their tether cannot be doubted. The U-boat was a decisive weapon – for the other side.

War in the air had been prophesied ever since Francesco de Lana in 1670, urgently in the years before 1914 by H. G. Wells and others, and aerial bombardment of British cities had become a practical possibility from the moment that Blériot flew the Channel in 1909. The Germans believed that they had a terrifying engine of war in the Zeppelin airship, which bombed Antwerp in the opening days of their offensive and was capable of bombing London, as it did from April 1915. The Army was responsible for the air defence of Britain but sent all its forty-eight available planes to France to act as scouts and artillery observers over the battlefield. The Naval Air Division had been formed to fly seaplanes in support of the Fleet and the defence of the Channel ports, but Winston Churchill as First Lord of the Admiralty had collected a force of fifty fighter planes to defend naval installations in this country. With these he offered to take over responsibility for home air defence generally, which Lord Kitchener at the War Office reluctantly accepted. The Zeppelin proved to be a vulnerable monster. Naval aircraft destroyed six in the first twelve months, either by incendiary bullets in the air or by bombing in their sheds at Düsseldorf, Cologne, Cuxhaven and Lake Constance. By 1917 they were increasingly replaced by Gotha bombers, which were more difficult to shoot down.

The aeroplane, in spite of the prophecies, did not prove to be more than an auxiliary engine of war. In its first role as a reconnaissance scout and artillery spotter it offered the generals something they had never had before, direct observation of the enemy's dispositions and movements and of the accuracy and effect of long-range bombardment. It became important to monopolize this knowledge by command of the air. But the early plane was an ineffective fighting machine not because, as some romantics believe, opposing airmen were mutually chivalrous, but because it was so slow, unmanoeuvrable and ineffectually armed, with pistols and, later, side firing machine-guns of no great accuracy. Only a forward-firing gun could realize the fighting plane's potential, but this was frustrated by the danger of shooting off the propellor. The British solved the problem in 1914 by putting the propellor at the back of the engine of the two-seat Vickers Gunbus, with a machine-gunner in the forward seat, effective but too slow and cumbersome. The French in April 1915 solved it by firing the machine-gun through the propellor, fitted with metal deflector plates, of a Morane-Saulnier L, which shot down five German planes in three weeks. The Germans found the best solution, with an interrupter gear to synchronize the gun with the propellor, producing 'the Fokker scourge' which gave them domination of the air until the French and British adopted the same device in 1916. In aircraft speed, rate of climb and manoeuvrability, too, the Allied and German air forces leapfrogged each other in the struggle for mastery of the air, which continually oscillated between the two. If anything, the Germans had the better of it for most of the war, producing in the Fokker D.VII (1918) the best all-round fighter, and in the Junkers J.7-10 low-wing monoplanes (1918) the prototype of all the single-winged, unstrutted, all-metal planes ever since. The British, who at first had to rely on French engines, came to excel in engine-building, notably with the Rolls-Royce series, designed by Henry Royce himself, which founded the British leadership in the post-war aero-engine industry.

The importance of air power can be judged from the enormous growth in the numbers of aircraft, on the British side from about 100 in 1914 to 3,300 in 1918, and command of the air certainly played a significant part in the German spring and summer offensives and the final Allied offensive in 1918. It also played an important part in the Austro-German victories in Serbia, Bulgaria and Rumania in 1915 and 1916, and in the Allied counter-offensive in Macedonia in 1918, where fighter-bombers were far more effective than traditional cavalry in harrying an enemy in retreat along mountain roads. They also put panic into the retreating Turks in Palestine and Mesopotamia. But air power was not in itself decisive. It did not destroy the railways which were the key to the defence of the Western front. It did not enable the navies to annihilate each other: there was only one British aircraft in the air at Jutland and that did not find the High Seas Fleet. It certainly could not fulfil the dream of Sir Hugh (later Lord) Trenchard, Commander of the Royal Flying Corps and first Chief of Staff of the Royal Air Force when it was formed in November 1917, that strategic bombing could force an enemy into submission. On the home front bombing was feared but ineffective. In Britain throughout the War some 1,414 people were killed by bombs, in Germany 746, and the effect on the outcome was negligible. Compared with the impact on the nations' health and on war production of the British naval blockade and of the German U-boat campaign, the war in the air was irrelevant.

On and under the sea and in the air war must always be waged by machines, since men cannot survive and fight in these elements without them, and the admirals and air force commanders on both sides were professionally machine-minded. But on land most generals repudiated machinery except for the purpose of carrying the troops and their weapons to the battlefield. Perhaps they thought mechanical aids unsporting, like riding to hounds on a motor bike; they certainly thought them no substitute for the traditional arms, the artillery for the preliminary bombardment to 'soften up' the defence, the infantry for the main assault to punch a hole through the enemy's line, and the aristocratic cavalry – beloved of all the generals, who were aristocrats by training if not by birth – to pour through the gap and exploit the victory. The trouble with this conception of warfare was that it had not kept pace with the weapons themselves, which had become infinitely more effective in defence than in attack. The enormous destruction wreaked by high explosive shells from heavy artillery did not obliterate a well-dug in enemy, but only warned him to reinforce that part of the line. As the bombardment ended, up rose the defenders out of their dug-outs to man the machine-guns which wiped out row upon row of attacking infantrymen, conveniently concentrated in the gaps blasted by the artillery in the barbed wire, before they could reach the defending trenches. One machine-gun cleverly sited could mow down 500 attackers. Even when the bombardment had reduced the trench system to a line of shell holes, the machine-gunners manned the craters. Flesh and blood were no match for this simple hand machine, which might be called the handloom of defensive war.

At this stage the automobile played little or no essential role

5a and b. Engines of War   1. A German biplane flying over a captured British tank. 2. The Battle of the St Quentin Canal, 29 September 1918: British tanks and American troops moving forward. *Photos: Radio Times Hulton Picture Library; Imperial War Museum*

6a. The Home Front   Women mechanics repairing a car, June 1916.
Photo: Radio Times Hulton Picture Library

6b. The Deadlock-breaker   A British tank moves forward past German
prisoners bringing in wounded on the Amiens–Roye road, 10 August
1918. *Photo: Imperial War Museum*

7. The People's Car Motor charabancs at Plymouth about to take
members of the Ancient Order of Foresters on their annual outing to
Dartmoor, 1922. *Photo: Radio Times Hulton Picture Library*

8a. The Baby Car 'Bright Young Things' after the ball in a 1922 Austin 7, November 1923. *Photo: Radio Times Hulton Picture Library*

8b. The Rival Trams were the cheapest form of urban transport and survived down to and beyond the Second World War. *Photo: by kind permission of London Transport*

in warfare. German motor-cycle troops, dismounting to fire their rifles, played a small but effective role in Belgium as scouts and dealt with ominous celerity with opposing cavalry. The Belgians replied with armoured cars, improvised Rolls-Royces hung with boiler plates and fitted with a machine-gun. The same makeshift device, eventually improved by a machine-gun turret, was adopted by the British Navy for the defence of the sea-plane base at Dunkirk, and proved very effective against German motor-cyclists and *Uhlans* (cavalry), until the Germans dug trenches across the roads to hamper their movement, thus turning the mind of Winston Churchill, First Lord of the Admiralty, to a trench-crossing vehicle. Such a 'landship' had been designed by Leonardo da Vinci, and forecast as recently as 1903 by H. G. Wells. Apart from this, the idea of an armoured fighting vehicle, immune from machine-gun bullets and able to cross trenches, was not merely known to the armies on both sides; it had been decisively rejected by every General Staff in the last decade before the War. The Austrians and the Italians had developed effective armoured cars for reconnaissance purposes, but military opinion everywhere rejected the concept of a 'battle wagon' as a primitive device reminiscent of the Assyrian chariot or medieval siege engine, rendered obsolete by modern shellfire.

The motor vehicle did have some acceptable uses in warfare. The car became the usual transport for generals on their front-line inspections. Motor cycles proved a more reliable means of communication on the battlefield than the field telephone, since cables had to be buried nine feet deep to be shell-proof. London buses carried the Expeditionary Force from their rail-heads to the front line at Mons. The famous 'taxis of the Marne' helped General Galliéni's Paris garrison to stem the German onrush in September 1914. But until its closing stage the First World War was a railway war. The railways moved the troops and their weapons and ammunition within marching distance of the front and helped to turn it into a war of attrition. The Western front settled down into a great mutual siege behind vast systems of 'field fortifications', multiple lines of trenches, dug-outs and gun-emplacements, up to seven miles in breadth, stretching over 425 miles from the Belgian coast to the Swiss frontier. If the railways piled up the shells and concentrated the troops for each offensive, they also enabled the defending side to rush reserves to the threatened part of the line, and plug the breach with fresh troops. Every breakthrough cost hundreds of thousands of lives, but even when successful could never be exploited. Before the cavalry could burst through into open country in the classic manner and attack the enemy from behind – a role which in the face of machine-guns or even resolute rifle fire they were totally unfitted for – the railways poured in their shoals of defenders to form a new front line a mile or two further back.

The nature of trench warfare on the Western front has been vividly described by Winston Churchill:

> The anatomy of the battles of Verdun and the Somme was the same. A battlefield had been selected. Around this battlefield walls were built – double, triple, quadruple – of enormous cannon. Behind these railways were constructed to feed them, and mountains of shells were built up. All this was the work of months. Thus the battlefield was completely encircled by thousands of guns of all sizes, and a wide oval space prepared in their midst. Through this awful arena all the divisions of each army, battered ceaselessly by the enveloping artillery, were made to pass in succession, as if they were the teeth of interlocking cog-wheels grinding each other.

The defenders were little better off than the attackers, except that they always inflicted more casualties. This is what the first day of the Somme was like for a German eye-witness (quoted by Churchill):

> At 7.30 a.m. the hurricane of shells ceased as suddenly as it had begun. Our men at once clambered up the steep shafts leading from the dug-outs to daylight and ran singly or in groups to the nearest shell craters. The machine-guns were pulled out of the dug-outs and hurriedly placed into position,

their crews dragging the heavy ammunition boxes up the steps and out to the guns. A rough firing line was thus rapidly established. As soon as in position, a series of extended lines of British infantry were seen moving forward from the British trenches. The first line appeared to continue without end to right and left. It was quickly followed by a second line, then a third and fourth. They came on at a steady pace as if expecting to find nothing alive in the front trenches . . . A few minutes later, when the leading British line was within 100 yards, the rattle of machine gun and rifle fire broke out from the whole line of craters . . . Red rockets sped up into the blue sky as a signal to the artillery, and immediately afterwards a mass of shells from the German batteries in rear tore through the air and burst among the advancing lines. Whole sections seemed to fall, and the rear sections, moving in close order, quickly scattered. The advance rapidly crumpled under this hail of shells and bullets. All along the line men could be seen throwing their arms into the air and collapsing never to move again. Badly wounded rolled about in their agony, and other less severely injured crawled to the nearest shell-hole for shelter . . . The noise of battle became indescribable. The shouting of orders and the shrill British cheers as they charged forward could be heard above the violent and intense fusillade of machine-guns and rifles and bursting bombs, and above the deep thundering of the artillery and the shell explosions. With all this were mingled the moans and groans of the wounded, the cries for help and the last screams of death. Again the extended lines of British infantry broke against the German defence like waves against a cliff, only to be beaten back. It was an amazing spectacle of unexampled gallantry, courage and bull-dog determination on both sides.

On that first day of the Somme offensive, 1 July 1916, the British lost 60,000 men, over 20,000 of them killed and the rest wounded or captured. In the whole month, they lost 171,000 men for a gain of $2\frac{1}{2}$ miles and a German loss of 52,000. In the whole offensive from July to mid-November, the losses by attack and counter-attack were more even: the French and British lost a computed 613,000 men, the Germans an estimated 650,000. This was what a war of attrition meant: buying one

German life at the cost of one British or French, and in an assault two or three attackers were lost for every defender. As Churchill pointed out, attrition even on this scale was not enough: allowing for the fresh yearly drafts of young German conscripts you had to kill, capture or permanently lame at least 700,000 Germans a year before making any progress towards wearing them down – and there was no guarantee that the Allied man-power would not be worn down first. The Allies made five great assaults in the years 1915 to 1917, the French in Champagne and Artois in the spring and summer of 1915 and again in Champagne in the autumn, the British and French on the Somme in summer and autumn 1916, the British at Arras and the French on the Aisne from April to July 1917, and the British at Passchendaele (Ypres) in the autumn and winter of 1917, while the Germans, admittedly engaged until late in 1917 on the Russian front (which, however, never occupied more than a quarter of their troops), made only one, at Verdun in the spring of 1916. This imbalance is reflected in the unequal losses: over the whole war on the Western front the Germans inflicted a loss of 7,644,000 killed, prisoners and wounded on the Allies, the Allies 4,846,000 on the Germans. Attrition worked against the Allies until the German spring and summer offensive of 1918, when 854,000 Germans were lost for 688,000 Allied soldiers, and it is probable that the German defeat owed more to their own attacks than to the counter-offensive of the Allies. Even in the last victorious offensive when vast numbers of prisoners were taken it cost 786,000 Allied losses to kill or capture 943,000 Germans.

Such losses, which meant that more than half the men who entered the line were killed, wounded or captured, could not be sustained without enormous strain on the nations suffering them. This was the first total war, in which almost every man and a large part of the women of the countries involved were drawn into the fighting or the war industries. At first the armies on both sides were flooded with enthusiastic volunteers. The European powers already practised conscription, but Britain was driven to it too by degrees: first under the guise of Lord Derby's scheme, October 1915, by which men 'attested' to be called if needed, and finally by full compulsion in January 1916.

The strain brought one great power to its knees in 1917. The Russians had fought valiantly and at one time came near to overwhelming East Prussia, but they were badly led, except for one general, Brusilov, who scored a notable victory against the Austrians in 1916. Not having the industrial or financial resources for a long war, they were always short of munitions, and the pressure of taxation and conscription became more than even their peasant millions could bear. The Tsarist autocracy only existed to protect the fatherland, and when it miserably failed to do this it collapsed. It was replaced, first by the 'bourgeois liberal' government of Kerensky in March 1917 (February by the old Gregorian calendar), and then in November (the 'October Revolution' by the old calendar) by Lenin and the Bolsheviks. Kerensky was an old-style patriot and still further exhausted Russia and his own political credit by one last, unsuccessful offensive. The Bolsheviks, to ensure their grip on what was left of the country, ended the war on terms very close to capitulation, and at Brest-Litovsk traded vast areas of Russian territory for a breathing space in which to consolidate the revolution.

The French, too, were nearly brought to their knees. The terrible conditions in the front line, the lack of decent food and the continual slaughter ordered by the generals provoked the famous mutinies of April to June 1917. Beginning amongst Russian troops formed out of deserters and prisoners from the compulsory German levies, the 'collective indiscipline' – refusal to reinforce the front line or advance against the German trenches – spread through fifty-four divisions of the French army. Only the prestige of General Pétain, victor of Verdun, who promised improved conditions, and the execution of 423 mutineers and the punishment of 23,000 others, prevented catastrophe. Fortunately, the Germans did not know about it at the time, or they would have attacked the French instead of the British.

Even the British government and people, safe behind the steel walls of the Navy, felt the strain. After the first year of patriotic volunteering, the slaughter at the front produced a gulf of mutual incomprehension between the people at home, the men too old to fight and the women bravely 'substituting' for men in the munitions factories, on buses, ambulances, refuse carts and other work, and the troops, blasted, gassed, shell-shocked and disillusioned by the total incapacity of the generals to find any alternative to the frontal assault. The change was measured by the transition in the poetry of war, from the eager martyrdom of Rupert Brooke – too many volunteers found a corner of a foreign field which was forever England – to the sense of appalling futility of Wilfred Owen and the bitter irony of Siegfried Sassoon:

> Squire nagged and bullied till I went to fight
> (Under Lord Derby's scheme). I died in hell
> (They call it Passchendaele); my wound was slight,
> And I was hobbling back, and then a shell
> Burst slick upon the duck-boards; so I fell
> Into the bottomless mud, and lost the light . . .

At the top, the mutual incomprehension was the other way round. Sir Douglas Haig and the generals called for more troops, guns and shells, and used Lord Northcliffe and the press to put pressure on the government, while the politicians were appalled at the slaughter. The shell shortage and his own manifest distaste for war brought down the prime minister, H. H. Asquith, and split the Liberal Party, replacing him in December 1916 with David Lloyd George, a brilliant war premier who produced the munitions and tried to hold the generals in check to let the Germans batter themselves to death.

In the stalemate on the Western front there was an obvious need and a frantic search for some new weapon or strategy to break the deadlock. The Germans tried poison gas, which they first released against the British at Ypres on 22 April 1915. But gas, though a barbarous and revolting weapon against the unprotected soldier, 'flound'ring like a man in fire or lime', was double edged, especially to a user like the Germans in the lee of the prevailing winds, and easily countered by masks and protective clothing, and became no more than a wretched nuisance like the lice and rats of the trenches.

The Allies with their naval power tried to break the deadlock by turning the flank of the enemy. They considered an attack on Germany through Denmark and the Baltic. In 1915 they attempted an attack on Constantinople through the Dardanelles, to knock Turkey out of the fight, release the Russian armies in the Caucasus for the main struggle against the Germans and the Austrians and to roll up the Austrian flank through the Balkans. But the scheme, conceived by Churchill and the politicians, was botched by the admirals and generals, who failed to strike when the Turkish defences were weak and persisted too long when they became strong. Their failure cost Churchill the Admiralty – though he came back into the War Cabinet as Minister of Munitions in July 1917 – and the flank attack was reduced to a series of small wars on the Greek frontier with Serbia and Bulgaria, in Palestine and Mesopotamia (modern Iraq).

The deadlock breaker, when it came, was to be a new engine of war, a fighting version of the automobile, able to resist machine-gun and rifle bullets, crush barbed wire, cross trenches and penetrate the enemy lines without preliminary bombardment or massive loss of life. The idea of the tank, as we have seen, had been rejected before the War by every general staff. In October 1914 a few junior officers in Britain continued to urge it, Colonel Swinton, Colonel Hankey and Captain Tulloch, but it was rejected by Lord Kitchener in December. Fortunately, Winston Churchill at the Admiralty, pondering on the problems of how to get the Dunkirk armoured cars to cross trenches dug across the roads and how to transport 15-inch siege howitzers across country, became interested in 'special mechanical devices for taking trenches'. Having read Colonel Hankey's rejected paper, he told Prime Minister Asquith in January 1915:

> It would be quite easy in a short time to fit up a number of steam tractors with small armoured shelters, in which men and machine guns could be placed, which would be bullet-proof... The caterpillar system would enable trenches to be crossed quite easily, and the weight of the machine would destroy all wire entanglements. Forty or fifty of these engines prepared secretly and brought into position at nightfall could advance quite certainly into the enemy's trenches, smashing away all the obstructions and sweeping the trenches with their machine-gun fire and with grenades thrown out of the top.

Ignored by the War Office, Churchill discussed with Major Hetherington of the Dunkirk naval armoured car squadron a plan for a 'land battleship' with enormous 40-foot wheels. Finally, in February 1915 he set up a Landships Committee of the Admiralty and allocated £70,000 on his own responsibility for the construction of prototypes.

The experiments came to fruition after Churchill left the Admiralty, in 'Little Willie' (December 1915), essentially a square box of armoured plate on caterpillar tracks, and in 'Big Willie' or 'Mother' (January 1916), the familiar rhomboidal shape with caterpillar tracks carried over the top for better trench-crossing, and guns in sponsons projecting from the sides. The latter tank, Mark I, the mother of all the tanks used in the First World War, was demonstrated to the generals in February 1916, and so enthused Haig that he asked for as many as could be built in time for his summer offensive on the Somme. A programme of 150 was put in hand, seventy-five 'males' with two 6-pounder cannon and four light machine-guns, seventy-five 'females' with four heavy and one light machine-gun. The code-name 'tank' was invented by Sir Edgar Jones of the Ministry of Munitions, to disguise their purpose and mislead enemy agents. The first fifty-nine tanks landed in France in

August 1916 in the second month of the battle of the Somme. The thirty-five which reached the front were sent in twos and threes straight into the mud and shell holes of the bogged-down battlefield, against the wishes of their commander, Colonel Swinton, who wanted a mass attack on a fresh front without preliminary bombardment. In spite of the vile conditions, thirty-one of them succeeded in crossing the German trenches, and captured or put to flight thousands of Germans. One tank alone, a 'female' with machine-guns, captured 1,500 yards of trench, eight officers and 362 men for the loss of five British lives.

The moral effect of these monsters, blundering on in the face of bullets and grenades, was even greater than the physical, and many Germans surrendered without a fight. The eight men inside each tank, three to drive (including one brakesman for each track for steering purposes) and five to fire the guns, were overheated and deafened by the 105-h.p. Daimler engine, flecked by the deadly splash of white-hot metal from the armour plate as bullets struck the outside, and in constant peril of being blown up by shell-fire or roasted alive by petrol flames. Their initial success could not be exploited, since they could only travel at 4 m.p.h. and for only a few miles, and there was as yet no equivalent engine of war for the cavalry role of breaking through into open country and taking the enemy from behind. Moreover, the secret was out. The French, who had been experimenting independently, soon produced hundreds of the tiny Renault two-man tanks. But the Germans believed that shellfire would always defeat the tank, and never built enough of their own to use with effect against the Allies. It became obvious that the tank could only be used successfully in a mass attack on firm new ground without preliminary bombardment. This was tried at Cambrai on 20 November 1917, when in one day 474 British tanks, mostly the more manoeuvrable Mark IVs, penetrated six miles of the German trench system, and took 10,000 prisoners and 200 guns for the loss of 1,500 British casualties. The cavalry burst through the breach but were soon shot down by the machine-guns, and the German reinforcements counter-attacked to even the score in prisoners and captured guns.

The solution to the problem of exploiting the breakthrough was the cavalry tank, a lighter vehicle of higher speed and longer range which could burst through the gap made by the heavies and harrass the enemy before he could regroup and plug the hole. This was the medium tank Mark A, nicknamed 'the Whippet' which, manned by a driver and two machine-gunners, could travel at 8 m.p.h. over a range of 80 miles. In appearance it was the first modern tank, with a turret (non-revolving) overtopping low caterpillars. It proved itself in one day in 1918, when seven Whippets overran three German battalions, entrenched to the south of Villers-Cotteret.

The tank also proved itself in defence, and helped to defeat the German 1918 offensive. The Germans belatedly built a few tanks of their own, twenty massive A7V assault vehicles, each with a crew of eighteen, a 57-mm cannon and six machine guns. On 24 April 1918 they sent in fifteen of them together with thirty captured British tanks at Villers-Bretonneux against thirteen British tanks, and won the first and only tank battle of the War. But the Germans never had more than a handful, forty-five at the end of the War against nearly 10,000 of the British, French and Americans.

The German spring and early summer offensive of 1918 had carried them, by sheer weight of numbers and guns brought back from the victorious Eastern front, to the line of the Marne, where they were halted again as in 1914. On 18 July General Mangin counter-attacked with 330 little Renault tanks, and drove them back three miles on a thirty-mile wide front. This was the turn of the tide, though it took several weeks to be certain. Then, at Amiens on 8 August General Rawlinson, with no artillery preparation, sent in 600 tanks, which in less than two hours took 16,000 prisoners and over 200 guns, and by mid-day cavalry tanks and armoured cars were running free nearly ten miles behind the German line. The French, without tanks, advanced half as far. The British advance brought the railway junction at Chaulnes, the key to the defence of the German line, within artillery range. General Ludendorff, the German commander, wrote: 'August 8 was the black day of the German Army in the history of this war . . . The Emperor told me later on, after the failure of the July offensive and after August 8, he knew the war could be no longer won.'

The deadlock had in fact been broken. After this the advance was pressed forward relentlessly before the Germans could dig themselves in again. Wherever there was a hold-up, the tanks were brought up and forced a way through. Whenever the troops got too far ahead of the tanks, as the Canadians did at Drocourt-Quéant, the same old slaughter by machine-gun and rifle took place. The Germans were pressed back upon the arc of railway just to the west side of the broken, wooded country of the Ardennes, nearly impassable to heavy road traffic. Once the junctions serving this arc at Aulnoye and Mézières were cut, something like three quarters of the German army in France would be cut off from supplies and reinforcements. On 11 September the Allies began a three-pronged assault towards these junctions, the French and Americans towards Mézières, the British towards Aulnoye, and the British, French and Belgians towards Ghent, the key to the railways serving the Flanders front. By 29 September the German High Command decided to sue for peace.

Meanwhile, Germany's allies, no longer sustained by continuous military aid, were collapsing. The Austrians were routed by the Italians, British and French on the Italian front, the Austrians and the Bulgarians by the 'Salonika army' of Serbs, Greeks, French and British in the Balkans, the Turks by General Allenby in Palestine and by General Marshall in Mesopotamia. The Turks were allowed an armistice on 31 October, the Austrians on 4 November.

In late October and early November the German war machine collapsed. Ludendorff, the only general who wished to fight on, was forced to resign. The battleship crews mutinied rather than obey Admiral Scheer's order to sail and challenge the Grand Fleet in a suicidal battle. The government fell to a socialist revolution in Berlin, the Kaiser and his heir fled to Holland, and the few remaining German generals signed the armistice on terms close to complete surrender in the forest of Compiègne at 5 a.m. on 11 November.

The victory, after the millions of killed and wounded sacrificed on both sides, had been won by less than 15,000 engines of war: about 5,000 British tanks, 3,500 French (mostly light two-man Renaults) and 5,200 American (all but fifteen of them supplied by the French). If the War had gone on, there would have been in 1919 some 7,000 British tanks, 8–10,000 French and 10,000 American, against 800 German ones – an imbalance which would have made the victory still more total, and destroyed the absurd legend that Germany was not beaten in the field. The credit for the victory must go to the armoured fighting vehicle. Unfortunately, the old, unregenerate Germany lived on to a hideous resurrection, when the tank, wielded with horrific genius, would once more display its power of winning decisive victories.

FURTHER READING

A. J. P. Taylor, *The First World War: An Illustrated History* (Penguin, 1966)

Cyril Falls, *The First World War* (Longmans, 1960)

Sir Llewellyn Woodward, *Great Britain and the War of 1914–18* (Methuen, 1967)

Correlli Barnett, *The Swordbearers: Studies in Supreme Command in the First World War* (Penguin, 1966)

Winston Churchill, *The World Crisis* (Odhams Press, 1939)

Arthur Marwick, *The Deluge: British Society and the First World War* (Bodley Head, 1965)

B. H. Liddell Hart, *The Tanks: The History of the Royal Tank Regiment and its Predecessors* (Cassell, 1959)

J. F. C. Fuller, *Tanks in the Great War, 1914–18* (Murray, 1920)

Kenneth Macksey and H. J. Batchelor, *Tank: A History of the Armoured Fighting Vehicle* (Macdonald, 1970)

Armin Halle and Carlo Demand, *Tanks: An Illustrated History of Fighting Vehicles* (Patrick Stephens, London, and Edita, Lausanne, 1971)

R. M. Ogorkiewicz, *Design and Development of Fighting Vehicles* (Macdonald, 1968)

R. M. Ogorkiewicz, *Armoured Forces: A History of Armoured Forces and Their Vehicles* (Arms and Armour Press, 1970)

Douglas Orgill, *The Tank* (Heinemann, 1971)

Sir Julian Corbett and Sir Henry Newbolt, *History of the Great War: Naval Operations* (5 vols, Longmans, 1920–31)

Sir Walter Raleigh and H. A. Jones, *History of the Great War: The War in the Air* (6 vols, Clarendon Press, 1922–37)

C. H. Gibbs-Smith, *Aviation: An Historical Survey from its Origins to the End of the Second World War* (Science Museum, 1970), ch. xv

4. PEACE WITHOUT PROSPERITY

The jubilant crowds who celebrated the Armistice on 11 November 1918 had only one thought in mind: to get back to peace and prosperity as soon as possible. 'Recovery' and 'reconstruction' were the catchwords, which meant the restoration of pre-war economic conditions when Britain still led the world in manufactured exports, shipping, ship-building, insurance, banking and foreign investment. A spending spree by people long deprived of luxuries and the replacement of clothes and household goods brought on a great boom. What the *Economist* called 'a craze for speculation' seized business men who paid unheard of sums for cotton mills and other factories in the staple industries, in an orgy of mergers and amalgamations. Prices raced upwards as too much paper money chased too few goods. Finally, in 1920, the boom burst, prices began their long inter-war decline, and Britain sank into depression. By June 1921 there were over two million unemployed, and the figure was never again to fall below a million between the Wars.

There was in fact to be no turning back to the pre-war world, either to the prosperity which most business men remembered or to the lower depths of poverty experienced by a third or more of the working class. For one thing, the War saw to that. Though in itself it started nothing, except perhaps 'daylight saving' (British Summer Time), it accelerated all the economic, political and social trends of the previous fifty years, and exposed British industrialists and workers to the realities of a world economy they no longer dominated. Apart from the appalling human cost – three quarters of a million Britons killed plus another 200,000 from the Empire, the 'lost generation' mourned by some politicians and even more by the record number of surplus women – the War had cost much less than had been feared. To pay for it we sold off about £300 millions of overseas investments more than we bought, about $7\frac{1}{2}\%$ of our holdings of £4,000 million. We had lent some £350 million more to our allies, especially Russia, France and Italy, than we borrowed, mainly from the United States; since some of them, notably Russia, defaulted, we paid back slightly more than we received. The biggest cost was the more than tenfold increase in the National Debt, from £706 million in 1914 to £7,876 million in 1920, but this was an internal transaction which did not affect our international position. Its main effect was a large increase in taxation, about a third of the inter-war budget going to pay the interest – paying the rich in fat pounds for lending patriotically in thin ones.

The main cost of the War was in lost markets. Other countries were forced to make goods Britain could no longer supply, or get from her better-situated allies, the United States and Japan. It thus exposed the weakness of Britain's pre-war economy, her too great dependence on traditional manufactures, cotton and other textiles, coal, ships and heavy engineering such as railways, and on exports to the diminishing number of non-industrial countries which produced only food and raw materials. These were to suffer most from the depressed world economy. The prices of food and raw materials fell further and faster than those of manufactured goods. Thus the terms of trade turned against the poorer countries, which had to pay more of their goods for the same amount of ours – about one quarter more in the 1920s, two fifths more in the 1930s. Their poverty, and the competition of others for their markets, were the most important reasons for the mass unemployment in Britain. At the same time their loss was our gain: cheaper food and raw materials helped us to pay our way in the world and even to raise our living standards.

The peace treaty compounded Britain's economic difficulties. Whatever the rights and wrongs of Versailles – it was probably too mild rather than too harsh, since an Allied occupation of Germany, as in 1945, might have securely established democracy there and rebuilt German industry on peaceful lines – reparations harmed the victors more than the defeated. If paid in full they would have stimulated German industry into gigantic growth and undermined British and French industry and exports. As it was, the treaty combined maximum irritation to German pride and desire for revenge with minimum effectiveness either in recompensing the victims of war or in preventing the revival of German militarism. In the end, after nearly wrecking their economy by inflation, the Germans with the aid of American loans and investment paid only one third of the £3,000 million reparations to Britain and France. Even at this rate, they contributed something to depression and unemployment in Britain, though not nearly so much as the unsettled state of world trade and the longer-term causes of Britain's decline.

It was not so much that Britain had changed as that the world had changed around her. She had been overtaken by 1900 in productive capacity by the United States and Germany, though the change had been disguised by her continued dominance of international trade and investment. The War ruthlessly exposed her Achilles' heel, her dependence on imports for half her food and most of her raw materials and thus on exports of cotton goods, coal, ships, railway engines and rails, and other products of nineteenth-century industry, demand for which was now falling. We did not produce enough of the new products, light engineering, fine chemicals, durable consumer goods like motor cars and radios, for which demand was rising. In 1929 42% of our exports of manufactures were in the group which had expanded least since 1913, compared with 27% of German and 17% of American exports. Our share of world manufactured exports shrank from 27·5% in 1911–13 to 23·8% in 1921–5 and 18·5% in 1931–8. Our share of exports of all kinds declined from 14% in 1913 to 11% in 1929 and 10% in 1937. Since world trade was growing only slowly in the 1920s and declining in the 1930s, the volume of our exports (allowing for declining prices) shrank by 13% to 1929 and by a further 15% to 1937.

The stagnation of world trade affected Britain more than any other great trading nation, since not only did we live more by trade but made up our customary deficit on the visible trade in goods by invisible exports of shipping, banking and insurance services, all of which suffered when world trade was depressed. Free trade suited us best, but the free trade area had been shrinking since the 1880s and now disappeared altogether. Britain herself, having rejected tariff reform at the elections of 1906 and 1910, accepted it by the back door in 1915 with the McKenna duties of $33\frac{1}{3}\%$ on 'luxuries' such as clocks, watches and motor cars, ostensibly a temporary measure to save shipping space. Far from being abandoned, they were extended in 1921 to safeguard key industries against foreign 'dumping'. Philip Snowden, that stout socialist defender of nineteenth-century capitalism, abolished them in 1924, only to see Churchill restore them the next year to pay for Chamberlain's pensions scheme. Free trade was officially abandoned by the National Government in 1932, a sacrifice to the world slump which protection could only extend. When world trade, still rising in the 1920s, actually shrank in the 1930s, the British balance of payments for the first time since Waterloo went into the red.

Since great power status in international politics ultimately rests on relative economic strength, Britain's position in world affairs was also declining. The most striking evidence of this was the Washington Naval Treaty of 1922, by which the Royal Navy at last abandoned the 'two-power standard' (equality with the next two navies put together) and accepted equality in capital ships with the United States. It also allowed the next naval power 60% of the American or British battle strength (the famous 5:5:3 agreement), which in effect gave Japan local supremacy in the Far East, with disastrous results in the Second World War.

Britain of course needed a navy more than any other great power, for the defence of her shipping life-lines and her still vast and sprawling Empire, swollen by the mandated ex-German colonies in Africa and the Pacific and ex-Turkish provinces in the Middle East. Some of these, South-West Africa, New Guinea and Papua, had been mandated to South Africa and Australia, but the self-governing dominions were also defended largely by the Royal Navy. The Empire had remained a source of strength up to and during the War, when imperial troops, especially Anzac and Indian, had played a considerable part and sustained about a fifth of the casualties on the British side; and in the increasingly protectionist pre-war world economy India and the colonies had taken an increasing share of our trade, while the dominions still held out some hope of fulfilling Joseph Chamberlain's dream of imperial free trade.

After the War, however, the Empire began increasingly to seem a liability, destined for ultimate self-government, and meanwhile a drain on British troops and resources. The white Dominions had already made it clear that imperial preference meant preferential tariffs for their food and raw materials in the British market but not for British manufactured goods in competition with their infant industries. The independence of the Dominions as 'autonomous and equal communities within the British Commonwealth of Nations' was recognized by the Mackenzie King formula in 1926 and confirmed by the Statute of Westminster in 1931. The Ottawa Conference of 1932 at last arrived at imperial preference not by reducing tariffs within the Commonwealth but by raising them still higher against outsiders. This merely diverted a limited amount of British trade with foreigners to the Commonwealth and contributed to the partition of the world into hostile trading blocs.

Meanwhile, the emancipation of the white Dominions stimulated other colonies to demand self-government. In India Gandhi perfected the technique of civil disobedience which was so effective against a morally vulnerable democracy. India was promised dominion status by the Labour Government in 1929, and the Government of India Act in 1935 gave 'responsible government' to the provinces. Egypt became theoretically independent in 1922, Iraq in 1930, but both remained in leadings strings as British protectorates. The other colonies were almost all placed on the same escalator, at various stages of 'responsible' and 'representative' government leading to future independence. Empire had been a by-product of leadership in industry and commerce; when that leadership was lost it became a luxury we could not afford, like a house too large for our income.

In one area Britain cut her losses altogether. Ireland had been promised Home Rule before the War, at the risk of civil war between the Catholic majority and the Protestants of Ulster. After the Easter Rising of 1916 the British government offered Home Rule for the twenty-six mainly Catholic counties at once, leaving the position of six counties of Ulster to be decided after the War, but then played into the hands of the extremists by watering down the terms and finally withdrawing the offer. When the War ended, Catholic Ireland seized independence for itself. The seventy-three Nationalist MPs elected in 1918 refused to take their seats at Westminster and set up their own parliament and government in Dublin. After a brutal and squalid civil war, the British government recognized the Irish Free State in 1921 and granted it dominion status within the Empire. After a further civil war between those Irish

Nationalists who accepted the treaty and those who refused to abandon Ulster even temporarily, Eire settled down to a sullen and anti-English independence which ignored the Commonwealth, except to break the last formal link with it in 1937 – though the border remained to tie the two countries to a common future of strife.

At home the War had produced great changes in the structure and management of industry, most of them temporary but nonetheless influential for the future. Under the pressure of increasingly total war, the government had gradually taken direct control of almost every sector: munitions, heavy engineering, coal, ship-building, aircraft and vehicle manufacture, food supply, shipping, railways and canals – everything which remotely affected the supply of war materials. The proportion of the national income passing through the hands of the government rose from under a tenth (£198 million out of £2,265 million in 1913) to nearly three fifths (£2,579 million out of £4,372 million) in 1918. The form of control varied but for the most part it was a voluntary partnership which the state operated through the previous owners and managers. The railways, for example, were run by a Railway Executive Committee composed of the general managers of the ten biggest companies. Labour was also controlled, mainly to organize the replacement of men recruited or conscripted for the forces, which obviously required the acceptance by the skilled trade unions of unskilled 'dilutees' and women workers. The trade unions, like the managers of the industries taken over, thus became partners of the government. This led on the one side to a doubling of trade-union membership, from under four million in 1913 to over eight million in 1919, and a consequent increase in their power and respectability, and on the other to resentment of government control, which kept wages down and undermined old differentials, and of the official trade-union leadership, and a consequent rise in the power of the local shop stewards.

After the War, under the overwhelmingly Conservative coalition of 1918–22, there was a rush to unscramble the omelet of state controls, and most of them were abolished by the summer of 1921. But the omelet could only be cut up, often into much larger pieces than before, and industry was never the same again. The railways were reduced from 120 to the four great companies of 1923 (excluding the London Underground network). A majority of the 1919 Royal Commission on the Coal Industry, chaired by Sir John Sankey, recommended nationalization, but the mines were returned to their old owners, along with their bad old industrial relations and the new demand by the miners for public ownership. Many other industries, not so completely taken over and therefore more easily unscrambled, got a taste of the benefits of large-scale organization and mass production, like the motor car manufacturers who went over to munitions, tanks or aero-engines, and thus intensified the trend towards amalgamation.

The increased responsibility of the trade unions was recognized by the setting up in 1920, on the recommendation of a war-time committee under the chairmanship of J. H. Whitley, Deputy Speaker of the House of Commons, of fifty-six 'Whitley Councils' of employers and workers' representatives for over three million workpeople – though these did very little except for government employees. The increased power of the trade unions was manifested in the increased number of strikes, including damaging strikes by railwaymen in 1919 and coal miners in 1921, either of which could have led, through the machinery of the 1914 triple alliance of miners, railwaymen and transport workers, to a general strike.

The political Labour movement had also benefited from the War. In spite of the pacifism of Ramsay MacDonald, the Labour Party under his successor Arthur Henderson got its first taste of power in Asquith's coalition government of 1915, still more in Lloyd George's of 1916, when Henderson, mainly to conciliate the trade unions, was given a place in the five-member War Cabinet. Even Henderson's resignation in 1917 over his support for the international socialist peace conference in Stockholm benefited the party: it preserved its reputation as the party of peace, and enabled him to reorganize it for the post-war return to party politics and, with the aid of Sidney Webb, to draw up the constitution of 1918 which marked the beginning of Labour as an independent party instead of a pressure group acting on the Liberals.

What benefited Labour most was the break-up of the Liberal Party, which never recovered from the split inflicted by Lloyd George's palace revolution of 1916 and Asquith's vengeful intransigence. Whether a stronger party with a more powerful social base could have recovered under more reconcilable leaders is a debatable question: the Liberal Party had been declining since the 1870s in its hold upon the propertied classes without permanently consolidating its hold upon the organized working class. But the ambition of Lloyd George for office and of Asquith for revenge ruled out conciliation until it was too late. In British politics third parties are squeezed between the upper and nether millstones of government and opposition, and once the Liberals allowed Labour to gain second place they were squeezed out of the power game.

If British politics had been completely class-based, the Labour Party should have had a permanent majority from 1918, when the working class were rewarded for their support for the War by the final establishment of universal manhood suffrage. Not only did a large fraction of the working class continue to vote Conservative, but the Reform Act also enfranchised women over thirty (followed by those over twenty-one ten years later), and more women than men vote Conservative. Labour took office but not power in the minority governments of 1924 and 1929–31. The Conservatives remained continuously in power, though not always in office, and curiously content to serve under coalition prime ministers like Lloyd George (1918–22) and Ramsay MacDonald (1931–35).

Women were also rewarded with the Sex Disqualification

Removal Act of 1919 which, with exceptions like the clergy, the stock exchange, the coal mines and the front-line army, opened every occupation to them. In practice it chiefly benefited single middle-class women, since married women continued to be excluded from the civil service and most other professions while working-class women had always worked in every manual occupation from which they were not excluded by legislation or by the power of the craft unions. In fact, liberation for working-class wives and mothers then meant not the freedom to work but the opportunity to stay at home and look after their families without exhausting themselves, an opportunity provided by higher wages for husbands. Despite the temporary increase in women's employment during the War, there were fewer women at work in 1921 than in 1911, and because of unemployment the proportion hardly changed between the Wars.

The War was also praised or blamed for a supposed revolution in 'morals', meaning relations between the sexes. Certainly, the absence from home of millions of men and women in the forces and munitions factories had provided more opportunities for extra-marital sex and temporary increases in illegitimate births and venereal disease, but those mainly middle-class moralists who saw a permanent deterioration in 'morals' must have been extraordinarily ignorant of the sexual customs of the Victorians and Edwardians. Some upper- and middle-class women were perhaps liberated by war-work and the decline of the chaperon. The real moral revolution, if there was one, was in the decline of the flagrant unabashed prostitution of the pre-war world. The plush, aristocratic bawdy houses of the West End of London never regained their Edwardian splendour, the 'pretty horse-breakers' no longer flaunted in Hyde Park their expensive charms and the equipages of their rich or noble protectors, and the swells and clubmen of St James's no more expected to buy a working-class woman they met on the street for half a crown. A new egalitarianism and self-respect, reinforced by the rise in real wages, had put an end to that particularly repulsive form of class exploitation. Prostitution and mistress-keeping still survived of course, but they were more secretive and shame-faced than in good King Edward's golden days.

The moralists were misled, perhaps, by the extraordinary revolution in women's fashions, the greatest change in human dress since the fashion cycle began in the fourteenth century. In 1916 women's skirt-lengths for the first time in history rose permanently above the ankles – ostensibly to make it easier to drive ambulances and dust-carts and work in factories, but who can say from what psychological depths so profound a change welled up? This, surely, pointed to one of the most important turning points in modern society, woman's liberation from the subordinate role, at once hobbled, mysterious and coquettish, allotted to her by the overbearing, exploiting and prurient male. Nothing so superficial and temporary as a war could account for it. It had roots in the liberation by work outside the house from total dependence on the family income, in the emancipation from continual child-bearing by the contraceptive movement of the late Victorian age, and in the transformation of leisure by the bicycle, mixed bathing and other outdoor sports in the genera-tion before the War. Indeed, the essential principle, the declara-tion that women had legs and could stand up for themselves, was signalized by the leisure clothes of that pre-war generation, above all by the breeches worn for cycling and the shape-revealing costumes for sea-bathing. After the War the very short skirts, well above the knee by the mid-1920s, worn with flesh-coloured 'art. silk' (rayon) stockings and eye-catching suspenders, were almost a retrograde step, since along with the flat-chested, boyish figures and the exaggerated make-up they seemed to say that women, having abandoned both their maternal and servant functions, had been reduced to doll-like playthings of their playboy mates. Perhaps they symbolized a revulsion from motherhood witnessed by the fall in the birth rate, but this became a cult only for the irrelevant and diminishing leisure class. In the 1930s women began to look womanly again, without

91

returning to the monumental matronliness of Victorian dress.

The fall in the birth rate was a pre-war trend which the War undoubtedly accelerated. The army's concern with venereal disease, which kept more troops out of the front line than any other cause, led from 1917 to the issue of sheaths, and familiarized millions of men with the practice of birth control. After the War Dr Marie Stopes in *Married Love* (1919) familiarized millions of women with contraceptive methods, though it may be doubted whether she was the prime mover in so fundamental a social change. The desire to have children and the desire to limit their number are powerful forces which operate at a level beneath the threshold of historical evidence, and the supply of contraceptive knowledge is less important than the demand for it. Whatever the ultimate cause, birth control seems most often to have been associated with rising living standards and the desire to share them with fewer children. Between the Wars the middle-class ideal of a house, two babies and a baby car began to spread, if only as an ideal, to the working class.

For whatever reason, the average British family declined in size from 3·4 children in 1900–9 to 2·1 in 1930. The decline in the birth rate led population experts to fear for the future of the nation, and Enid Charles forecast, on two different assumptions, a British population decline to 24·4 million, or even to 5·3 million, in 2035. Worst still, while professional men, employers and salaried workers had less than two children (1·65–1·75), manual workers had nearly three (2·7) and labourers over three (3·4), differentials which were used to argue (somewhat arrogantly) that the more intelligent and better educated were becoming a smaller fraction of the population. But people are not statistics and when the smaller family had worked its way down through the social scale the birth rate would stabilize in all classes a little above the inter-war figure.

One other demographic change coincided with the War. Until then, Britain (and Ireland still more) had been a major exporter of people. Millions of emigrants left the British Isles in the Victorian age, chiefly for the United States but also for the white Dominions. In the last three years before the War this traffic reached a peak, with an average of 464,000 emigrants a year. After the War, with the United States operating a tight quota system and depression elsewhere discouraging movement to new jobs, emigration shrank to a trickle, and then in the 1930s was swamped by the immigration of about half a million Jewish and political refugees from Hitler's Europe. This change in the direction of migration contributed a little to the unemployment of the period, but also brought new energies and skills which were to contribute to the recovery of the British economy and not least, in the shape of many scientific ideas including the theory of the atomic bomb, to the winning of the Second World War.

Finally, the War accelerated the building of the welfare state. Lloyd George promised the returning troops in 1918 'a fit country for heroes to live in'. The first problem was how to enable demobilized heroes without jobs to live at all. As early as 1915 it had been decided to support unemployed ex-servicemen by 'out-of-work donations' from the national exchequer, and in 1918 these were extended to all workers covered by the 1911 health insurance scheme (most manual and lower-paid non-manual workers), and allowances added for dependants. It could only be a temporary measure, however, and in 1920 unemployment insurance was extended to all manual and other low-paid workers except agricultural labourers, railwaymen, nurses, domestic servants and civil service employees, dependants' allowances being added the following year. This came just in time for the 1921 slump and the beginning of mass unemployment.

There remained the problem of the long-term unemployed, who fell out of insurance benefit after six months and were paid 'uncovenanted benefit', later 'extended benefit' and 'transitional payments' (the notorious 'dole') on a means test, or reverted to poor relief, from 1929 'public assistance'. To relieve the local

authorities in the depressed areas where long-term unemployment was concentrated, the Unemployment Assistance Board
was set up in 1934 to pay the dole from 1936 from national
funds. The means test was deservedly hated, since it required a
man to run down almost all his savings and to rely on his chil-
drens' earnings, thus encouraging lies and family strife. Yet it
was more generous than the old Poor Law, and enabled the
long-term unemployed to survive without the alternative of
starvation or the workhouse which had been their lot before the
War.

The old Poor Law itself was gradually broken up, as envisaged
by the Minority Report of the Poor Law Commission of 1909,
and finally transformed on the terms recommended by the
Majority. The aged poor, partially removed since 1908 by the
non-contributory pensions at seventy, were more largely covered
by the contributory, insurance-based pensions between sixty-five
and seventy for all manual and lower-paid non-manual workers
paying national health insurance, introduced by Neville Chamberlain in 1925. By the same Act, widows and orphans of
insured workers also received pensions. 'Voluntary contribu-
tors', self-employed shopkeepers, craftsmen and the like on
small incomes, were brought in in 1937. Blind persons were
given pensions at fifty in 1920, and removed from public
assistance altogether in 1938. By 1942 the Beveridge Report on
Social Insurance and Allied Services could say that provision
was made for 'most of the many varieties of need through inter-
ruption of earnings and other causes that may arise in modern
industrial communities', the chief exceptions being industrial
injury insurance, family allowances, death grants, and medical
treatment for the dependants of insured workers.

The Poor Law itself was officially ended in 1929, with the
abolition of the boards of guardians and the transfer of their
responsibilities to the new public assistance committees of the
county and county borough councils. Apart from the long-term
unemployed and the still extant workhouses and orphanages,

these included some 540 hospitals, sanatoria and other medical establishments, and the local authorities became responsible for nearly twice as many patients as the voluntary hospitals. The best of these were transferred to the health committees of the local authorities, but most remained under public assistance, often still attached to the workhouses out of which they had grown. Here, nevertheless, was the nucleus of the future National Health Service.

'Homes fit for heroes' Lloyd George had not promised, but the War had introduced rent control of working-class housing (in 1915 to placate munitions workers in Glasgow) and raised expectations that could only be met, when control discouraged the private landlord, by the state. Housing legislation since 1890 had encouraged slum clearance and replacement by local authorities. Now Christopher Addison's Act of 1919 required them to make up the deficiency of houses due to lack of building during the War and provided a Treasury subsidy for the purpose. John Wheatley's Act under the 1924 Labour Government went further and introduced a long-term plan of subsidized 'council houses' under which half a million houses were built. Although council building was cut back during the slump, the local authorities built 1·4 million houses, subsidized private builders 430,000 and unsubsidized builders over 2·5 million between the Wars.

In education there was some extension of the slight trend towards equality begun by the state secondary schools of 1902 and the scholarship system of 1907. In 1918 H. A. L. Fisher's Act raised the school-leaving age to fourteen and allowed local education committees to raise it to fifteen and to provide part-time 'day-continuation' classes for adolescents as well as nursery schools for under-fives – permissions which very few of them took up in that age of continual economy cuts. In 1926 the Hadow Committee, inspired by R. H. Tawney, reported in favour of 'secondary education for all' by the transformation of the senior elementary schools into 'modern schools' with 'parity

95

of esteem' with the grammar schools. When joined to the technical schools recommended by the Spens Report of 1938, this was to lead to the tripartite system under the Butler Act of 1944. But between the Wars almost the only educational progress was in the expansion of scholarships from the elementary to the grammar schools, and even these were subjected to a parental means test in 1931 by which rather more than half the pupils paid all or part of the fees. Free meals and milk were expanded for needy children, cheap milk was provided for all children from 1934 and the school medical and dental services were extended, as were welfare clinics for babies and expectant mothers. All these contributed much to a visible improvement in child health and physique: twelve-year-old schoolboys in Lincolnshire and Northampton in 1933 were two inches taller and five to seven pounds heavier than in 1913.

Altogether, government and local authority spending on the social services went up dramatically, from £74·6 million in 1913 to £382·4 million in 1935, and from 5·5% of the national income in 1913 to 13·0% in 1938. Taxation increased accordingly, both indirect taxes, on drink, tobacco, petrol and oil, motor cars and imported manufactured goods, and direct taxes, especially income tax. The standard rate of income tax went up from 1s. 2d. in 1913 to 6s. in the pound in 1918, and it never again went below 4s., being generally between 4s. and 5s. after 1922. Surtax and death duties were also raised and more steeply graduated. According to C. L. Mowat, in 1913 the working class paid more in taxes than they received in social service benefits; by 1925 they paid only 85% of the cost and by 1935 only 79%.

Yet it would be a mistake to suppose that the redistribution of income by taxation was entirely one way, from the rich to the poor. A large part of the social insurance benefits were paid for by the wage-earners themselves, more if the employer's contribution is regarded as part of the remuneration of labour. Although most wage-earners did not pay income tax until 1940, indirect taxation weighed more heavily on them than on the middle class, and the flat-rate health and unemployment insurance stamps were a regressive poll tax which took a much larger proportion of the wages of the lowest-paid. Altogether, the working class, all of whom fell into the income groups below £250 a year, paid a larger proportion of their incomes to the state than the middle class, between £250 and £1,000 a year (e.g. in 1930–1 11·0% of £100 and 9·6% of £200 as against 4·5% of £500). Nor did all the benefits go to the poor: housing subsidies went to the better-off working class and lower middle class who could afford council rents (higher than slum rents), and subsidized mortgages and grammar-school and university education mostly benefited the middle class, interest on the National Debt was paid by the taxpaying majority to the rich minority, while social insurance was largely a redistribution from the wage-earners in work to those out of it through sickness, unemployment or old age.

The inter-war period is rightly remembered for mass unemployment, for the waste of human skill and effort which it represented, for the demoralization of men living year after year on the 'dole', for the frustration of teenagers who left school only to 'sign on' at the employment exchange, for the shabby, down-at-heel drabness of the distressed areas with their filthy streets, mouldering houses and flaking paint, for the sheer boredom of men in cloth caps, mufflers and threadbare clothes standing on corners watching the ragged children play. This was the age of Walter Greenwood's *Love on the Dole*, of George Orwell's *The Road to Wigan Pier*, of Ellen Wilkinson's *The Town that was Murdered* (Jarrow, consigned to economic death by the closure of its shipyard). After 1920, unemployment never dropped below a million in the 1920s or a million and a half in the 1930s. It reached a peak during the great slump of 23% in August 1932, nearly 3 million workers. Since not all workers were insured, and many married women, school leavers and others did not claim benefit, the true figure may have been as high as

3·75 million. The insured unemployed remained at over 2 million until 1935, with some recovery to 1937, but rose again in 1938 and were only brought down below a million in 1940.

Unemployment was heaviest in the traditional export industries, coal mining, iron and steel, shipbuilding and textiles, and lightest in the new, mainly light industries and services serving the home market, motor car manufacture, light engineering, radios and vacuum cleaners, food canning and preparation, hotels and catering, shops and wholesale distribution, and in house building. This meant that it hit the old industrial areas, the North East, Lancashire and Yorkshire, Scotland, South Wales and Northern Ireland, harder than the Midlands and the South East, where the new consumer-oriented industries chose to go to be near the rich middle-class markets of London and the more prosperous South. In 1932, for example, the percentage unemployed in Scotland (28·5%) and the North East (27·7%) was twice as high, in South Wales (36·5%) nearly three times as high, as in London (13·5%).

Not surprisingly, observers like J. B. Priestley in his *English Journey* found two Englands, one the depressed industrial North, standing amongst the grim, silent factories and grimy terraced houses, the other the prosperous, suburban England of the South, with its new housing estates and 'by-pass variegated' villas, motor cars and fitted carpets, cocktail parties and country clubs. The contrast was overdone: there were stockbroker belts in North Cheshire as well as in Surrey and country towns taken over by company directors in Wilmslow and Altrincham, Harrogate and Stirling as well as in Sevenoaks and Weybridge; and there were slums and grime in the working-class areas of London and other southern towns. But it was justified in that a disproportionate share of the prosperous middle class and of the workers in the new and expanding industries lived in the South and Midlands, and a disproportionate share of the unemployed and low-paid workers of the declining industries in the North and West.

Hence, too, the drift of population was from the latter to the former, the reverse of the drift from the Industrial Revolution down to the First World War which had followed the new factory industry to the coalfields. Now the migrants swarmed to the new light industries and service trades which, because of the easy distribution of power by the electricity grid, gravitated towards the outskirts of the southern conurbations. The South East and the Midlands took 3 million out of the $3\frac{1}{2}$ million increase in the population between 1921 and 1938. The drift, not enough to cure the problem of regional unemployment, aggravated the problems of the distressed areas. It consisted of the young and vigorous, and left behind the middle-aged, sick and elderly, who became a greater burden on local relief, social and medical services. It further reduced spending in the local shops and left empty houses and lower property values in the old areas, reducing rent and rate income and the capacity of the local authorities to support social and other services. Thus the depressed areas became still more depressed in a vicious downward spiral of decay.

The policies of all the governments between the Wars seemed designed to aggravate the depression. The orthodox economists they consulted all held to the Gladstonian axiom of public finance: leave money to fructify in the pockets of the people. The government's duty in an economic crisis was to cut public spending, reduce taxes, keep a balanced budget, and wait for consumers to spend and business men to invest again. J. M. Keynes and Ernest Bevin argued unsuccessfully before the Macmillan Committee on Finance and Industry of 1929–31 that governments should do the opposite: spend more on public works and social benefits than they collected in taxes ('deficit spending'), so directly stimulating private spending and investment. Instead, every recession led to cuts in government spending: in 1922 to 'Geddes' axe', cuts in social services, education, the civil service and naval building recommended by a committee of businessmen chaired by Sir Eric Geddes, the first Minister of Transport; and in 1931 to the cuts, recommended by the notorious committee under Sir George May, Secretary of the Prudential Assurance Company, in the salaries of civil servants, postmen, teachers and other government employees and in unemployment benefits. It was this last cut which split the second Labour government and brought it down.

Government policy in the late 1920s even prevented Britain getting a full share of the one short-lived boom in world trade. Churchill's return to the gold standard at pre-war parity ($4·80 to the pound) in 1925 was acclaimed as a restoration of Britain's dominating financial position of 1913. In fact, it overvalued the pound by about 10%, thus making our exports dearer and more difficult to sell. The worst effect was on the coal industry, still heavily dependent on exports, in which wages made up most of the selling price. The miners were 'crucified upon a cross of gold'. To keep the price of coal down to a competitive level their wages were cut, which led by inexorable steps to the coal strike, and, when the TUC supported the miners, to the General Strike of 4–12 May 1926. In the railway age a general strike would have brought the nation to its knees. In the automobile age fleets of lorries, some manned by middle-class volunteers, students, clerks and business men, kept essential supplies moving. Churchill tried in his bellicose way to turn it into a military confrontation between the strikers and the government, calling out troops and armoured cars to protect the food convoys. The only tangible results of the General Strike, however, were the discrediting of syndicalist ideas of direct action by trade unions for political ends, the vindictive 1927 Trade Union Act which by making members 'opt into' instead of out of the political levy reduced union subscriptions to the Labour Party, and (after their six-month strike) the bitter determination of the miners to pursue the nationalization of the mines.

If we failed to benefit as much as some other countries from the boom of 1925–29, we did not suffer so catastrophically from the great slump of 1929–33. Unemployment, which never reached

3 million in Britain, approached 13 million in the United States and 6 million in Germany. In the first it evoked Roosevelt's New Deal programme of public works and 'deficit spending'. In the second it brought Hitler to power on the cry of work for all by road building and rearmament. Even in Britain the government at last began to pass legislation to alleviate the plight of the distressed areas. Development and improvement acts for the 'Special Areas' were passed in 1934, 1936 and 1937. Under these, two Commissioners (one for Scotland and one for England and Wales) and four Special Areas Reconstruction Associations were set up for four distressed areas – the middle industrial belt of Scotland (excluding Glasgow), West Cumberland, Tyneside and most of Durham, and most of Glamorgan and Monmouthshire – to encourage firms to invest there with the aid of Treasury loans and grants which came to amount to nearly £2 million. William Morris, now Lord Nuffield, did more: his Nuffield Trust gave £2·2 million for the same purpose. Yet the effects were negligible. By September 1938 only 14,900 new jobs had been created for the estimated 2–400,000 'surplus workers' of the Special Areas.

Recovery, partial though it was in the 1930s, was due to two main causes: an expansion of consumer demand induced by the still lower prices of the slump itself, and rearmament, begun in earnest in 1936. In addition, the 1930s saw one of the biggest housing booms on record: helped by cheaper materials and the government's cheap money policy (with the bank rate at 2% – one of the few government measures which had much effect), 2·7 million houses were built, most of them for sale to owner-occupiers with cheap mortgages from the booming building societies. Government spending on rearmament increased twelve-fold between 1935 and 1939 and stimulated expansion in coal, steel, ship-building and engineering. In the end, it was rearmament on a massive scale which cured the Depression – but that was only when we were fighting for survival in 1940.

Yet in spite of mass unemployment, the inter-war period was

101

much more prosperous than its reputation implies, at least for those in work, the great majority of the occupied population, and their families. Living standards made steady progress, as real national income per head recovered its pre-war level by 1923 and then rose by 30% by 1937. The salaried middle class, civil servants, teachers, managers and clerks had never had it so good: their fixed salaries rose in value as prices fell and they found they could buy houses, small cars, household gadgets and furniture as never before, and could afford longer holidays at home and abroad. The number of cars in use, for example, increased from 186,801 in 1920 to 1,056,214 in 1930 and 2,034,400 in 1939, enough to provide for most middle-class families. Similarly, real wages for those in work rose by 1938, according to different estimates, to between 20% and 30% above the pre-war level – most probably by about a quarter. Something must be deducted from this to allow for increased unemployment, but something must also be added for the greater social services and subsidies of the 1930s: according to estimates for 1937 unemployment deducted about $7\frac{1}{2}\%$ while social services added $12\frac{1}{2}$–15% to real wages. At the same time working hours became shorter by about an hour a day, and under an act of 1938 a week's holiday with pay became normal for most workers.

Even the unemployed, though more numerous, were better off than the 'able-bodied poor' before the War. They had to be, for political reasons: the whole working class now had the vote, and the unemployed were better organized, through the National Unemployed Workers' Movement (1921) and many local Labour parties, to publicize their plight by demonstrations and hunger marches. The hated means test at least had the merit of being intended, if not always successfully, to raise the long-term unemployed above the poverty line. Second looks at towns originally surveyed before the War showed that grinding poverty in the old sense had been halved at least. In Bolton, Northampton, Reading, Stanley and Warrington the proportion of working-class families in poverty had fallen between 1910–13 and

1924 from 12·6% to 6·5%, in York between 1899 and 1936 from 15·5% to 6·8% and in London between 1889 and 1930 from 37·3% to 9·1%. This did not, of course, mean that hardship had disappeared. On a new 'human needs' standard Rowntree found that in York in 1936 nearly a third of working-class families (31·1%) and over half (52·5%) of their children, were below the line, three quarters of them because of earnings or unemployment pay too low for the number of dependants. The old poverty line was certainly too low, and even the new left only a tiny margin for the comforts of life, but there can be no gainsaying that the worst kind of poverty had diminished.

In the 1920s the world seemed to be heading for peace; in the 1930s it began once more to head for war. The Japanese seizure of Manchuria in 1931 followed by full-scale war with China in 1937, Mussolini's attack on Abyssinia in 1935, the Spanish Civil War of 1936–39 in which Italian Fascist and German Nazi troops openly fought on Franco's side and Russian, French and British volunteers more furtively on the Republican, above all the aggressive opportunism of Hitler in seizing or acquiring by bluff and threats the Rhineland, Austria, Sudetenland and Czechoslovakia, all pointed with increasing certainty to a second world war.

The inter-war period, then, was an age of paradox: a peace which became increasingly an armed truce between world wars, and an age of depression which brought higher living standards to most people in Britain – not quite peace, and not wholly without prosperity. Part of the second paradox was that the new mass production industries, which held the best promise of work and higher living standards for all, themselves contributed to the unemployment: their very efficiency and high productivity, more output by fewer workers, meant that they absorbed fewer of the unemployed than they would otherwise have done. In the next chapter we shall look at the economic and social implications of mass production and the motor car.

103

FURTHER READING

C. L. Mowat, *Britain Between the Wars* (Methuen, 1955)

A. J. P. Taylor, *English History, 1914–45* (Clarendon Press, 1965)

David Thomson, *England in the Twentieth Century* (Penguin, 1965)

Sidney Pollard, *The Development of the British Economy, 1914–50* (Arnold, 1962)

W. A. Lewis, *Economic Survey, 1919–39* (Allen & Unwin, 1960)

William McElwee, *Britain's Locust Years, 1918–40* (Gaber, 1962)

Maurice Bruce, *The Coming of the Welfare State* (Batsford, 1961)

Derek Fraser, *The Evolution of the British Welfare State* (Macmillan, 1973)

A. H. Halsey, ed., *Trends in British Society Since 1900* (Macmillan, 1972)

M. Abrams, *The Condition of the British People, 1911–45* (Fabian Society, 1945)

A. M. Carr-Saunders and D. C. Jones, *Social Structure of England and Wales* (Clarendon Press, 1927, second ed. 1937)

G. D. H. and M. I. Cole, *The Condition of Britain* (Gollancz, 1937)

J. Montgomery, *The Twenties* (Allen & Unwin, 1957)

M. Muggeridge, *The Thirties, 1930–40, in Great Britain* (Hamish Hamilton, 1940)

R. Graves and A. Hodge, *The Long Week-End* (Faber, 1940)

A. L. Bowley and M. H. Hogg, *Has Poverty Diminished?* (King & Son, 1925)

Sir H. Llewellyn Smith, *et al.*, *New Survey of London Life and Labour* (King & Son, 9 vols, 1930–35)

B. S. Rowntree, *Progress and Poverty: A Second Social Survey of York* (Longmans, 1941)

5. THE AUTOMOBILE AND MASS PRODUCTION

The reason why Britain between the Wars could experience both high unemployment and rising living standards can be summed up in two words – mass production. For the same reason Britain experienced the first Industrial Revolution, with productivity and living standards rising fourfold during the nineteenth century, and in this century so far national income per head has more than doubled. Although we are no longer the richest country in the world, we are far richer today than when we were the top nation, and still amongst the minority of advanced industrial countries with living standards five or more times the world average.

Mass production, the secret of industrialization and economic growth, is not new. It was described by Adam Smith in 1776 in relation to pin-making, in which one unskilled workman 'could scarce, perhaps, with his utmost industry, make one pin in a day, and certainly could not make twenty', but ten practised workmen could make about 48,000 pins a day. The division of labour led to an increase in dexterity, a saving of the time lost in changing from one kind of work to another, and 'the invention of a great number of machines which facilitate and abridge labour, and enable one man to do the work of many'. Here, indeed, were all the elements of modern mass production except one: powered machinery. Adam Smith's machines were for the most part powered by the men themselves: only the drawing of the wire and the grinding of the point would perhaps be driven by a water wheel. Steam engines, so unfamiliar that he called them 'fire engines', were then only used for pumping purposes and almost never for driving machinery. When powered machinery was introduced in the nineteenth century, a thousand men could make over four tons of pins, or about half a billion, a day.

Powered machinery and the division of labour enabled 750 operatives in a steam mill of 1827 to spin as much cotton yarn as 200,000 hand-workers on the old spinning wheel. Even continuous-flow production came in as early as the 1780s, with Oliver Evans's water mill in Pennsylvania and the Albion steam mill in London, in which the grain flowed by gravity through all the processes of milling and emerged as sacks of flour, and with the 'power-loom brewers' like Thrale, Whitbread and Barclay who applied the same methods to the brewing of London porter. Conveyor-belt production can be traced back to the Fourdrinier paper-making machine of 1808, which produced paper in an endless roll, and to the Royal Navy's mechanized bakery for ships' biscuits at Deptford in 1833. Still more important, the interchangeability of parts, by which an intricate mechanism can be assembled from any set of precision-made components, was introduced by Eli Whitney of New England in the late 1790s for the manufacture of muskets and by Samuel Bentham and Marc Brunel in 1802 for the production of pulley blocks for the Royal Navy. Even automatic control mechanisms, including the punched cards and paper tape of the modern computer, find their progenitor in the Jacquard loom of 1804, in which the pattern of the cloth was determined by the holes punched in a continuous line of cards. Computers themselves were anticipated by Charles Babbage's 'difference engine' of 1834.

Modern mass production, however, in the sense of complex, precision-made machines produced by the thousand in a continuous stream, was undoubtedly pioneered by the automobile industry in the twentieth century. (By contrast the aircraft industry is almost a hand-made, 'workshop' industry: only 500 aircraft were constructed in Britain in 1969 and only 246 in 1972.) A motor car is the largest, most complex precision-made product the average consumer ever buys. The average car contains about 2,500 different parts, most of them several times over, and the whole vehicle consists of up to 20,000 'bits'. Most of them are of metal and machined to fine tolerances of a few thousandths of an inch, so that they will fit together without any further adjustment than the minimum of welding, riveting, screwing or bolting. Car manufacture is largely a process of assembling parts which are mostly bought from outside suppliers. As much as three quarters of the cost of a mass-produced car may consist of bought-out components, from the body which accounts for about 40% of the total to the dipstick at a few pence. Most firms make their own engines but buy outside the brakes and steering gears, clutches and propellor shafts, wheels and tyres, electrical parts and instruments. Some of the component manufacturers, such as Lucas (electrical equipment) and Dunlop-Pirelli (tyres and wheels), are as large as the car manufacturing companies themselves, if not larger. Every day at the British Leyland Austin works at Longbridge or their Morris works at Cowley 500 or 600 trucks arrive with components from 4,000 suppliers. Ford and Vauxhall (General Motors) make rather more of their own parts or get them from subsidiaries, Chrysler rather less. But whether bought out or made on the premises the thousands of components must all be put together in the fastest possible time in order to make a car at a price which the average customer can afford to pay.

The earliest cars were, of course, hand-made and, although crude 'horseless carriages' with none of the modern fittings and comforts, cost from £200 to £600, or from three to nine years' wages for a skilled car-worker. At that stage cars could be bought only by the rich, who had always been able to buy the labour of several other people. It was soon recognized, particularly in the United States where a large scattered population of modestly prosperous farmers and small business men had a need for a personal road vehicle and the means to pay for it if the price were right, that only volume production, already familiar in the manufacture of boots, sewing machines, typewriters and canned meat, could bring the car within reach of a mass market. Repetitive precision engineering and the system of interchangeable parts were the obvious solution, and could dramatically lower the cost. On this system Ransom Olds made 2,500 of his little Oldsmobile runabouts in 1902 and 5,000 in 1905. Similarly in Britain, the Standard Motor Company was founded in 1903 to manufacture cars from standard, interchangeable parts. Most American and British manufacturers, with the exception of specialists like Rolls-Royce and Lanchester, followed their lead, but it was an American, Henry Ford of Detroit, who made the breakthrough into modern mass production.

Henry Ford was a small farmer's son from Dearborn near Detroit, who learned to be an engineer by repairing clocks and watches and watching self-propelled steam threshing machines. His first job with the Michigan Car Company, which made railroad trucks, taught him the essentials of flow-line production:

Everything goes in one direction. At one end of the yard are the materials. The wood leaves the lumber pile, is shaped in the woodworking shop, and arrives at the setting-up shop. The iron at the same end of the premises divides into two streams of completed work, one being the wheels, the other the soft castings. Both streams, however, unite in the machine shop, and from there the wheels, trucks and other iron parts meet the wood in the setting-up shop, and are united in completed cars, which are pushed forward, still in the same direction, to the paint shop, where they receive the finishing touches, and emerge from the other end of the premises ready for the rail.

This system of manufacture, albeit of a much less sophisticated product, contained all the essentials of the assembly line which Ford introduced in 1913.

From the beginning Ford was fascinated by the idea of quantity production. He thought of mass-producing clocks and watches, but rejected it as likely to saturate the market too quickly. After selling his first 'quadricycle' in 1896 he said, 'It was not at all my idea to make cars in any such petty fashion. I was looking ahead to [large-scale] production.' The Ford Motor Company, founded in 1903, set out to reduce the price of a car from $2,500 (then £520), which was usual, to $500 or less, which the Model T arrived at by 1914. As Ford replied to a critic around 1910,

> I am going to democratize the automobile. When I'm through everybody will be able to afford one, and about everyone will have one. The horse will have disappeared from our highways, the automobile will be taken for granted, and there won't be any problem.

Mass production was achieved by stages. From the first 11,000 Fords manufactured in 1903 the system of interchangeable parts and an efficient flow of work through the factory were in operation. In the purpose-built factory at Highland Park in 1910–14 the raw materials for the foundry were fed in at one end, other components at the sides, and castings, chassis, bodies, and all other parts carried by crane to the machine shops and other processing departments. The work flowed along subsidiary lines within the different departments, and chutes and conveyors carried the components between floors, these streams all finally converging into the main river, along which the chassis were pushed until they reached the final stage of assembly, to emerge complete and ready for the road at the far end.

It was a small step from this flow-line system, moving jerkily by crane and muscle power, to the key innovation, the assembly line. Ford and his managers got the idea from the Chicago meat-packing factories where a pig was carried by overhead trolley and *disassembled* by a series of butchers each cutting one part

109

away 'until there was nothing left but the squeak'. Early in 1913 they applied it first to the assembly of the magneto, which when carried out by one man took twenty minutes but when performed by twenty-nine men spaced along a moving belt was reduced to an average of five man-minutes. After further success with assembling the engine and the transmission, they applied it in the summer of 1913 to the assembly of the car itself. A motor-driven capstan and rope hauled a whole line of chassis continuously along the floor. Six assemblers moved along with each chassis, taking up parts from stockpiles supplied by side-conveyors or arriving by crane overhead. (At this stage the men moved with the work and were not forced to repeat the same tedious operation every few minutes.) By this means the average man-time for assembling one car was reduced from twelve and a half hours first to five hours fifty minutes, then to two hours thirty-eight minutes, and finally to one hour thirty-three minutes. A completed car came off the assembly line every ten minutes, then every five minutes, and finally every two minutes. Production rose from 78,000 cars in 1911–12 to 261,000 in 1913–14, and to 730,000 in 1916–17 – an average of over 2,500 cars every working day.

Ford had discovered what Marx called the enormous forces of production sleeping in the lap of social labour. In 1913–14 the Company's 261,000 cars were produced by 13,000 workers, while the 66,000 employees of the other 299 American car manufacturing companies produced 287,000. By 1914 Ford produced every second car in the United States, 96% of the cars in the low-priced category below $600. Ford in that year reduced the price of the Model T runabout to $440, raised his workers' wages from $2·30 to $5 a day, and still made a profit of nearly $25 million. When he started, the cheapest car at $650 cost more than two years' wages for a car worker. By 1914 a Ford worker could buy a Model T for less than four months' wages. In a decade the luxury of the rich had been brought within the reach of the wage earner. Ford had democratized the automobile.

In 1913 British car manufacturers produced only about 25,000 cars – one tenth of those produced by Ford, one twentieth of those produced in the United States, just over half of those made in France (45,000). The most efficient British producer was William Morris, who in 1914 built 1,300 cars at prices ranging from £175 to £225 – more than two years' wages for a car worker. Morris had the same aim as Ford, to cheapen the car by volume production and bring it within range of the mass market. When the Ford Company began to assemble cars at Old Trafford in 1910, it is surprising that it did not scoop the market for cheap cars as it had done in the United States. For this there are three main reasons. First, the social structure of Britain was not so open and democratic as the American, the initial middle-class market for cheap cars was much smaller, and wages were far too low at that time to make a working-class market a practicable goal. The Ford subsidiary, the largest plant in Britain, produced only 6,000 cars in 1914, and this was not enough to achieve the economies of scale of the assembly line's potential. Secondly, the War brought the McKenna duties of 1915 on imported cars, and behind this tariff barrier British car firms were able to compete successfully not only with American Fords but with other foreign makers. Thirdly, the horsepower tax, introduced in 1909 and raised in 1920, fell more heavily on large-engined cars like the Model T, even when produced in this country.

Between the Wars British production of cars (and commercial vehicles) rose from a few thousand in 1918 and 71,000 (24,000) in 1923 to 182,000 (56,000) in 1929 and a peak of 390,000 (118,000) in 1937, when Britain had become the second largest producer of vehicles in the world. Morris installed the assembly line and his production rose from 1,550 cars in 1920 to 55,600 in 1925 and to 104,000 in 1935, when the Morris group produced a third of the British output. He was followed by others, notably Austin, Ford, Singer, Vauxhall (acquired by General Motors in 1925), Rootes (the car distributors who took over Humber and Hillman about 1930) and Standard which, along with

111

Morris and Ford, came to produce over 90% of the output.

Assembly-line production yields an optimum return at about 100,000 cars a year. Line production of engines reaches the optimum at 400,000 a year, and tooling costs, above all for dye-pressed bodies, are recouped on a production of one million a year. The most efficient car firm, therefore, would be one like American Ford or General Motors, making a million or more cars a year in few models with two or three different engines and a limited range of bodies, though it could assemble cars at as many as ten assembly plants dispersed near the best markets. The largest British firms could not compete at this level, but they were still large enough to reap considerable economies of scale and drive their local competitors out of business, though they could have been much more efficient if they had not clung to a large range of diverse models. Between 1929 and 1934 the ten largest manufacturers increased their models from forty-six to sixty-four. This reflected the nature of the British market and British society, with its gradations of status: each manufacturer had to have a model for every niche in the social hierarchy.

Every niche, that is, from the middle class upwards. Between the Wars car ownership in Britain remained almost a middle-class preserve: only a few wage-earners, thrifty single men or working couples with two incomes, could afford a car, though a much larger number drove motor cycles and the poor man's family vehicle, the motor-cycle combination (with side-car). (Motor-cycle registrations reached a peak of 724,000 in 1930, nearly three quarters of the number of cars.) Nevertheless, mass production even on the smaller British scale brought the price of cars within reach of a growing segment of the population. The price of a small family car like the Austin Seven, the Morris Eight, the Ford Eight and the Standard Eight was halved, from about £225–£250 in 1922 to about £115–125 in the 1930s. For a short period in 1935–37 the Ford Eight was reduced to £100, but significantly failed to achieve the mass sales to justify so low a price, and it returned to the £115–125 price bracket.

Ultimately it was the market, not mass production alone, which set the limit to the output.

One British contribution to mass production was ahead of its time. At the Morris engine works in Coventry in 1923 F. G. Woollard installed a line of unmanned transfer machines for machining cylinder blocks, the first example of automation, but the experiment was far ahead of the control devices then available and the factory reverted to manned production. Transfer machines and other forms of automation had to wait for the computers and electronic control devices of the Second World War and after. When they came they were installed first where volume production most justified them, in the USA and the USSR.

The British car firms were, nevertheless, the most advanced producers in this country and when rearmament began in 1936 it was natural for the government to turn to them both for military vehicles such as tanks and armoured cars and for other weapons of war such as guns and warplanes. 'Shadow factories' were built alongside the car plants. Morris, now Lord Nuffield, set up Morris Mechanizations and Aero Ltd next door to his Wolseley plants in Birmingham to build fighter engines and develop a fast, light tank. He also built factories for the manufacture of Spitfire fighters, at thirty a week, and Bofors anti-aircraft guns. Other car manufacturers made similar efforts, and the Second World War became, as we shall see in Chapter Eight, a mechanized war between mass production economies.

The War diverted almost the entire productive capacity of the automobile industry to armaments, warplanes and military vehicles. In 1943 only 1,649 cars were assembled and in 1945 only about 17,000, although commercial vehicles, more closely related to military trucks, rose from their previous peak of 118,000 in 1937 to 122,000. Agricultural tractors, too, were made in quantity throughout the War in an effort to extend the acreage under crops and save man- and woman-power: 18,000 were built in 1945, the same number as in 1937.

113

At the end of the War, therefore, the British motor industry found itself in an exasperating position. The world was crying out for motor cars, but the industry had neither the capacity nor the supplies of steel and other materials to meet the demand. The European car makers had been all but destroyed, the Americans were pre-occupied with supplying their own insatiable market and the world shortage of dollars prevented them from seizing the export market, and the whole world lay open to the British car manufacturers. Yet their equipment was worn down and often inappropriate to peacetime production, and there was an acute shortage of materials, especially steel. The government, beset by the adverse balance of payments and the need to export to survive, forced the industry by means of purchase tax and a quota system to export most of its production. For a time three quarters of the cars produced went overseas, and over 90% of some models – such as the Jaguar XK 120 and Austin-Healey 100 sports cars for which the American demand was brisk. Meanwhile, the domestic market was starved, and second-hand cars were at a premium, fetching prices nearly twice that of new ones, which were restricted to doctors and other priority users: in 1951 a Hillman Minx cost £600 new, £1,000 second-hand. The car industry seized the opportunity to the limit of its ability. Car production passed the pre-war peak of 1937 in 1949 with 412,000, and in 1958 it passed one million. Commercial vehicles rose to a peak of 341,000 in 1955, and tractors grew steadily to 144,000 in 1957.

By the mid-1950s, however, the British car industry's troubles which might have been thought to be over, were only just beginning. Just when other old and new car-producing countries were recovering from the War and beginning to compete fiercely in some of Britain's best overseas markets such as Australia and South Africa, a series of economic crises forced the government to squeeze the home market and restrict the growth of car sales. In the 'stop–go' economic policies which bedevilled the fifties and sixties, purchase tax was raised and lowered with bewildering irregularity. Hire purchase was manipulated by varying both the percentage deposit the purchaser had to pay and the length of time in which he had to pay the remainder. Petrol tax and car licence duty were repeatedly raised, and for a time in 1956 petrol rationing, abolished in 1952, was reintroduced as a result of the Suez war and the closing of the Canal. The crises unfortunately coincided with the downswings in car sales, so that the recessions were deepened and prolonged.

The industry met the challenge of competition and economic crisis by the classic method of concentration and merger. Amalgamation was in any case one of the major trends of mass production, not merely of cars but of every other product and service from soap to banking, but the car industry and its allies, the component manufacturers and oil companies, led the way in size of company as they did in scale of production. The largest company in the world, General Motors of America, is a car producer, and nearly all the top twenty are either car pro-ducers, oil companies, component manufacturers or chemical producers with a large stake in supplying the car and transport industries. Between the wars the number of car-producing firms was reduced by bankruptcy and amalgamation from ninety-eight to twenty, and by 1938 six firms, Morris, Austin, Ford, Vauxhall, Rootes and Standard, produced 90% of the output. Since the Second World War, the independents have almost disappeared and four firms, British Leyland, Ford, Vauxhall and Chrysler – only the first British owned – produce about 98% of all British cars. These car assembly firms, it is true, depend for a large proportion of their components on thousands of suppliers but these in turn are dominated by a comparatively few giants: Dunlop-Pirelli, Firestone, Goodyear and Michelin in tyres; Dunlop-Pirelli again, Rubery Owen and Joseph Sankey in wheels; Lucas and AC-Delco (a subsidiary of General Motors) in electrical equipment; Girling (a Lucas subsidiary), Lockheed (a subsidiary of the American-owned Automotive Products), and Ferodo in brakes; Hardy Spicer and GKN in propeller shafts; Smiths in clocks and instruments; Triplex and Pilkington in windscreens and windows, and so on.

The process of amalgamation can best be illustrated by the series of takeovers and mergers which culminated in the union in 1968 of almost the whole British-owned part of the car-producing industry in the single firm of British Leyland. Leyland Motors itself was an outsider, a solid, dignified conservative truck and bus manufacturing company descended from the Lancashire Steam Motor Company of the 1890s. It expanded steadily in this lucrative and very stable market, tapping the upsurge of road transport of passengers and goods between the Wars and the demands of both Wars for trucks. After the Second World War, it launched a brilliant sales campaign under a bright ex-apprentice, Donald Stokes, who broke the rival Associated Equipment Company's monopoly of the London bus market, and sold buses and trucks indiscriminately to countries as politically diverse as South Africa and Cuba. In the five years 1947–52 sales trebled; by 1954 the profit reached £1 million and by 1957 £2 million. In 1953 Stokes was put on the board of directors.

Most of the growth had been by straightforward expansion of the Leyland works, with only an occasional takeover of smaller rivals, like the Albion and Scammell companies in the 1950s. By the early 1960s, despite its leadership in its own field, Leyland began to be concerned about its future and that of the whole British vehicle-building industry. Its chief rival Associated Commercial Vehicles (as the old AEC became when it absorbed the Crossley and Maudslay companies) looked round for a car-producing partner. It made a play for Rolls-Royce, and was in turn courted by the British Motor Corporation. This threatened to outflank Leyland and leave it isolated amongst still larger giants. Leyland looked round for a car-producing partner so as to complete its range and use its now powerful sales organization to better effect, and in 1961, after a whirlwind courtship, absorbed the Standard-Triumph company, the smallest of the volume producers. Then, to outflank BMC's bid to take over ACV, Leyland put in a counter-bid which, surprisingly, succeeded. Although it paid heavily for both acquisitions, Leyland in two bites raised itself from a small giant in the conservative heavy-vehicle-building industry to a large giant in the rough and tumble of the car industry.

Meanwhile, the British Motor Corporation, the largest car-producing company in Britain, which had brought together many famous British marques, including Morris, Austin, Wolseley, Riley, MG and Austin-Healey, continued to expand its empire. In 1966 it absorbed Sir William Lyons's Jaguar company, one of the two remaining large independents. Leyland acquired the other, Rover, more important for its utility vehicle, the Land-Rover, than for its cars. BMC was still very much the leading company, especially in car production, but it was in some difficulty over design policy and cost control, and the American-owned companies were eating into its share of the market. The American parent companies were increasing their control: American Ford bought up the whole equity of British Ford, and Chrysler increased its holding in Rootes and changed the name to Chrysler. To fight off the American invasion, the British government urged a merger between BMC and Leyland.

The final outcome was a cliff-hanging tussle of personalities for control of the projected giant company, which would become (after Volkswagen) the second-largest vehicle-producing company outside the United States, and the fifth-largest public company in Britain. On the one side was Leyland's Sir Donald (later Lord) Stokes, on the other BMC's chairman Sir George Harriman and J. R. Edwards, their chief engineering executive. The marriage brokers were Sir Frank (now Lord) Kearton, chairman of Courtaulds, in his capacity as chairman of the government's Industrial Reorganization Corporation, who arranged a government loan of £25 million, and the Prime Minister himself, Harold Wilson, who invited Harriman and Stokes to dinner at Chequers in October 1967 to persuade them

117

that a merger was essential for the good of the country. In January 1968 the merger was announced, with Harriman as chairman and Stokes (over Edwards's hostile opposition) chief executive. But before it could be ratified by the respective boards, the terms of the deal were undermined by the revelation that BMC's projected profits had been grossly over-estimated, and the Leyland directors forced a renegotiation which resulted in Harriman's (and ultimately Edwards's) resignation and left Leyland in a controlling majority.

The resultant giant combine controlled 40% of the home market in cars and 35% of that in trucks and buses. It had a capacity of over a million cars and over 200,000 commercial vehicles a year, worth £1,000 million in sales and a gross profit of £50 million. In May 1973 Lord Stokes announced a massive new investment programme for British Leyland of between £400 and £500 million by 1978, including the rationalization of production and a reduction in the number of models. But it was all to no avail. British Leyland's problems, above all of over-manning and low productivity compared with its competitors at home and abroad, caused a financial crisis which by the spring of 1975 forced the government to come to its rescue with a massive investment of £1,400 million to save the last remaining British-owned section of the motor industry. The price was a majority share of the equity by the government, in effect nation-alization on the British Petroleum model. Whether this will solve the British car industry's troubles remains to be seen. Since 1960 foreign cars have increased their share of the British market from about 10% to over 30%, with a far from corresponding increase in British exports. As the backbone of British industry are exports, the collapse of the car industry could mean the collapse of the economy.

Today the British motor vehicle-building industry employs about half a million workers and could produce two million cars and half a million commercial vehicles a year, though it rarely works at full capacity. In the record year 1964 it produced

118

1,867,640 cars and 464,736 commercial vehicles, but by 1970 it was down to 1,640,966 and 457,532. 1972 was another record year, with 1,921,311 cars and 465,776 commercial vehicles, but the oil crisis and the economic recession have hit the industry hard once more. Meanwhile British production, never more than a fraction of the American, has been overtaken by the German, Japanese and French. In earlier years this could be blamed on the advantages of defeat in war, their need to start from scratch with brand new factories and machinery and with an artificially low rate of exchange which automatically reduced their prices. But now it is undoubtedly due to their much higher productivity and efficiency and Britain's failure to keep up with them. British car makers, both management and workers, must share, along with governments of both parties who failed to solve the almost continuous economic problems of the country since the War, the responsibility for the industry's poor performance.

The reasons are easy enough to point to, but enormously difficult to eradicate. They are partly the problems which beset all modern industrial systems based on mass production: the material problems of quality control and poor products; the organizational problems of maintaining output at optimum levels and selling it effectively enough and with sufficient after-sales service to make a profit and provide for expansion; the imaginative problems of designing an efficient and popular commodity which can be manufactured cheaply in quantity; the socio-political problems of making a safe, clean product safely and cleanly, without causing intolerable injury or death or polluting the environment; and above all the human problems of doing all this without dehumanizing the labour force and fomenting bad industrial relations, stress diseases in managers and workers, and distress and unhappiness generally.

Since all these problems have to be faced by mass production industry everywhere, however, the reasons are also in part peculiar to Britain. Managements here have manifestly been less successful in solving their problems. In the first ten post-war

119

years of near monopoly in the export field, quality control was lax and British cars got a bad reputation for reliability and after-sales service which they are only now beginning to live down. British manufacturers made, and still make, too many models, and thereby throw away a large part of the advantages of volume production. Volkswagen became the biggest car manufacturer outside the United States by concentrating on one model. The American 'big three', General Motors, Ford and Chrysler, make no more than half a dozen each. British Leyland, with an output far smaller, makes about sixty, and though some, like the Austin, Morris and Wolseley Minis, are the same basic model with minor variations of styling and performance, others like the Rover and Triumph 2000 series or the Allegro, Maxi and Marina are widely different models aiming at substantially the same market. Not surprisingly, British Leyland has a larger ratio of workers to output than the American-owned companies, Vauxhall, Ford and Chrysler, and far larger than the Germans and Japanese. With some notable exceptions, too, new designs have been unimaginative and slow to appear. Even the revolutionary front-engined, front-wheel drive series from the Mini to the 1800 were designed without much thought about production difficulties and cost control, with the result that the first Minis leaked rainwater into both the engine and passenger compartments, and the 1800s were too heavy for their engine power and too costly at their scheduled rate of production. Much less attention has been paid by British than by American producers to the problems of safety and pollution, with the paradoxical result that British exported cars are now being forced to conform to higher standards than those sold on the home market. Finally, by far the worst feature of the British car industry is its record of industrial relations. To understand this we must return to the disadvantageous aspect of mass production and its effect on the human beings who operate it.

What Henry Ford did not bargain for when he invented the car assembly line was the deadening effect of repetitive work on the workers themselves; or, if he did, he thought that high wages would be sufficient compensation. In one sense he was right: at the high wages car manufacturers were able to pay out of the vast yields of mass production, there has never been any shortage of car workers. Between the Wars, many unemployed miners, textile operatives and steel workers of the north and west, and many employed workers too, flocked to the car plants of the Midlands. Since the War the new car plants on Merseyside and in Scotland have similarly attracted workers in any numbers they required. Yet the boredom and psychological oppression of repetitive work have shown themselves in other ways. The mind-deadening automatism of the assembly line may indeed produce more mental and psychosomatic illness, high blood pressure, stomach ulcers and other stress diseases and so a far higher rate of absenteeism than days lost by strikes.

More attention has been concentrated on the bad industrial relations in the car industry, which has replaced the coal mines as the leading industry for industrial disputes. Losses through strikes were blamed for the declining profits which robbed BMC of equality in the merger with Leyland, and for the troubles at Rootes, which led to the take-over by Chrysler in 1967. Industrial relations at Fords have been the most notorious of all, and led to a court of inquiry under Lord Cameron in 1957 which revealed that the Briggs body plant alone had had 237 stoppages in the previous eighteen months. Vauxhall have a better reputation for good relations, attributed to paternalistic management and a smaller number of competing trade unions, only two as against the twenty-two at Fords and seventeen at British Leyland, but even Vauxhall in recent years have had a rising number of stoppages.

The high rate of industrial disputes in the car industry is often blamed on 'militant' shop stewards and politically motivated 'agitators' affiiliated to the Communist Party and splinter parties still more left-wing and 'irresponsible'. But this explanation puts the cart before the horse. In the first place, the number of Communists, Trotskyists and Anarchists is tiny, and even though they exercise influence out of all proportion to their numbers, they are still a small minority of the shop-floor leadership: at the British Leyland Austin works at Longbridge in 1972 only twenty out of 750 shop stewards were members of the Communist Party, and another half-dozen belonged to Trotskyist groups. In the second place, 'militants' can only exploit pre-existing industrial discontent. It is the nature of the work on the assembly line and the methods used to wring more production out of fewer workers which produce the original discontent. Endlessly repetitive work, the breakdown of tasks into ever simpler, shorter, more frequently repeated operations, the speeding up of the line so that each repetition comes round faster, the psychological pressure that arises from the sense that if one slackens pace neighbouring workers will lose time and wages, the feeling that one is tied to an inexorable juggernaut which will not wait for ordinary human functions like blowing one's nose or going to the lavatory, build up into a hatred of work and of the supervisors and managers who organize it. This can often find no relief save in the safety valve of the industrial stoppage. As one Ford worker at Dagenham put it,

> You're doing the same job, week in, week out, you can't leave the job for a change, there is the continuous repeated movement, your mind is miles away – I used to think of the [football] pools – you have that impersonal ruddy feeling and no pride in your job. Somebody gets on top of you, you get niggly. That's how it starts.

'It' might be a row with the supervisor ending in a punch-up; a deliberate act of sabotage as the only way to halt the inexorable pace of the assembly line; or a strike by a few dozen operators throwing thousands more out of work.

Even when, through patience and self-restraint on both sides, stoppages are avoided, the quality of the cars produced may suffer from the carelessness which comes from boredom and forgetfulness. A weld is missed here, a rivet there, a screw somewhere else, and the car develops a fault which the inspectors miss and the customer ultimately pays for. Friction between different workers, different departments, and between the production staff and the inspectors, adds to the causes of industrial discontent and disputes. On top of all this, the large number of competing trade unions in British car firms, by contrast with the one or very few in American and Continental plants, make negotiation and settlement of disputes more complex and hazardous here than elsewhere. Hence a large part of the difficulties of British industrial relations.

The remedies are not to be found only in an improvement of management techniques and a streamlining of trade-union representation, although these would undoubtedly help. Ultimately the solution lies in the reorganization of mass production so as to abolish or minimize short-cycle repetitive work and to give the individual worker a greater share of responsibility and sense of achievement. One line of advance is towards automation, to give the machines the tedious, heavy, dirty and repetitive work and to reserve for the human worker the creative functions of design, maintenance and overall control. Since the War the rapid development of computers and transistorized control systems has enabled both the Americans and the Russians to build automatic factories for such complex components as engine blocks and pistons, and British and West European firms are following on behind. More recently, individually programmed machines controlled by miniaturized computers can bring the benefits of automation within reach of the smaller firms and processes. If the manufacture of prefabricated timber buildings at Melksham, Wiltshire, can be automated, there is hope for the British car industry to compete in automation with its American and Japanese rivals.

Automation may in the short term cause unemployment, but in the long term it cannot do so without destroying itself. When a Ford executive told Walter Reuther, the American trade-union leader, that he was going to have trouble collecting union dues from a line of transfer machines, Reuther replied: 'You are going to have more trouble selling them automobiles.' If and when automation gets to the stage of replacing most productive workers, the problem will become one not of production but of distribution – distribution of work, especially in service industries such as administration, education, entertainment and the like, distribution of leisure in larger amounts to everybody instead of in enforced idleness to the unemployed, and distribution of income from the vast yields of automated production not to the few who own the transfer machines but to the majority who alone can consume enough of the output to keep the system going. A society which cannot solve this problem of distribution will soon destroy itself.

However, since not every process of production, and probably last of all car assembly, can be automated, a more promising line of advance is to fit the work to the worker instead of the worker to the work. At the Swedish Volvo works at Kalmar the traditional assembly line has been replaced by teams of 10–25 workers who organize the production of cars or sub-assemblies to suit themselves. Electric battery-driven carriers take the cars from one group to the next, and each team can decide how to share out the tasks in their process, and can see and feel responsible for their part of the completed car. Volvo have introduced the scheme to make it easier for workers to find meaning and satisfaction in their work, but they have also benefited from an improvement in quality and in industrial relations. Oddly enough, this is a return to Ford's original conception of the assembly line in 1913: a team of six assemblers moved along the line with each chassis, and saw its construction through from start to finish. Such a return might not only restore the quality of pride in workmanship but give the worker some sense of sharing responsibility for his work.

The Swedish government has also introduced in 1973 representation of employees on the boards of companies, which Volvo has had since 1971. A similar system is being introduced in the European Economic Community and is envisaged in the new Industrial Relations Bill before the British Parliament. Worker participation in management, offered by Chrysler and a requirement of the deal between British Leyland and the government, might go a long way towards solving the almost insuperable problems of industrial relations in the British motor industry.

Outside work, the main effect of mass production has been to increase material affluence, not least amongst the production workers themselves. Car workers are amongst the highest-paid manual workers, and at upwards of £60 per week (over £3,000 a year) can earn more than many middle-class non-manual workers, such as school-teachers and bank-clerks. They spend their money on cars, colour television, refrigerators, record players, fitted carpets and increasingly on owning their own houses and on foreign holidays. As one Ford worker put it in the early 1960s, 'They express their rise in class by boasting about material things.' This has led many observers to suppose that they are becoming more middle-class in other ways. According to a Ford shop steward, 'I've seen the change in blokes, a change in their political thinking. The system forces them to buy houses, and then they identify themselves with a group higher than the workers.' Some political sociologists have put down the electoral success of the Conservatives since 1951 to the *embourgeoisement* of the working class, and cited the car workers as the prime example of manual workers who have cut their roots in the Labour-voting, collectivist proletariat. Such sociological evidence as there is, however, suggests that this is far from the truth. The affluent workers of Luton in 1963–64, according to Goldthorpe and his colleagues, displayed a greater membership of trade unions and a larger propensity to vote Labour than the national average for the working class.

The reasons are not far to seek. Class is not, and never has been, merely a matter of income size. Security, future expectations for oneself and one's children, and style of life generally

125

have always been equally if not more important. The same Ford shop steward who saw house ownership as a step towards middle-class pretensions went on,

> Mind you, they're only middle-class through overtime. Their earnings could burst any time. Don't forget that overtime also deprives our fellows of those delightful leisure-time pursuits – freemasonry, Rotary, tennis and golf, though I must admit we're making some headway down at the golf club.

Insecurity, loss of overtime and loss of earnings through strikes or unemployment are an omnipresent fear of the affluent worker's life which mark him off indelibly from the professional and business middle class. The constant threat of income collapse makes most middle-class aspirations and assumptions unattainable: long-term thrift and planning, private education, private medical treatment, even the certainty of holidays. 'There's always a strike just before the holidays', one Ford worker complained, and another, 'I can't afford to risk going away. As soon as you save a bit, there's trouble and bang goes your money.' Economic insecurity and industrial unrest find their antidote in intensified working-class solidarity, trade unionism and Labour voting.

The remedy for working-class insecurity is not just middle-class incomes but middle-class conditions of employment, in other words, to professionalize the proletariat. This solution is already in process of adoption in the United States, Western Europe, the Soviet Union and Japan. American car workers have a trade-union-negotiated guaranteed year's wage, which is what but a professional salary? German workers are guaranteed 65% of their earnings by the state when sick or unemployed. Russian car workers are ensured full employment and large payments during illness. Japanese car workers have their jobs for life and are provided by the paternalist employer with every amenity from holiday homes and leisure clubs to complete medical care. Is it a coincidence that Britain has the lowest level of economic security for the car worker of any major industrial country and also the highest level of industrial unrest in its car industry? Perhaps that is why the human problems of mass production have been more keenly felt here than amongst our competitors.

FURTHER READING

George Maxcy and Aubrey Silberston, *The Motor Industry* (Allen and Unwin, 1959)

Graham Turner, *The Car Makers* (Eyre and Spottiswoode, 1963)

Graham Turner, *The Leyland Papers* (Eyre and Spottiswoode, 1971)

Allan Nevins, *Ford: The Times, the Man and the Company* (Scribner's, New York, 1954)

P. W. S. Andrews and Elizabeth Brunner, *The Life of Lord Nuffield* (Blackwell, 1955)

Alfred Plummer, *New British Industries in the Twentieth Century* (Pitman, 1937)

S. Lilley, *Automation and Social Progress* (Lawrence & Wishart, 1957)

S. Lilley, *Men, Machines and History* (Lawrence & Wishart, 1965)

W. H. G. Armytage, *A Social History of Engineering* (Faber, 1961)

J. H. Goldthorpe, David Lockwood, Frank Bechhofer, Jennifer Platt, *The Affluent Worker: 1. Industrial Attitudes and Behaviour* and *2. Political Attitudes and Behaviour* (Cambridge University Press, 1968)

Huw Benyon, *Working for Ford* (Allen Lane, 1973)

6. THE CAR AND THE COMMUNITY: I. BETWEEN THE WARS

The most visible effect of mass production and the rise of living standards in this century has been the crowding of our roads and streets with motor traffic. But the social effects of the motor vehicle have been far more profound than the congestion of our towns, the pollution of city air or the appalling danger and injury to life and limb. The automobile in its various forms has transformed the way we live and the way we work and spend our leisure. Above all, it has determined where we live and work, and so the shape and character of the human community.

How far-reaching these changes were first became apparent between the two World Wars. Between 1919 and 1939 the number of motor vehicles on the roads increased nearly tenfold, from 330,518 to 3,148,600. Cars increased nearly twentyfold, from 109,715 to 2,034,000. The rest were chiefly motor cycles, which rose from about a quarter of a million to a peak of nearly three quarters of a million in 1930 and then fell back to less than half a million; goods vehicles, which grew, to the dismay of the railways, from about 98,000 to 488,000; and buses and coaches, which increased from about 42,000 in 1919 to over 52,000 in

1930 and then stabilized, but which had an effect on social life and the community out of all proportion to their numbers.

At the same time, horse-drawn vehicles almost disappeared: though some brewers' drays and horse-drawn delivery vans, including 24,000 railway vehicles, could still be seen on the streets in the 1930s, the number of horse-drawn carriages licensed, 437,000 in 1903, shrank to 23,000 by 1933. The horse, which had been the mainstay of civilization for over 5,000 years and even survived the coming of the railways, now became only a pet for children and a sport for grown-ups. The electric tramway after enjoying a great boom reached its maximum extent of 2,600 miles in 1924 but between then and 1933 about a third of the track was abandoned. British Electric Traction, the largest private operator, and most of the municipal transport departments, transferred their investment into buses, and the noisy, comfortless but much-loved tram disappeared from many cities altogether.

The horse and the tramcar were doomed, but the railways, also under severe competition, fought back. There the competition was less for existing traffic than for the increase which greater mobility of people and goods brought with it. Compared with the pre-war peak of 1,550 million passengers in 1913 traffic on the railways did not fall even in the Depression, and rose to 1,819 million by 1937. Goods traffic fell drastically, but chiefly in coal and minerals, little of which went by road, and shrank, mainly because of the decline in heavy industry and coal exports, from 297 million tons in 1913 to 247 million tons in 1937. General goods carried by rail fell from 68 million tons in 1913 to 61 million in 1924 and 50 million in 1937. But the railways failed to get their share of what increases there were. Only a small proportion of the 6,664 million passengers by bus and coach in 1937 could have gone by rail, since most of them went short distances not served by railway stations, but Dyos and Aldcroft estimate that road transport deprived the railways of more than 200 million passengers, and Walker concludes that in 1935 about 100 million tons of freight went by road of which about 45–50 million could have gone by rail – as much as then went by rail apart from coal and minerals.

The railway companies argued that the competition was unfair, because they had to maintain their permanent way plus bridges, crossings and stations (although the motoring lobby claimed that motor taxation more than covered the maintenance and construction of roads); because their rates were controlled by a tribunal under the 1921 Act (although, since the companies never achieved the 'standard revenue' allowed by the Act, their charges were never in fact reduced by it); still more because their 'common carrier' obligation did not allow them to pick and choose their traffic as the road hauliers did, or vary their rates according to what the traffic would stand (although they could and did charge different rates for different classes of goods, such as coal and minerals, and made special agreements at favourable tariffs with individual traders). The solution which they proposed to the 1929 Royal Commission on Transport was that competition should be made fair by restricting the number of road carriers of passengers and goods and making them pay a larger share of the upkeep of the roads. This solution was adopted by the Road Traffic Act of 1930 and the Road and Rail Traffic Act of 1933, but it did not solve the railways' difficulties.

Their real problem was that they were badly organized for the automobile age. They had too many lines and too many stations in small communities better served by road; steam locomotives were too slow to accelerate from frequent stops, and local trains were mostly too infrequent for the new mobility demanded; goods traffic was bedevilled by small wagons, often without modern brakes so that they could not run at speed, by short hauls between too many centres with frequent breaking and making up of trains at numerous marshalling yards, so that a journey which took less than a day by road could take a week by rail; and there was the special difficulty of the privately owned wagon, which cluttered the system as it ran back empty to its

131

base and delayed the transition to modern rolling stock and methods of handling, such as larger, high-speed wagons and the container system. On top of this, the companies chose their managers from sound but conservative engineers, who resisted technological change such as electrification or diesel operation and had little concern for the commercial aspects of transport. They pursued outdated technological ambitions like the world speed record for steam locomotives, but did not calculate the costs of the separate areas of operation, such as branch-line working or excursion traffic, so as to know which of them were paying their way and worth continuing. As a result the cuts they made in fares and freight rates, which in theory should have enabled them to compete effectively with bus fares at about 1d. per mile and with road haulage over about fifty miles, failed to make the necessary profit.

The 'Big Four' companies which took over the whole railway system from their 121 predecessors in 1923 – the 'Big Five' if we include the London Underground Group taken over by the (nationalized) London Passenger Transport Board in 1933 – certainly improved the speed and efficiency of the railways between the Wars. They improved and standardized equipment to reduce maintenance costs, rationalized construction and repair works, reduced administrative costs, and made pooling agreements to reduce unnecessary competition where their regions overlapped. Operating expenses fell by about £29 million between 1924 and 1938, which further economies raised to £46 million a year. The London, Midland and Scottish Railway reduced its locomotives by 24% between 1923 and 1935, and in the 1930s introduced sixty-six new express trains operating at start-to-stop speeds of over 60 m.p.h. The London and North Eastern Railway achieved the world steam speed record of over 120 m.p.h. in 1938 with the *Mallard* hauling the 'Flying Scot', and its 60 m.p.h. expresses increased from twenty-five in 1934 to 107 in 1938, cutting 2 hours 15 minutes off the London–Edinburgh run. Between 1930 and 1933 about 900 miles of branch line were closed. On the freight side, express goods trains were introduced, and the use of containers rose from 350 in 1928 to 15,500 ten years later. Motor vans and lorries, 10,000 of them by 1938, gradually took over railhead distribution from the horse.

The most impressive advance was the electrification of most of the Southern Railway's network. Before 1923, apart from the London Underground, there were few electrified lines in Britain. The Southern invested £21 million in raising its electrified mileage from 17% in 1929 to 60% in 1938, by which date it and London Transport accounted for 800 out of 900 electrified miles in Britain. The great majority of these lines were in the London commuting area, where the dense traffic made the acceleration and frequency of the electric train particularly useful, and where road congestion ensured that suburban railways had an essential role. But, apart from a few suburban lines in North London, Tyneside, Manchester and Glasgow, the other companies resisted the 1931 Weir Committee's proposal for main-line electrification, chiefly because of the high capital cost, the conservatism of steam-minded managers and, it was said, the opposition of coalowners on the railway boards who seemed unaware that almost all electricity was produced from coal!

The railways also went into road transport themselves. They were amongst the earliest to operate motor buses, as we have seen, chiefly for feeder services or tourist trips in remote areas. Between the Wars, apart from acquiring the long-distance removal firms of Pickfords and Carter Patersons in 1934 and their own local delivery vehicles, they took little part in road haulage, but they became by far the biggest investors in bus operation. Their interest began slowly. For most of the 1920s, apart from the London Underground Group, which already owned the London General Omnibus Company and the lion's share of London's buses, and the Great Western, which introduced over 100 services with over 300 buses between 1922 and

1928, they took little part. But in 1928 they obtained general powers of road operation, and began to buy substantial share-holdings in the larger regional bus companies, such as the Tilling and British Automobile Traction group of companies, Crosville, Northwestern and Midland Red. By 1933 they had invested nearly £10 million in bus undertakings, and had a stake in perhaps half the buses in the country. But in no case did the railways' share exceed 50% of the equity and the railway directors on their boards were instructed not to interefere with their operations in a way that might be interpreted as unduly favouring the railways. Thus the railway companies failed to gain anything from their investment except a financial return which, it was argued, was less than it would have yielded if invested in improving the railways themselves. The railways survived to fight another day, but they neither found a new role nor tried to beat road transport on its own ground.

Meanwhile, the internal combustion engine showed its versatility by its application to a vast range of peaceful uses: to fight fires, to water and clean the streets, to drive cranes, bulldozers, earthmovers, road rollers and air compressors for pneumatic drills, to carry liquids in bulk, wet concrete and larger loads than ever went by rail, to deliver goods from house to house, to sell ice-cream, coffee or hot-dogs at street corners, to ferry the sick to hospital and the dead to the grave. It ploughed and cultivated the soil: the few thousand agricultural tractors introduced in the First World War grew to 55,000 by 1939. It even invaded the railways, in the form of the diesel shunting engine and the petrol railcar, but only as experiments until the diesel locomotive appeared in quantity after the Second World War.

It also launched itself into a new dimension of transport with the legal commencement of civil flying on 1 May 1919 and the founding of the first two scheduled airline companies, G. Holt Thomas's Aircraft Transport and Travel Co. Ltd, and Handley Page Ltd. But the history of British civil aviation between the Wars was nothing like the success story of the motor vehicle.

The planes were too small and uncomfortable, the fares far too high (about £12 return London–Paris in the 1930s compared with £5 15s. by first-class rail and boat) to attract enough passengers to make a profit without government subsidies. Imperial Airways, the prestigious public corporation founded in 1924 – and along with the British Broadcasting Corporation one of the first examples of the modern nationalized industry under the guise of a 'public corporation' – was subsidized, but not to the extent of the French and other Continental airlines, and while it certainly pioneered the longest routes in the world (8,359 miles to Johannesburg and 11,600 miles to Melbourne) its passenger traffic rose only from 10,321 in 1924 to 66,324 in 1935, and it only survived by means of its politically precarious subsidy. So, for that matter, did British Airways, formed by the merger of a number of unsubsidized companies in 1935, and supported by the government until it amalgamated with Imperial to form the British Overseas Airways Corporation in 1940. Passengers carried between Britain and the Continent rose from 42,000 in 1930 to 161,000 in 1938, when 60% flew in foreign aircraft, more heavily subsidized. Internal air services, in a small island with good, fast railways, were even less successful. A score of companies had come into existence by the 1930s, but their passenger traffic grew only from 3,260 in 1932 to 147,500 in 1938. The amount of freight carried was even less impressive, only 2,000 tons in 1938, but a breakthrough was made in the mail service, which rose from 28 tons in 1928 and 200 in 1935 to nearly 3,000 tons in 1938, when most of the first-class external letter mail went by air, chiefly in British aircraft. Apart from the overseas airmail, flying had little impact on society between the Wars.

The inter-war period, then, saw the triumph of the internal combustion engine over all its rivals. It was not, of course, so signal a triumph as in the United States, where the number of motor vehicles registered reached 26·5 million as early as 1929, one car to every five Americans, and the number of air passengers passed half a million by 1930 and 3 million by 1940. In Britain by 1939 there was still only one car for every twenty-four people, but there was hardly a family some of whose members did not travel regularly by bus or occasionally by coach. The motor vehicle dominated not only the roads and streets, with its noise, smell and danger to other road users, but also a large part of the public controversy, legislation and fiscal policy of the country.

The car itself, though no longer a luxury, was still very much a middle-class amenity. The British Motoring League in 1919 could look forward eagerly to 'motoring for the million', but a million still did not mean the mass of the population. In 1927, when there were three quarters of a million cars on the road, the Society of Motor Manufacturers and Traders pessimistically forecast that car ownership was nearing saturation point: the cost of buying and keeping a car would confine it to about the top third of the income-tax paying class, or a maximum of about a million. In the event, that number was reached by 1930 and doubled by 1939. But it was still confined to the middle class and a very few highly paid manual workers with working wives and/or the children off their hands. The average price of a car declined steadily from £684 in 1920 to £279 in 1930 and £210 in 1938; more significantly, the price of the new, small, cheap cars such as the Austin Seven or the Morris Eight came down from £225–£250 in 1922 to £115–£125 in the 1930s, and for a time in 1935–37 the Ford Eight sold for £100; but with average male manual earnings at 55s. 6d.–57s. 6d. (£2·77½–£2·87½) per week a car represented nearly a year's income for the average worker. In addition, the motor tax at £1 per horsepower from 1921 to 1934 and 15s. (75p.) thereafter, plus compulsory third-party insurance (introduced in 1930) and petrol tax (abolished in 1920, reintroduced at 4d. a gallon in 1928 and raised by stages to 9d. a gallon in 1938), helped to put car ownership beyond most workers' pockets.

The interwar period was therefore the great age of middle-class motoring. The roads outside the great cities were freshly tar-macadamed and comparatively uncongested. Prices were falling faster than middle-class incomes, leaving more disposable wealth to spend on pleasure, including cars, which were falling in price faster than most commodities and at the same time becoming more comfortable, reliable and easier to maintain. The new hire purchase and cheap credit for those with secure incomes made them still easier to acquire. Amenities for the motorist, such as wayside petrol pumps, pubs and hotels (often revived coaching inns), 'roadhouses' and 'country clubs' newly built for the motoring clientele, proliferated. A wholly new and delightful mobility became an expected part of middle-class life, freedom to live where one liked within motoring distance of work or of the railway station, freedom to visit friends, to get to the shops, the theatre, the golf club, the racecourse or the new cinemas without consulting a timetable, to enjoy the hills, the countryside or the seaside without elaborate planning, or merely to 'take a spin in the car' at a moment's notice. For the fortunate minority the motor car brought a new way of life and a new sense of liberty.

For some, motoring became a passion. Motor rallies organized by the Royal Automobile Club or local clubs, surreptitious road racing especially after the 20 m.p.h. speed limit was abolished in 1930, track racing at Brooklands, Donington Park and other circuits, the annual Motor Show at Earl's Court to see the latest models and accessories, all helped to glamorize the motor car and make it a symbol of prestige for the status-conscious. For the rest, the motor car was a means to other pleasures. Picknicking, camping and caravanning became fashionable at one stage of the family life-cycle; at another, for the younger generation of the well-to-do, the 'bright young people' of Evelyn Waugh's and Aldous Huxley's novels, the car was the indispensable adjunct of courtship and the more frivolous pastimes of the age – as one percipient flapper remarked, 'You can't do *anything* without a car.'

There was, unfortunately, a darker side to the pleasures of middle-class motoring. Road casualties mounted at an appalling rate. Full figures were not kept until 1928, when 6,138 people were killed and 164,838 injured on the roads. They reached a peak in 1934 with 7,343 killed and 238,946 injured – a record of deaths not surpassed in peacetime until 1964 when there were five times as many vehicles on the roads – but fell back by 1938 to 6,648 killed and 233,359 injured under the road safety campaign to which we shall return. Since the car driver was armoured and most of the victims were defenceless pedestrians and cyclists – in 1938 4,447 out of the 6,648 killed and 139,900 out of the 233,359 injured (and many of the rest motor cyclists) – and, if only for demographic reasons, mostly from the working class, while their assailants were labelled 'middle-class killers', the result might easily have been a species of class warfare. Since most magistrates and most juries were middle-class it became increasingly difficult to convict motorists for dangerous or negligent driving, while as William Plowden shows the average fine for all driving offences was little more than £1 and for dangerous driving only about £5. Not only were life and limb held cheap but the motoring lobby was insolent towards its victims. Col. Moore-Brabazon (later Lord Brabazon of Tara), one of the leading motoring spokesmen, burst out in the House of Commons in 1934: 'Over 6,000 people commit suicide every year, and nobody makes a fuss about that.' The Society of Motor Manufacturers and Traders described the Pedestrians' Association campaign against blood-stained roads as 'hysterical'. The Pedestrians' Association, by contrast, could by 1938 point to '100,000 killed and 3 million injured on the roads of Great Britain since the Great War'.

The motoring organizations opposed almost every attempt to improve road safety. The RAC and the AA condemned all speed limits, the driving test, compulsory insurance, pedestrian crossings, most punishments for driving offences, especially imprisonment and suspension of licence, the frequent publication of accident figures and any means, such as 'speed traps' or motorized patrols, by which the police might try to enforce the law. They attributed most accidents to 'human error' (56%), but chiefly by non-motorists, pedestrians, cyclists, animals or farm-carts, to bad roads (12%) or 'acts of God' (14%). The only remedy they offered for the toll of death and injury was increased expenditure on road construction and improvement to 'make the road safer for the motor vehicle' rather than for human beings.

The roads were, indeed, greatly improved between the Wars, though few new ones were constructed and none at all exclusively for the motor vehicle. Although the special 'motor road' was mooted by the Road Board in 1909, the inter-war Ministry of Transport set its face against motorways, and preferred to concentrate on the improvement of the general, all-purpose road. No one before Sir Alker Tripp, the Assistant Commissioner of Metropolitan Police, who published his famous little book on *Town Planning and Road Traffic* in 1942, thought in terms of segregating the motor vehicle from other road users, either on rural motorways or by pedestrianized areas of towns. The Road Board of 1909 and its successor the Ministry of Transport from 1919 thought in terms of classification of the existing roads (introduced in 1920, with 50% Exchequer grants to local authorities for class I and 25% for class II roads, raised to 60% and 50% in 1929, and finally 100% grants for the 4,500 miles of 'trunk roads' from 1936), of improving curves and cambers, widening bridges, providing overtaking lanes ('suicide strips') and, very occasionally, dual carriageways. New roads mainly took the form of by-passes, such as the Kingston and Exeter by-passes, and a few major links and reconstructions like Western Avenue, parts of the Great North Road (A1) and the Shrewsbury–Holyhead Road, and the Glasgow to Edinburgh and Inverness roads. It was all little enough: only 4% was added to the road mileage between 1899 and 1936.

The existing roads were improved in unspectacular but vital

ways. The familiar white lines, continuous on curves and broken between hazards, appeared. Road margins were more clearly defined. Direction and traffic signs multiplied, including the important 'halt' and 'slow' signs (now 'stop' and 'give way'). Traffic signal lights at intersections made their timely appearance from 1929, and the famous 'Belisha beacon' pedestrian crossing (named after the Minister of Transport, Hore-Belisha) from 1936. A few cycle paths appeared, and roundabouts became common, though not the more expensive flyover, which made its first appearance on the Winchester by-pass. Altogether, motoring became within the limits of the age easier, faster and safer. But the limits of the age can be seen from Osbert Lancaster's phrase for a familiar kind of middle-class villa, 'by-pass variegated'. Until the Restriction of Ribbon Development Act, 1935, not only villas but shops, factories, schools and, unbelievably, riding stables were allowed to set up on major roads with no limit on the exit of pedestrians and vehicles on to them.

Yet, despite the motoring lobby's talk of 'class hate', motoring and road safety did not become issues in the class war. In the first place, the predominantly middle-class government did not automatically side with the motorists. On the contrary, politicians like Churchill, Baldwin and Neville Chamberlain brought up in the railway age still tended to regard the motor car as a luxury of the wealthy – 'Would you', asked Churchill in 1925, 'propose to build joy roads to Brighton or Ascot at a time when you could not afford to build cruisers?' – and motorists as 'voluntary taxpayers' who ought to pay for their pleasure and the nuisance they caused. They thought it 'nonsense' to regard as valid for all time the pledge which Lloyd George had given in 1909 and Austen Chamberlain confirmed in 1920 that motor taxation would be entirely spent on the roads. At the Exchequer Churchill made a series of 'raids' on the Road Fund (transfers to general expenditure) in 1926–29 and Neville Chamberlain continued them in 1935–37. The motoring lobby continually upbraided the government for 'breaking its pledge' and the magazine *Motor* protested in 1927 that motor taxation had become 'a form of super-tax imposed on a class'. In Churchill's view, 'the motorists of every class, whether the owner of the Rolls-Royce or of the humble motor-bicycle, are amongst the most lucky and fortunate specimens of the many classes from which they spring'. This continual bickering between the politicians responsible for road policy and the motoring organizations gave the impression that the government put the public interest above that of the middle-class motorist.

In one respect it did, in the road safety legislation of the 1930s. After the 20 m.p.h. speed limit was abolished for cars and motor cycles in 1930 and raised for some classes of commercial vehicle, there was a surge in road casualties which led to the introduction of the 30 m.p.h. limit in built-up areas in 1935. The 1930 Act also introduced compulsory third-party insurance, set standards and penalties for careless and dangerous driving, and laid down maximum hours for drivers of public service and goods vehicles – fatigue, as in the early days of the railways, being a common cause of accidents. The 1934 Act introduced the driving test for all new drivers, raised the penalties for reckless or dangerous driving, and required a special driving licence and test for drivers of heavy goods vehicles. At the same time an important road safety campaign was mounted by the police in conjunction with the National Safety First Association (a body which was regarded by the Pedestrians' Association as in the pay of the motoring organizations since it received £1,000 in 1934 from the Motor Legislation Committee), and the 'safety-first' policeman became a familiar figure in the schools. The road safety posters helped to keep the roads out of class politics. In the second place, the working class had enough to think about in the 1930s with unemployment and depression, not to mention war and the mounting threat of war in Spain, China, Abyssinia and Hitler's designs on Austria, Czechoslovakia and Poland. Thirdly, enough working men had motor cycles or that substitute for the family car, the motor cycle combination, to bring motoring within reach of the working class. Fourthly, and most important, the majority of the working class had already experienced an improvement in mobility and the amenities of life from the advent of the motor bus and coach and, indirectly at least, from the services of the commercial goods vehicle.

The motor bus and coach were far more important in their social effects for the mass of the population between the Wars than the car. The long-distance coach in its 'liner' form for inter-city travel was cheaper if slower than the railway, and in its 'special' or charter form for day trips, works outings, football and other sporting excursions, it was the poor man's leisure vehicle. Private coaches licensed by the Metropolitan Police increased from 347 in 1928 to 1,762 in 1930, and a census in Central London in September 1930 showed 3,500 express coaches, including the new Green Line buses, passing each way. Throughout the country express services and excursion coaches competed with the railways and provided cheap trips to see relatives or to the seaside and countryside for the motorless majority. The coach and bus improved enormously in comfort, with better springing, upholstered seating, and windscreens for the drivers. In ordinary stage bus operation the 1920s saw a great expansion: the number of operators increased more than tenfold, from 331 during the War to 3,962 in 1930. It was a time of free-for-all competition in which large numbers of small men who could raise enough capital to buy a single bus – many of them ex-soldiers with gratuities – set up wherever they saw a demand for passenger transport. Such 'independents' with five vehicles or less came to constitute 90% of the operators and own 40% of the buses. They pioneered the concept that every town, suburb and village should be linked by motorized public transport and forced the larger operators to provide better services and compete in areas which they had neglected. The municipal authorities, many of which had tramways which they now began to abandon, also went into bus operation on a large scale, and the number of towns with municipal bus undertakings expanded from eighteen during the War to ninety in 1928. Though their fleets were larger than the independents', averaging fifty-four vehicles in 1931, and the traffic denser than in the rural areas, they accounted in 1933 for only one in eight of the buses and less than a quarter of the passengers.

The regional companies, the Midland Red, Southern National, Eastern Counties, North Western, and so on, were the biggest bus operators by far. Through their Provincial Omnibus Owners' Association founded in 1913 they divided up the whole country into non-competing territories. Only 10% of the operators but owning 60% of the vehicles, they were mostly controlled by a smaller number of holding companies, notably Tillings and British Automobile Traction Ltd, which came together in 1928 to control over twenty regional companies, British Electric Traction, which migrated from tramways to control a further twenty-seven, and Scottish Motor Traction, which came to dominate bus operation north of the border. It was in these territorial companies, and particularly in the Tilling-BAT group, that the railway companies invested from 1928 onwards.

The area companies soon came to terms with the local authority undertakings, usually leaving the short-distance traffic within the town boundary to the municipal buses in exchange for a monopoly of the outer suburban and rural services. But the independents presented a different sort of challenge and were not to be put down without a fight. From 1919 J. M. Hudson, an ex-Merchant Navy engineer, ran buses from Ellesmere Port to Chester in opposition to Crosville Motor Services, and started a 'war' which ended in dangerous driving and road accidents. In Stoke-on-Trent the BET subsidiary, Potteries Electric Traction, played a game of 'racing', 'chasing' and 'leapfrogging' with the ninety buses of its twenty-five rivals along the main route through the Five Towns. In London the near-monopoly of Lord Ashfield's Underground Group, including the original London General Omnibus

Company, was broken from 1922 by Arthur Partridge's 'Chocolate Express' and a host of imitators, 200 of them with 500 buses by 1924. In almost every urban area the competition of the independents, labelled 'pirates' by the big companies, extended services and cheapened fares at the expense of wasteful operation and sometimes danger to the travelling public.

Against the resulting 'chaos' the government felt obliged to act, first in London, then nationally. The London Traffic Act, 1924, introduced the licensing system by which the Metropolitan Police Commissioner could limit the number of bus operators and the routes they could operate. The ultimate solution to London's public transport problem, inaugurated by the socialist Herbert Morrison and the capitalist Lord Ashfield in 1933, was nationalization by public corporation in the shape of the London Passenger Transport Board. The licensing system was extended on the recommendation of the Royal Commission on Transport, 1929, to the rest of the country by the Road Traffic Act, 1930, under which regional traffic commissioners licensed not only operators and routes but also the fitness of vehicles, and the drivers and conductors, who now came to wear the familiar numbered badge. The result of the new system was to freeze the status quo, or rather to give advantage to the incumbent licensee especially if he were a large operator. The commissioners applied the principles of priority, protection and public need: that is, the right of the first-comer to protection from competition unless the newcomer could prove there was a public demand for his service. The existing operators and the railway companies had the right to object at the public hearings on new applications, few of which succeeded. Consequently, the growth in new vehicles, so headlong in the 1920s, slowed down to just over 3,000 between 1931 and 1938 and, as the large companies continued to buy out the small, now more desirable for their coveted licences, the number of operators shrank from 6,434 to 4,798. At the same time, however, there was an undoubted improvement in the standard of comfort and service, in the regularity and reliability

144

of the timetables, and in the co-ordination between different companies and areas. The relative provision of public road transport was much larger and more widespread in the 1930s than it is today, since a larger proportion of the population was dependent upon it to get to work and play.

The road transport of goods had a less obvious but nonetheless important effect on the distribution of the population. Road haulage after the First World War was an even more open field than the bus service for the independent operator, aided by the Ministry of Munitions which sold off 20,000 vehicles at throwaway prices, and apart from a score or so of large firms it continued to be dominated by the small man throughout the inter-war period. The number of goods vehicles more than trebled, from 98,000 to 348,000, between 1919 and 1930. Most of these were used by manufacturers and traders for carrying their own goods, and the average haulier was a small man owning no more than three vehicles and often driving one himself. Many only made a profit by overworking themselves and their men, not to say their vehicles, many of which were found by the Royal Commission on Transport, 1928–31, to be unfit for the road. The Royal Commission recommended the licensing principle for road haulage as well as for buses, as also did the Salter Conference convened by the Ministry of Transport in 1932. The Road and Rail Traffic Act, 1933, introduced the modern system of licensing: 'A' licences for public carriers for hire, 'C' licences for private carriers carrying their own goods, and 'B' licences for mixed carriers. 'C' licences were issued freely, but 'A' and 'B' licences very sparingly, and after 1935 their numbers actually fell. But the number of goods vehicles continued to rise, if more slowly than before, from 348,000 in 1930 to 488,000 in 1939, and more and more manufacturers and traders delivered their own goods.

The impact of the motor vehicle between the Wars on the distribution of the population between regions, between town and country and between city centre and suburb was immense, and yet almost no account was taken of it in the town and country planning legislation of the period. Land-use planning was one thing, traffic planning another, dealt with under separate laws, mainly concerned with police control of parking, road obstruction, traffic speed and flow, and so on. Traffic, indeed, was thought of as an inevitable nuisance, which had to be at once nursed and controlled, like a wilful and unruly child. The aim was to smooth the passage of the motor vehicle between and through towns and villages and to reduce its inconvenience when stationary by parking restrictions. Since motorways were ruled out by government policy, the main roads (class I arterial roads from 1920 to 1936 and trunk roads thereafter) went from town centre to town centre and through all the villages in between.

The only answer to congestion was the by-pass, hundreds of which were constructed, though never enough to solve the problem. The notion that it was towns themselves which generated traffic, and that the larger the town the more of its traffic was making for destinations within it and so could not be by-passed, did not occur in official thought until a Ministry of Transport report of 1946 which showed that, while four fifths of the traffic in towns under 10,000 population and two thirds in towns of 10,000–50,000 could be by-passed, in towns over 50,000 more than half the traffic was making for destinations within the urban area itself and, in conurbations of over half a million, more than 90% of the traffic was self-generated. Thus the road network was firmly based on the nodal points formed by hundreds of towns and thousands of villages, with a few inadequate by-passes and ring roads round favoured places.

Since all roads in the new classified system led ultimately to London, on the national scale the road system reinforced the drift of industry and population from the depressed North and West towards the prosperous Midlands and the South East. London and the Home Counties and the counties around Birmingham, with about 35% of the population of England and Wales, took 70% of the national increase in population between

146

the Wars. Most of the increase went to the suburbs of the 'conurbations', Patrick Geddes's word for the urban sprawl which was developing around every great city. The sprawl was itself a product of the motor vehicle. In the railway age the city's business and industrial district had packed tight around the central railway stations, surrounded by dense working-class terraces and by looser belts of lower-middle-class suburbs to the limit of the horse bus and the tramcar (about 4–5 miles), while the upper-middle-class suburbs had been strung like tight little beads on the strings of the radiating railways. In the automobile age the flexibility of the bus, the car and the goods vehicle enabled the city and the suburb to burst like a poppy-head, scattering its seeds into every available space around and between the urban centre and the surrounding towns and villages. Light industry based on electric power, like motor manufacture itself, radios, telephones, and consumer durables of all kinds, could migrate to the edges of the urban area, as in north-west London, the Great West Road, the car-building belts of Birmingham and Coventry, and so on. New housing, partly under the influence of the garden city and garden suburb movement, inevitably went to the suburbs, particularly to those suburban estates of uniform semi-detatched houses, 8–12 to the acre, with their small, attractive gardens and tree-lined avenues but often with no shops, public houses, churches or amenities of any other kind, which characterized urban development after the First World War.

Between the Wars over 4·3 million houses were built in Britain, mostly on estates of this kind. About a third of these, 1·4 million, were council houses built by the local authorities with government subsidies, partly to replace slums demolished in the town centres, partly to house the increase in population which, with the stagnation of private rented accommodation, could not be housed by private enterprise. New standards of internal amenities – bathrooms and internal lavatories and at least three bedrooms per house – and of external space – no more than twelve or fourteen houses to the acre – meant that the slum dwellers and their newly married children could not be rehoused where they came from but had to go to new estates on the edge of town. The council estate became a poor imitation of the private estate, usually built on a more generous scale, at eight or ten to the acre, for owner-occupiers on building society mortgages. The chief difference was that the council estates with their narrow roads and no garages made no provision for the motor car. Since they had, if anything, even fewer amenities than the private estate, they were entirely dependent, for access to work, secondary schools (infant schools were amongst the few amenities provided), shops and leisure facilities, on the ubiquitous motor bus.

Even the private estates were more dependent on the bus than on the car. By no means all the aspiring middle-class families could afford a car, and even in those who could only one member, usually the father who used the car to go to work, was fully mobile: the mother went to the shops, the children to school, both to the doctor, the hospital, the town hall, library and other central facilities by bus. On both private and council estates the isolation was mitigated in other ways by the motor vehicle: the travelling shop, the mobile library, the milk, bread and ice-cream vans, and the delivery van from the town shops with items of furniture and equipment impossible to take by bus.

Meanwhile, the well-to-do who could easily afford motor cars also broke out of the iron mesh of the railways, to live not merely an outer suburban but an ex-suburban life. The prosperous villa of the successful Victorian business or professional man had generally been within walking distance of the suburban railway station. Now it could be anywhere within daily driving distance of the station or of the city itself. The upper middle class began to invade the quiet villages off the railway lines, and to colonize the open countryside and steal its finest views. At the time when so many squires were selling up their estates and country houses, quasi-squires, with their weekday foot in the city

148

and their weekend one on the land, swept in to replace them. The 'stockbroker belts' of Surrey and Kent, Warwickshire and the Cotswolds, mid-Cheshire and the Wirral, and around Harrogate and Stirling thickened and stretched, and acquired the golf courses, tennis clubs, country clubs and all the motorized amenities of the automobile age.

The suburban explosion nearly doubled the built-up area of the country, from about 6% to about 10%, for a population increase of only about 10% – so loose was the texture of the new urban sprawl. Until the later 1930s, despite the 1919 and 1932 Acts, there was almost no effective planning control, and housing spread wherever the motor vehicle could go. Some of it went to the unmade lanes and tracks of what Colin Buchanan has called 'sporadic development', a patchwork of bungalows, smallholdings and scruffy plots on moors and commons. Outside the private and council estates, the commonest form of expansion was ribbon development, Whereas the railway had concentrated the suburb around the station the motor car and bus strung it out along every accessible road, thus adding to the congestion and dangers of the main traffic arteries. Even the by-passes were invaded, stultifying their main function of speeding the through traffic. A halt was called to this disastrous march of random building by the Restriction of Ribbon Development Act of 1935. It required that all future development within 220 feet of the centre of a classified road should be subject to the approval of the highway authority, in addition to that of the planning authority under the 1932 Act. Unfortunately, it also empowered the highway authority to lay down with Ministry of Transport approval a 'standard width' (of 60, 80, 100 feet, etc.) for any existing or 'proposed' road, without consulting the local planning authority. This made hay of integrated control, and further widened the gap between traffic and land-use planning.

The only integrated planning between the Wars was done by the voluntary garden city and suburb movement founded by

Ebenezer Howard around 1900. The First Garden City Ltd had been started at Letchworth in 1903 and Hampstead Garden Suburb followed in 1907. The second garden city was begun at Welwyn in 1920. They found imitators in Wythenshawe and Speke, new towns built by Manchester and Liverpool Corporations in the 1930s – though until well after the Second World War they lacked town centres and were indistinguishable from large council estates, except for a small industrial estate. But the movement bore the stigmata of its birth in the railway age – Ebenezer Howard's designs envisaged his new towns as satellites linked by rail to their parent cities – and the garden cities, still less their debased imitations in the semi-detached housing estates, made no concession, apart from the occasional cycle path, to the needs of the motorized society.

The inter-war period thus brought to only semi-conscious birth the motorized community of the automobile age. Its characteristic form of development was the conurbation, the growing together of towns, suburbs and bus- and car-linked villages in one vast urban sprawl. The conurbation, metropolis or, in its most gigantic form, the megalopolis, is an octopus whose arms are the ribbons of development, arteries the main radial roads and suburban railways, and nerves the telephone wires which link the offices, factories, shops and homes in a network of instant communication. Although few of its inhabitants know more than a handful of the rest by name, it is a real community, since each is dependent on all the rest for the mutual services vital to his survival and way of life. In a strange way it offers more freedom and choice than smaller, traditional communities, since one is less dependent on immediate neighbours and freer to choose one's friends, work and pleasures from a much wider area. But all of this was at an unplanned and immature stage of growth between the Wars, and an environment deliberately geared to the motor vehicle was still in the future.

FURTHER READING

C. D. Buchanan, *Mixed Blessing: The Motor in Britain* (Leonard Hill, 1958)

H. J. Dyos and D. H. Aldcroft, *British Transport: An Economic Survey from the Seventeenth Century to the Twentieth* (Leicester University Press, 1971), Chapters 11, 12, 13

D. H. Aldcroft, *British Railways in Transition: The Economic Problems of Britain's Railways since 1914* (Macmillan, 1968)

Kenneth Hudson, *Air Travel: A Social History* (Adams & Dart, 1972)

R. E. G. Davies, *A History of the World's Airlines* (Oxford University Press, 1964)

John Hibbs, *The History of British Bus Services* (David & Charles, 1968)

C. F. Klapper, *The Golden Age of Tramways* (Routledge, 1961)

William Plowden, *The Motor Car and Politics, 1896–1970* (Bodley Head, 1971), Part Two

William Ashworth, *The Genesis of Modern British Town Planning* (Routledge, 1954)

Sir Montague Barlow, *Report of the Royal Commission on the Distribution of the Industrial Population* (Cmd 6152, HMSO, 1940)

Sir Alker Tripp, *Town Planning and Traffic* (Arnold, 1942)

G. E. Cherry, *Urban Change and Planning: A History of Urban Development in Britain since 1750* (Foulis, 1972)

7. THE ROAD TO THE SUN

'Holiday making', wrote Charles Booth in the final volume of his famous social survey of London in 1903, 'is spoken of as "one of the most remarkable changes in habits of the last ten years," and the statement is applicable to all classes.' Holidays, however, even for the working class of the East End of London, were much older than that and began before the railways, with trips by horse and cart to the country and steamer trips down the Thames to Greenwich and Gravesend. The cause of the increase in holidays at the turn of the century was not the motor car or motor coach but that remarkable increase in real wages which resulted from the great fall in prices in the last quarter of the nineteenth century. The twentieth century was to see an unprecedented growth in holidays away from home, and the motor car and its offshoots, the motor cycle, the motor coach and the aeroplane, were to play the leading role in their direction and location. The road to the sun has been opened to ever greater numbers by the automobile.

The redistribution of leisure in this century has gone much further than the redistribution of income. The wholly leisured rich who still dominated society down to the First World War

153

have all but disappeared and have been replaced by hard-working managers and professional men who often take their work home with them, while the working class, and especially the increasing proportion of white-collar workers, enjoy ever shorter hours of work and progressively longer holidays. Most workers before the First World War worked a basic nine or more hours a day for a 5½-day week, some like shop assistants and clerks much more. Between the Wars basic hours were 8–8½, but overtime added an hour or more to these. Since the Second World War basic hours have declined from 44·4 a week in 1951 to 39·9 in 1973, with overtime from 47·8 to 45·6, while many office workers work 37 hours a week or less. According to a North West Sports Council survey in 1969, they have over-taken their bosses in their enjoyment of leisure: 'the most surprising result is that high socio-economic status is associated with a relatively small amount of available leisure time'.

A week's holiday, unpaid, was the norm for most manual workers, apart from bank holidays, before the First World War, though some white-collar workers got two. Between the Wars most of the former still got one, though an increasing number got two, but the striking change was the Holidays with Pay Act, 1938, which increased the numbers receiving payment from about 1½ million in the 1920s and 4 million in 1937 to over 11 million in 1939. Since the Second World War most workers have achieved at least two weeks' paid holiday, and in the early 1970s, partially under the influence of the European Common Market where holidays are longer than in Britain, there has been a further change in the direction of three or four weeks.

The numbers taking a holiday away from home have grown less fast, since many people either cannot afford or do not wish to stay away from home. As late as 1937 only about 15 million (including families) went away for a holiday, or less than one in three of the population. Nearly 1½ million Britons travelled abroad, perhaps about a million of them on holiday. After the War, about half the adult population went on holiday in

1951, 59% in 1970 and 63% in 1973 (of whom 20% took two or more holidays, defined as four or more nights away from home). The third or more who did not take a holiday were mainly old-age pensioners, parents with very young children, and families in the manual socio-economic groups (C2, D and E). Those who did go created an all-time boom in the number of holidays, rising from 26·5 million in 1951 to 48·8 million in 1973. They also spent record amounts of money, rising from £380 million in 1951 to £1,750 million in 1972, or from £11 per holiday maker in Britain to £25.

If we add to these the foreign visitors to the United Kingdom, 6·5 million of them in 1972 who spent £518 million, holiday making, like the motor industry, is very big business. And the two are increasingly interconnected. Whereas before the First World War the great majority of holiday makers went by train, between the Wars an increasing minority went by car and a substantial minority which grew into a majority by road (including the poor man's car, the motor coach). Since the Second World War the proportion of holiday makers in Britain going by rail has shrunk from 47% in 1951 to 12% in 1972, while those by car have risen from 27% to 70%, and those by motor vehicle (car, bus or coach) from 53% to 85%. Of those going abroad in 1973 only 15% took their cars, mainly due to the increasing popularity of the airborne package tour: the proportion going abroad by plane rose from 40% in 1960 to 71% in 1973.

The motor vehicle had a greater impact on the type and destination of holidays than on the numbers taking them, which with higher living standards would have risen considerably in any case. The railways had tended to concentrate provision for holidays in a comparatively small number of large resorts. Not that the Victorian resorts catered uniformly for the undifferentiated masses: each had its own 'social tone' and attracted, according to season and local geography, its own subtly graded spectrum of the social strata, the higher classes going to Bournemouth, Torquay, Scarborough and Southport throughout

155

the season, the lower to Blackpool, Southend, Skegness and Rhyl in the high season only. But the motor coach, which carried over 82 million passengers by 1937, and still more the motor car gave a new lease of life to the smaller and remoter resorts, and hundreds of decayed fishing villages along the coasts of Yorkshire, East Anglia, West Wales and the South West suddenly found themselves the object of the motorized tourist looking for peace and beauty off the beaten track. It took some time for the trend to establish itself, and between the Wars the larger resorts benefited from the cheap fares of the coach and long-distance service bus and scarcely felt the competition of the smaller places: in 1938 Blackpool still had 7 million visitors, Southend 5½ million, Hastings nearly 3 million, Bournemouth and Southport 2 million each, and Eastbourne over 1 million. But the strength of the trend since the Second World War can be seen from the rise in the popularity of the South West and Wales, even as they lost most of their railway services and they came to rely increasingly on the motor vehicle: the proportion of tourists taking their main holidays in the West Country rose to 21% in 1965 and to 26% in 1973, and in Wales from 9% in 1951 to 14% in 1973 – a total of 40% in the two areas with fewest large resorts and most coves and seaside villages inaccessible by rail. By contrast, according to an English Tourist Board survey, Blackpool still received a large proportion of its 2·6 million staying visitors and 3·4 million day trippers in 1972 by rail, most of them from the lower socio-economic groups in which car-owning was less frequent.

Before the First World War, as we have seen, the motor car was a rich man's toy while between the Wars it was a middle-class delight. The roads were, however, used by more than the rich and middle classes. Cycling began for the well-to-do and energetic in the late Victorian age but soon became democratized, and the Cyclists' Touring Club was founded as early as 1878 to encourage the provision of modest accommodation at fixed prices. It reached a peak membership of 60,449 in 1899 and though it declined to 18,227 in 1910, unorganized cycling thrived down to the 1960s, until the roads became so choked with cars as to make cycling miserable. With the oil crisis, it is now enjoying a revival, and the cycling lobby is demanding separate amenities. Hiking, a more democratic version of the Victorian intellectuals' walking tour, became a craze between the Wars enshrined in a popular song, and in the form of 'hitch-hiking' to shorten the more boring parts of the journey made use of the motor car and lorry. Camping, until recently mainly associated with walking and cycling, became increasingly popular. It was catered for by the Camping Club of Great Britain, founded in 1901, and by similar bodies providing sites in the 1930s for as little as 8d. (3·3p.) a night per head. The Youth Hostels Association, founded in 1929 and with nearly 80,000 members by 1939, provided bed and breakfast for walkers and cyclists for as little as 2s. 6d.(12·5p.). In recent years camping and still more caravanning, with either towed or fixed-site caravans, have come to be more associated with car ownership. In 1972 camping accounted for 5% of all holiday accommodation in Britain, towed caravans for 3% and fixed caravans for 11%. If we add rented flats and cottages no less than a quarter of all holiday makers went in for do-it-yourself accommodation. Since more than half stayed with friends or relatives or in a second home (holiday cottage or flat), less than a quarter stayed in hotels and guest houses, a surprising comment on the change in holiday habits during this century.

A further 3% stayed in holiday camps, an inter-war innovation, though even they may be said to derive from the convalescent homes for sick workers provided by some Victorian trade unions and business firms and for children by local authorities and charities. Before the First World War the Workers' Travel Association, the Co-operative Holidays Association and its 1913 offshoot the Holiday Fellowship provided non-profitmaking guest houses at cheap prices, but the first modern holiday camp is claimed to be the one built at Lowestoft in 1924 by the Civil Service Clerical Association for its members. In the early 1930s Cunningham's Camp for young men at Douglas, Isle of Man, was probably the first such camp open to the general (male) public, but the pioneer of the holiday camp as we know it, providing every possible facility for the whole family within the perimeter fence, was undoubtedly 'Billy' Butlin who opened his first camp at Skegness in 1937. It was so successful that it was extended the next year and a further one opened at Clacton in 1939, and more at Filey, Pwllheli, Minehead and elsewhere since the War. He stimulated many imitators, like Travco Ltd, jointly owned by the Co-operative Wholesale Society and the Workers' Travel Association, Thomas Cook Ltd and the London, Midland and Scottish Railway who opened a jointly owned camp at Prestatyn in 1939, Pontin's who began one at Heysham, and even Lambeth Borough Council, which planned a camp for 400 at Herne Bay. By 1939 there were up to 200 camps with accommodation for 30,000.

The original camps were famous for their 'camping spirit', the mixture of compulsory, regimented, noisy, vulgar if innocent fun jollied along by professional cheer-leaders, Butlin's 'redcoats' and their like. They were not cheap, but considerably more expensive than the typical working-class boarding houses, and attracted the lower-middle-class clerk and shopkeeper more than the manual worker, but once inside everything from the mass catering to the dances, swimming pools, funfairs and competitions for the most beautiful girls or the knobbliest male knees was free and, a boon for families, there were safe crêches and playgrounds for babies and children. It was not an institution for the motorist, any more than the traditional holiday resort, and most campers arrived by train or coach. If it had any relevance to the motoring age it was, like the mass holiday resort, to keep the non-motoring majority out of the competition for the smaller, less accessible resorts – which were becoming overcrowded by the motorists and still more, like such tiny Cornish resorts as Newquay and St Ives, jammed by their vehicles.

More recently, the holiday camps have joined the modern trend towards self-catering and have begun to provide chalets with kitchenettes instead of compulsory mass dining. In a similar way, the hectoring regimentation and compulsory fun of the redcoats has largely been abandoned for a freer, more easy-going, take-it-or-leave-it provision of a wide range of facilities. They have even exploited the modern airborne search for guaranteed sunshine on the Mediterranean, with such typically English institutions as the Pontinental camps in Majorca.

Holidays abroad have boomed in the twentieth century even more than holidays in general. While holidays in general nearly doubled, the number of foreign holidays more than quintupled between 1951 and 1973 from 1·5 million to 8·3 million, and the amount of money spent rose from £60 million to £830 million, or from £41 to £96 per holidaymaker, four times as much as at home. Once the prerogative of the rich on the aristocratic grand tour, foreign holidays were facilitated for the middle class by the railways and steamships and by the 'package tour' pioneered by Thomas Cook. He began his foreign tours in 1855 with trips to continental capitals and soon he was organizing tours to Switzerland, Italy, America, Egypt and Palestine, and even around the world (1872). Like Butlin he found imitators: Dean and Dawson (1871), the Polytechnic holiday organization (1872, separated from the College in 1911), Sir Henry Lunn (1892), and many others. Cook's organized the first motoring tours to the Continent from 1902. Since then the foreign package tour, at first by train and boat, later by coach and boat and more recently by charter plane, has gradually ousted the independent tour for most winter sports and seaside holidays: between 1960 and 1973 package tours (including cruises) rose from 30% to 63% of all foreign holidays. The convenience of the package tour, the certainty of what you have to pay, the saving of trouble in putting together the arrangements for transport and accommodation, and the provision of guides and interpreters all help to account for their popularity. But the key

159

reason for their triumph is their cheapness, which enables the holiday maker to get full meals and accommodation in a resort a thousand or more miles away for not much more than the cost of travel by scheduled services. This in turn derives from the economics of transport and above all of air travel: a charter plane with a guaranteed payload can offer tickets at half the price of a scheduled service with its risk of empty seats. On the other hand, competition cut profit margins so fine that even the largest tour operators were in danger from any unforeseen hazard. When the oil crisis in 1974 increased costs and cut bookings by 30%, several large operators, including the huge Court-Line-Horizon-Clarkson's group, went out of business.

One form of package tour which burgeoned between the Wars was the sea cruise, expanded to make use of the surplus shipping of the 1920s and still more of the world slump of the 1930s. In 1937 about 55,000 passengers travelled on British vessels cruising to Mediterranean and European ports. Some cruise lines sought a specialized clientele, like Swann's guided tours to classical Greece or Wayfarers' 'cruises with books', 'with music' or 'with drama'; but most were floating holiday camps for the well-to-do, with all the usual pastimes of the bored and boring rich. Since the War, cruises, especially of the fly-and-sail type in the Mediterranean or Caribbean, have sustained their popularity, mostly in non-British vessels to avoid British taxation and marine safety laws and working conditions, though being even more dependent on fuel costs they have been hit harder than other package tours by the oil crisis.

Though the British pioneered holidays and particularly holidays abroad, they are no longer the leaders in the field. The Americans and Canadians, the Germans and the French have overtaken them, and the Japanese are rapidly catching up. Holiday making is a function of economic development and is dependent on the surpluses generated by high productivity and a positive balance of payments. In the world-wide boom since the War there has been a phenomenal increase in international tourism, from 25 million arrivals in 1950 to 181 million in 1971. Not surprisingly, the overwhelming majority, 96%, of this traffic originated in Europe and North America, two thirds of it in Europe since the Americans and Canadians each have half a continent to themselves and only a small minority (still a large number) travel abroad, while three quarters of all international tourists come from only twelve countries: USA, Germany, France, the United Kingdom, Canada, Belgium, the Netherlands, Italy, Switzerland, Sweden, Denmark and Austria. Two countries alone, USA and Germany, with less than 8% of the world's population, provide 40% of international tourists. Europe is even more important as a tourist centre than as a generator of tourism: three quarters of the world's tourists arrived there in 1971. The number visiting Britain (some of them partly on business) increased more than tenfold, from 618,000 in 1950 to 6,730,000 in 1970.

Such figures raise the question of whether the intense international competition for tourists, backed by government agencies and advertizing campaigns, is worth it. Some countries, such as Spain and the Caribbean states, have become dangerously dependent on tourism for their balance of payments. Yet there are grave doubts whether tourists do not cost more, in imports of their special foods and other needs, in diversion of capital from more rewarding investment and in distortion of the labour market towards unskilled and season service trades, than they are worth. Moreover, the pressure of tourism on the environment and other amenities of the home population is incalculable, especially in a small, overcrowded island like Britain. Since the foreign tourists concentrate on a few centres, notably London, Windsor, Stratford, Oxford and Cambridge, they add to the expense and traffic congestion of these places and raise costs for everyone else. That is why some commentators like Sir George Young think that tourists should now be discouraged, at least from overcrowding the more traditional attractions, or diverted to areas which are not so hard-pressed. But this may only add to the congestion of Devon and Cornwall, Wales and the Lake District. The kind of visitor who comes to Britain from America or the Continent is not seeking the sea and sun, and it is highly unlikely that he will be attracted in large numbers to the places where the hotel beds are available, such as Blackpool, Brighton or Bournemouth.

British holidaymakers in this country still far outnumber both those going abroad and foreign tourists coming here. Pressure on the environment comes more from the natives than from overseas visitors, and more from changing patterns of leisure than from the traditional holiday maker, concentrated as he tends to be in certain areas and in three or four months of the year. One feature is the taking of second holidays (of four nights or more), a recent phenomenon which rose from about 7% of the adult population taking two or more holidays (out of the 56% who took holidays at all) in 1966 to 20% (out of 63%) in 1973. Another trend is the number of winter package holidays, mostly abroad, which rose from under 7,000 in 1963–4 to 600,000 in 1971–2. Second holidays tend to be spread more evenly round the year than main holidays, those in this country to be somewhat nearer home, and to involve still more the use of the family car and self-catering accommodation, including second homes and caravans, or staying with friends and relatives. They mainly reinforce the second and more important feature, the use of longer weekends to enjoy holiday trips all the year around. This explains the popularity of the second home, country cottage, seaside flat or fixed caravan, of the towed caravan and of the small boat, sailing dinghy or cabin cruiser, either towed behind the car or moored as a floating second home. Caravans and small boats are one of the growth industries of the age, and almost as good an index of prosperity as national income itself.

The most important feature of modern leisure, however, is the sheer mobility provided by the motor vehicle. Probably the commonest outdoor leisure-time activity is going for a drive in the car: 58% of the population did so at least once a month in 1970, and this varied only from 62% in the professional and managerial and in the skilled working class to 49% in the semi-skilled and unskilled, the latter figure being lower only because of the lack of cars. What people did on these trips varied little with age or class: according to the first National Recreation Survey in 1967, they mostly went to the countryside (34%) to a well-known beauty spot or simply somewhere to picnic and look at a view or play a game within sight of the car, to the seaside (28%), either a large resort with all the usual holiday attractions or a secluded beach for sun and sea bathing, or to a town (24%) to shop or see historic buildings or museums or 'just to look around'. The rest (14%) went to visit country houses or historic sites, to watch sporting events such as football matches or gymkhanas, or to visit friends and relatives. There was little difference between city and small town or country dwellers, except that fewer large town dwellers went to visit another town, and for obvious geographical reasons Liverpudlians went more to the seaside and Mancunians more to the countryside.

Amongst the commonest objectives of the day tripper is the country house or garden open to the public, of which there are now more than 800. In 1971, according to the British Tourist Authority, 20 million visits were made to stately homes, a quarter of them by overseas tourists. At an average of 20p. a head they paid £6 million for their private view of the way the rich once lived. The top six in order of known popularity were Lord Montagu's Beaulieu which with its motor car museum attracted half a million visitors, the Earl of Warwick's Warwick Castle, the Marquess of Bath's Longleat with nearly 300,000 visitors to the house and nearly a million to the safari park, the Earl of Harewood's Harewood, the Duke of Marlborough's Blenheim Palace, and Lord Astor's Hever Castle. The Duke of Bedford's Woburn, with its 12,000-acre estate, £2 million picture collection, safari park, funfair and multiple attractions might

163

top the list, but 'we do not disclose our figures to anyone': over 1·3 million came to see the game reserve in 1970. In the safari parks at Woburn, Longleat, the Earl of Derby's Knowlsey and elsewhere, the motor car is a vital necessity: the free-ranging lions and other dangerous beasts can be viewed only from the safety of a travelling glass and metal cage. Many other stately homes have added to the historical charms of elegant furniture, beautiful pictures and fine gardens the contemporary catch-penny attractions of funfairs, sideshows, child-bearing model railways and the like, so that it is difficult to distinguish their drawing power from that of the popular seaside resorts.

Other day-tripping rendezvous include the railway museums at York, Swindon and Carnforth (and the late and much lamented transport museum at Clapham); the tramway museum at Crich near Matlock; those delightful narrow-gauge railways kept alive by enthusiastic volunteers, the Ffestiniogg, Talyllyn and Vale of Rheidol Railways in Wales, the Ravenglass and Eskdale in the Lake District, the Bluebell in Sussex, the Keighley and Worth Valley in Yorkshire, and so on. But the great majority of day trippers simply go for the beauty and fresh air and often make for the nearest place where they hope to find them. In the overcrowded South East, where open fells and national parks are scarce, this often means the remaining scraps of common land like the London commons, Ashdown Forest, Bagshot Heath, Burnham Beeches and Epping Forest. Large areas of open land as well as over 200 historic buildings have been preserved for the public and posterity by the National Trust, founded in 1895 and now grown to about a quarter of a million members owning 356,000 acres (1969) – about 1% of England and Wales. The Trust was built up to this size by the suburban motoring class, according to its historian 'modest people who since the last war have discovered in motor cars the pleasures and beauties of the coast and countryside'. The problem, as a government white paper put it in 1966, 'is to enable them to enjoy this leisure without harm to those who live and work in the country, and without spoiling what they come to the countryside to seek'.

Government policy has only recently begun to face up to this problem. For half the twentieth century it was content to leave the conservation of the rural landscape and access to the country-side to the National Trust, which with the help of tax concessions became the largest landowner after the crown and the state, and to the Council for the Preservation of Rural England founded in 1926. Only after the Second World War did the government begin to play a direct role in conservation, with the National Parks and Access to the Countryside Act, 1949. Under this ten national parks were designated between 1950 and 1955, all of them in the highland northern and western half of England and Wales: Northumberland, the Lake District, the Yorkshire Dales and North York Moors, the Peak District, Snowdonia, the Pembrokeshire Coast and Brecon Beacons, Exmoor and Dart-moor. They were mostly mountain and high moorland, in the words of John Dower's 1945 Report 'extensive areas of beautiful and relatively wild country' in which landscape beauty was more strictly preserved than under the 1932 and 1947 Town and Country Planning Acts, public access was amply provided, wild life and historic places and buildings of architectural interest were specially protected, while existing farming use was effectively maintained. Almost all the area was in fact being farmed and much of it in enclosed fields. Only a minority was fully open to the public, either as traditionally open moorland and fells or subject to access agreements negotiated by the local park authorities.

Partly to redress the balance towards the south and east twenty-seven Areas of Outstanding Natural Beauty covering 4,464 square miles, nearly 8% of England and Wales, were also designated, without the local machinery of the National Parks but subject to similarly strict planning control: the Solway Coast and the Forest of Bowland (North Lancashire) in the North; the Anglesey, Lleyn Peninsula and Gower coasts in

Wales; Cannock Chase, the Shropshire and Malvern Hills and the Cotswolds in the West Midlands; the Quantock Hills, most of the Devon coast, and parts of the Cornish moorland and coast in the South West; and the Dorset and South and East Hampshire coasts, the Isle of Wight and Chichester Harbour, the Surrey Hills and Kent and Sussex Downs, the Chilterns, Dedham Vale and the Norfolk and Suffolk coasts and heaths in the South and South East. In addition to these are the Green Belts around the major conurbations and the rather amorphous Areas of Great Landscape, Historic or Scientific Value, both designated under the 1947 Planning Act. All told, some two fifths of England and Wales are subject to active conservation. All these areas have been brought under the umbrella of the Countryside Act of 1968 and of the Countryside Commission, which has succeeded the National Parks Commission with a larger budget and wider powers, though still inadequate to the purpose. The Forestry Commission began to set up Forest Parks in the 1930s, beginning with Argyll (1935), the Snowdonia Forest Park (1937) and Dean Forest Park (1938); Grizedale, for example, on the shores of Lake Coniston, has nature trails, forest walks, 'photo-safari' viewing points, a wild-life centre and deer museum.

A recent development under the 1968 Act is the purchase by local authorities of country parks, real parks for the use of the public, with car parking, picnic places, toilets and other facilities, designed chiefly for the motorist, like Cheshire's Wirral Way (1969), Derbyshire's Elvaston Castle (1970) and Lancashire's Beacon Fell (1970). For the unmotorized pedestrian and pony-trekker are the Long Distance Footpaths scheduled under the 1949 National Parks and Access to the Countryside Act, like the Pennine Way, Offa's Dike Path, the South West Peninsula Coast Path and the North and South Downs Ways.

The amount of beautiful countryside opened up in recent years to the public and especially to the motorist is considerable, but in relation to the pressure of demand it is inadequate. The problem, in the words of Lord Sandford's Committee on the National Parks, 1974, is that the motorized public 'have begun to destroy the very qualities they have come to enjoy', by their congestion, noise, litter and, unavoidably, the mere tramp of feet which destroys vegetation and erodes the soil. It can be graphically illustrated from one area which the construction of motorways had put under hugely increased pressure. The Lake District was and is a primarily farming area with exceptional attraction for the mountaineer, fell walker, rambler, natural historian, view-seeking motorist and pursuer of every kind of water sport from angling to water-skiing. Since the closing of most of the railway lines most of these must, and would in any case, come by road. When the roads, developed by metalling the original farm lanes and tracks, failed to cope with the traffic, the first instinct of the motoring lobby was to demand and of the local authorities to provide improved roads by widening, straightening, dual carriageways, village by-passes and all the usual devices designed for increasing and speeding the traffic flow. It soon became obvious, however, that such a policy was self-defeating. The better the roads the higher the speeds and the larger the volume of traffic, so that people rushed in ever larger numbers to the already overcrowded beauty spots and on the way had no time to enjoy one of the main pleasures they came for, namely to enjoy the view. As a report on *Traffic Management in the Lake District* put it in 1972,

It is now generally accepted that in the Lake District, as in any National Park, the conservation of environmental quality should take precedence over the desire to save a few minutes in travel time. So far as tourists are concerned, once they are within the Park it has been established that their desire is to find pleasant roads with good scenery rather than to find the shortest possible route between any two points. To travel on winding roads, up hill and down dale, is part of the pleasure of arrival in the Park, in contrast to the need for speed in reaching it from the large urban areas. Thus it follows that roads for tourists inside the Park can be, and should be,

167

quite different in character from the main national and regional roads which lie outside it.

The report went on to suggest a function-based hierarchy of roads designed to restrict the flow of traffic to what the park and its environment could cope with without degenerating into a congested, polluted rural slum.

One beauty spot where such restriction has already been introduced at weekends is the Goyt Valley in the Peak District National Park. This involved banning through traffic altogether and providing a free mini-bus service through the valley from paying car parks. An interim report for 1970–71 showed that 45,000 people visited the valley during the experimental restricted periods and more than four out of five favoured the scheme which provided 'a pleasant easy walk in peaceful and attractive surroundings; and removal of the eyesore of parked cars on the open and exposed picnic site'. Such schemes, which are bound to proliferate, are a rural version of the urban pedestrian mall and might solve the problem of particular beauty spots. But the conservation of wider areas of beauty and special quality may demand more drastic measures, such as the charging of tolls for admission to national parks and other desirable areas. Such measures would add little to the cost of the day trip, already high with the new cost of fuel, and would afford much-needed revenue for the national park and other local authorities towards providing better amenities for the motorist.

The motor car has become the most influential factor affecting the use of leisure in the twentieth century. The Government Social Survey's *Planning for Leisure*, 1969, found that 'car-ownership was associated with a much higher level of activity' in all sports and games for all age groups over twenty-two. Although this was partly related to higher income in the car-owning class, it was not entirely so. As we have seen, the higher socio-economic groups did not have more leisure: a car enabled them to take more advantage of it. The situation of most golf courses, for example, makes a car essential, but even for cheap sports with local facilities such as athletics, fell-walking or fishing the car is the most common means of transport to the point of activity. For increasing numbers of people, fuel crisis permitting, the automobile is the open sesame to health, fresh air and recreation, as well as the road to the sun.

FURTHER READING

J. A. R. Pimlott, *The Englishman's Holiday* (Faber, 1949)

Γ. W. Ogilvie, *The Tourist Movement* (King & Son, 1933)

A. J. Norval, *The Tourist Industry* (Pitman, 1936)

Elizabeth Brunner, *Holiday Making and the Holiday Trades* (Oxford University Press, 1945)

Sir George Young, *Tourism: Blessing or Blight?* (Penguin, 1973)

J. Allan Patmore, *Land and Leisure* (David & Charles, 1970; Penguin, 1972)

Michael Dower, *Fourth Wave: The Challenge of Leisure* (Civic Trust, 1965)

Michael Smith, Stanley Parker, Cyril Smith (eds), *Leisure and Society in Britain* (Allen Lane, 1973)

K. K. Sillitoe, *Planning for Leisure* (Government Social Survey, HMSO, 1969)

British Travel Association and University of Keele, *Pilot National Recreation Survey* (University of Keele, 1967 and 1969), Nos 1 and 2

North West Sports Council, *Leisure in the North West* (NWSC, Salford, 1972)

British Tourist Authority, *The British on Holiday, 1951–73* (BTA, 1973)

British Tourist Authority *et al.*, *British Home Tourism Survey, 1972* (BTA and English, Scottish and Welsh Tourist Boards, 1973)

Ministry of Land and Natural Resources, *Leisure in the Countryside, England and Wales* (Cmnd 2928, HMSO, 1966)

Countryside Commission, *The Weekend Motorist in the Lake District* (HMSO, 1969)

H. Wilson and L. Womersley, *Traffic Management in the Lake District* (Wilson & Wormersley, 1972)

John Dower, *National Parks in England and Wales* (Cmd 6628, HMSO, 1945)

J. C. Miles, *The Goyt Valley Traffic Experiment, 1970–71* (Countryside Commission, HMSO, 1972)

8. MECHANIZED WAR

The Second World War was the first total war in history, in which whole populations, men, women and children, were in the front line and risked being killed like the troops themselves. This was because it was the first fully mechanized war, in which the warlike engines, winged as well as wheeled, could reach out beyond the front lines and strike at the main centres of population. The agent of this change was the automobile, the self-propelled fighting vehicle, the tank on the ground, the bomber and fighter plane in the air. We have already seen how the tank broke the deadlock of the war of attrition on the Western Front and gave victory to the Allies in the First World War. In the Second World War it was the Germans who first learned to use the tank, supported by air power, as the decisive weapon; the British and especially the French reverted to defensive trench warfare, albeit on the de luxe scale of the Maginot Line. Only when the British, Russians and Americans learned from the Germans the hard way how to use the tank and ground-support aircraft in larger and more effective numbers was victory theirs. The Japanese taught the Americans and British the power of the bomber against supposedly invincible naval forces, and were in their turn defeated, horrifyingly, by the bomber. Victory went in the end to the side which could build more planes and tanks and could use them more effectively.

It did not go, surprisingly, to the side which built the better tanks. In the escalation of firepower and armour which took place throughout the war Germany managed to keep one step ahead in tanks, though not in planes. In the closing stages the Tiger tank and the Jagdtiger self-propelled assault gun (tank destroyer) could still outgun any tank in the field, but they were too few, they outran their supporting tanks and infantry and were destroyed piecemeal. Victory went to the big battalions.

The causes of the war need not detain us long. While the First World War was to all intents and purposes an accident, admittedly amongst accident-prone powers, the Second World War was Hitler's war. The Italians and the Japanese were simply vultures in the wake of the triumphant German eagle. It was primarily a war of German revenge for the Treaty of Versailles and for German expansion, the search for *lebensraum*. A. J. P. Taylor has argued that Hitler had no precise plans of aggression but was an opportunist exploiting the fears and vacillations of his victims, and this is true. But to argue from this that the Second World War could have been avoided either by appeasing Hitler more abjectly or by standing up to him in concert would be naïve. It is like saying that a dangerous criminal could be stopped either by giving him what he declared he intended to steal (without saying precisely how) or by his victims outlawing and attacking him before he had proved himself by his actions to be a criminal.

There were good reasons why up to and including the Austrian and Czechoslovak (Sudetenland) crises of 1938 German demands should have been thought reasonable and in keeping with the League of Nations' principle of national self-determination. All that Hitler appeared to be demanding was that all the German-speaking peoples of central Europe should be embraced by the German Reich. Only with his entry into Prague in March

1939 did he go beyond this principle – and even then it could be argued that Czechoslovakia, with the secession of Slovakia, 'fell to pieces' and was in need of German 'protection'. Only then did the British and French governments come to believe that Hitler *was* a dangerous criminal who must be stopped and, divining that Poland was his next victim, gave that country the guarantee of aid which at Munich they had refused to Czechoslovakia.

The British and French had no means of enforcing that guarantee, and by the dismemberment of Czechoslovakia they lost twenty-six heavily armed divisions, replaced on the British side by only two additional divisions by the outbreak of war. While there is no adequate excuse in the 'purchase of time' argument for Chamberlain and the appeasers of Munich, some insight into their fearful reasoning is to be gained from what may be called the 'balance of terror' from aerial warfare as it presented itself to them in the autumn of 1938. In this two things stand out. The first is the belief in the destructive power of the bomber. British experts expected that any future war would begin with aerial attacks on defenceless British cities lasting sixty days, in which 'the bomber will always get through', killing 600,000 people and injuring twice as many more. It is true that British casualties in the event were far less than this – 60,000 civilians killed and 235,000 injured in six years of war – and that even the massive bombing campaign against Germany never reached the estimated scale of destruction; but there was no means of knowing that at the time and even the best-informed strategists believed the worst. The other was the preponderance of German air power, real or supposed. British experts were taken in by Hitler's boasting and believed that he would have 2,500 front-line aircraft, including 1,700 bombers, by the opening of 1939 and 4,000 by the autumn. Even if these numbers were grossly exaggerated, as they were, the disparity in air power was real enough. By the end of 1938 the RAF possessed 668 fighters, but only 100 of these were Hurricanes, even these inferior to the main German fighter, the Messer-schmidt 109, in speed if not in manoeuvrability, and only three Spitfires, the one undoubtedly superior British machine. The RAF had been founded on the principle of the deterrent bomber, but its 1,100-strong bomber force was much less of a threat to Germany than the Luftwaffe was to Britain since London was so close to Goering's air bases and the RAF could only reach most German cities by flying illegally over the Low Countries. The British government had a bomber force which did not deter and a fighter force deemed incapable of defending the country. Rearmament had begun effectively in 1936 and excellent fighters as well as the radar equipment to deploy them efficiently were in the pipeline and would come much nearer than anyone dared believe to redressing the balance by 1940, just when it was needed. But the fact remains that, in the light of the best judgement available of the balance of terror, Chamberlain at Munich had nothing to support any other policy than that of appeasement.*

Chamberlain's greatest mistake, it might be argued, was not the betrayal of Czechoslovakia but the futile support of Poland. The fact that Hitler unleashed his *Blitzkrieg* against Poland on 1 September 1939 is proof enough that standing up to him in concert was no deterrent. Only a massive collective defence of Poland by the British and French together with the Russians might have done that, and the Ribbentrop-Molotov non-agression pact of 23 August 1939 prevented it. Without Russian assistance Britain and France had no means of getting troops or munitions to Poland and made no attempt to intervene by air. The Poles were left to their own defences, which were not so unequal as was believed. They could, fully mobilized, have mustered 1,700,000 men, in forty divisions, with supporting cavalry, tanks and 377 aircraft, against, initially, thirty-eight German

*This paragraph is based on Malcolm Smith, 'The development of a theory of strategic airpower in Great Britain, *c.* 1934–39', Ph.D., University of Lancaster, 1975.

infantry and four armoured divisions (rising later to eight) and about 1,300 aircraft. Yet within a month the great Polish army had been destroyed. The Germans achieved this partly by surprise, attacking without a declaration of war, partly by outflanking the Poles from East Prussia, partly by the Polish high command's strategic mistake of holding their main forces on the frontier to be broken through and surrounded by the German spearheads, and partly by the stab in the back by the Russians who, in accordance with a secret clause in the pact, invaded their share of dismembered Poland on 17 September. But most of all they achieved it by a new style of mechanized warfare: air bombardment instead of artillery to soften up the defences and pave the way for advancing columns of tanks supported by motorized infantry to break through the front at several points, wheel round behind and encircle the defenders in easily mopped-up pockets.

This new, mobile technique, that of the Panzer army, was invented by Hitler's main tank-general, Guderian, and depended on a restructuring of the army around the tank. Instead of treating the tank as an adjunct to the infantry dispersed in 'penny packets' amongst them as in most armies including the British and French, the Germans built their armies around the *Panzer-divisions*, self-contained tank units with supporting motorized infantry, maintenance vehicles, supply lorries, petrol tankers, and everything else they needed on wheels, so that they could operate independently, cut gaps in the defences, race across country, surround the enemy and throw him into confusion. Ironically enough, Guderian had learned this technique chiefly from the writings of British tank experts, notably Major-General J. F. C. Fuller, Captain Liddell Hart and Major-General P. C. S. Hobart. But whereas Hitler and the German general staff had taken up Guderian's theories of warfare with enthusiasm as the key to their object of *Blitzkrieg* (lightning war), in Britain the tank experts had been deliberately ignored. Some of their ideas filtered through; the Army set up a separate Armoured Division and turned a number of cavalry formations into tank brigades, but the units were too small to emulate or oppose effectively the German Panzers.

When the so-called 'Phoney War' of the winter of 1939–40 came to an end with Hitler's invasion of Denmark and Norway in April and of the Low Countries and France in May, the Allies had still learnt nothing of the new style of warfare. It was not that they were unequal to the Germans either in men or in tanks. In France and the Low Countries against the Germans' 136 divisions and 2,700 tanks the Allies fielded 149 divisions (103 French, twenty Belgian, thirteen British and ten Dutch) and about 3,600 tanks (640 of them British). The quality of the armour was about equal: the 800 best French tanks, the Char B type, were as well gunned as the best German and more thickly armoured; the 100 British I (for Infantry) tanks could penetrate the German armour with their two-pounder gun but were safe from their return fire. The essential difference lay in their deployment. Whereas the British, French, Dutch and Belgians prepared for essentially static defensive battles, based on the infantry stiffened by tanks and artillery, with the commanders at fixed headquarters deep behind the lines, the Germans attacked with fully mobile armoured columns, with inspired commanders like Guderian and von Rundstedt up with the leading tanks, which cut great swathes in the defences and left the defenders high and dry.

The main German Panzer army broke through at Sedan, by-passing the Maginot Line which did not extend along the Luxembourg and Belgian borders, and fanned out in three fast-moving columns, one swinging left for Nancy to outflank the Maginot defences, one making straight for Paris, and one swinging right to reach the sea at Calais and cut off the British Expeditionary Force. 'Along the whole front,' wrote Guderian near Amiens on 21 May, 'the enemy is in retreat in a manner that at times approaches rout.' The BEF meanwhile had made the chivalrous mistake of moving forward to aid the Dutch and

Belgians, who were similarly cut up by Panzer armies and pounded by dive bombers and surrendered on 14 May and 28 May. The British army extricated itself, with the aid of the Navy and the famous 'little ships' under RAF air cover, by Operation Dynamo, the evacuation from Dunkirk. 338,000 soldiers, two thirds of them British and the rest French and other allies, were rescued from the Dunkirk beaches but they left behind most of their weapons and all their tanks, guns and heavy equipment. A further 192,000 men, 144,000 of them British, were later evacuated from Western France, making 558,000 in all, of whom 368,000 were British. In the whole campaign the British Army suffered 68,000 casualties, while at Dunkirk the Navy lost six destroyers with nineteen seriously damaged, and the RAF lost 474 planes. Almost the whole Army had been saved, but at the cost of their engines of war.

From the French surrender on 22 June 1940 Britain stood alone against an enemy who on land was now supreme. At sea, however, Germany was even more inferior than in the First World War. At the outbreak of war Britain had fifteen battle ships (with four building), six aircraft carriers (with six building), twenty-five large and thirty-eight small cruisers (with nineteen building), 168 destroyers and sixty-nine submarines. The Germans had only a handful of battleships and cruisers and, surprisingly, only fifty-six submarines, twenty-two of them ocean-going. In the early stages of the war, the Royal Navy concentrated on clearing the seas of German surface ships and enforcing the blockade, while the Germans built submarines to enforce the counter-blockade and starve Britain of food and war supplies. Down to the fall of France the British had the best of it, culminating in the sinking of the biggest battleship afloat, the *Bismarck*, crippled by torpedo bombers from the *Ark Royal* on 27 May 1940. By then the German Navy had only one battleship left, the *Tirpitz*, and she ended her days hiding in a Norwegian fjord, to be sunk by RAF bombers in the autumn of 1944. Although Britain's losses from U-boats and bombers were severe, she could afford them, while the effective German fleet after the Norwegian campaign was reduced to the *Tirpitz*, one eight-inch gun cruiser, two light cruisers and four destroyers. The French Navy might have fallen into their hands, but was either sunk by the British at Oran, scuttled or escaped to North and West African ports. The Italian declaration of war on 10 June 1940 brought a large modern fleet to the Germans' aid, but it was confined to the Mediterranean. The new U-boats began to make inroads into the merchant marine, and over 200 ships totalling 800,000 tons were sunk in the first ten months of the war (for the loss of twenty-three U-boats). But as a force able to mount and protect a sea-borne invasion the German fleet in the summer of 1940 was pathetically inadequate. Operation Sea Lion, the invasion of Britain, therefore hung on the balance of air power. If the Luftwaffe could destroy the RAF and prevent the Royal Navy interfering with the invasion fleet of 2,500 barges, tugs and other transports, the Panzer divisions would make short work of the twenty-five divisions, with pitifully few rifles and guns and the remaining 200 tanks of the British Army.

The Battle of Britain, from July to October 1940, was the first and only major battle to be won and lost entirely in the air. On the face of it the RAF was outnumbered. Against 2,830 German aircraft, more than half of them Messerschmidt fighters, the RAF could muster less than 700 fighters, most of them Hurricanes, inferior in speed and fire-power to the Messerschmidt 109s, and only one fifth of them the superior Spitfires. The RAF had almost as many bombers as the Germans but apart from attacks on the invasion barges and diversionary strikes against a few German cities these could have no effect on the main struggle for mastery of the air. Fighter Command, however, had advantages which in the end proved decisive. They were fighting on home ground, could fly more sorties per day than the Germans, whose covering fighters could afford only a few minutes in English air space before breaking off to refuel, and they could rescue more trained pilots, who were more valuable than the machines themselves. They also possessed radar, which could locate the bomber formations before they arrived and send up the fighters to meet them instead of wasting fuel and man-hours cruising in wait. And they were pitted in large part against slow-moving bombers which were comparatively easy to shoot out of the sky.

Even so, the battle was a near thing. If Goering had continued to concentrate, as he did for a time in early September, on knocking out the Kent fighter stations and radar masts, he could perhaps have won the day and opened Britain to invasion. The turning point came by an accident. On 24 August a dozen German night bombers sent to attack oil tanks and an aircraft factory near London bombed a residential area by mistake. Churchill immediately ordered a retaliatory raid on Berlin which infuriated Hitler, who ordered mass bombing raids on London and other cities, which began on 7 September. This, however unfortunate for the civilian population, came just in time to divert the Luftwaffe's main attention from Fighter Command, and allow it to restore its runways and put more fighters, now flowing from the factories at nearly 500 a month, in the air. Thanks to Beaverbrook's whirlwind methods at the Ministry of Aircraft Production, it actually had more aircraft at the end of the battle than at the beginning. German aircraft losses, though much less than claimed at the time by the RAF, were sufficiently heavy to give the Germans pause. Against 915 British planes shot down between July and October the Germans lost 1,733, most of them bombers with crews of five. By October it was too late for the Germans to land a force and conduct a campaign before the winter. On 10 August Hitler postponed Operation Sea Lion; on 12 October he cancelled it until the following spring. How far Hitler was in earnest about the invasion of Britain it is difficult to say. No doubt if it had become easy by the destruction of the RAF and the Royal Navy, he would have seized the opportunity. But his main aim seems to have been to persuade the British to sue for peace: 'I consider myself in a position to make this appeal since I am not the vanquished begging favours, but the victor speaking in the name of reason. I can see no reason why this war should go on . . .' His main weapon for this was the Blitz, the night raids on London and other cities which continued for months after the invasion was called off.

Air power, in conjunction with armoured columns, had proved decisive in Poland, Norway, the Low Countries and France. During the rest of the war it was to prove decisive in every other theatre of action. No campaign waged without mastery of the air was won and no campaign in which air superiority was fully secured was lost. On the other hand, the attempt to use air power as a decisive arm acting on its own, as in the German attempt to bomb Britain into submission in 1940–41 or in the Anglo-American bombing campaign to destroy German industry and morale, was a failure. After the fall of France Britain had no means of striking at Germany directly except from the air. Churchill wrote in July 1940:

> There is one thing that will bring Hitler down, and that is an absolutely devastating, exterminating attack by very heavy bombers from this country upon the Nazi homeland. We must be able to overwhelm them by this means, without which I do not see a way through.

In the absence of long-range fighter cover this meant night bombing, which in turn meant area bombing of civilian populations, since precision attacks on purely military targets were impossible except by daylight. In the years before the British (with the Americans) could return to Western Europe they put enormous resources into bombing Germany, rising to thousand-bomber raids on individual cities and causing massive destruction as in the man-made firestorms at Hamburg and Dresden which killed more people than the atomic bombs at Hiroshima and Nagasaki. No less than 120,000 planes were built in Britain during the War, most of them increasingly heavy bombers, from the Wellington to the Lancaster. They also invested great sophistication and ingenuity (as did the Germans) in radio-based navigation aids, such as the 'Gee' and 'Oboe' target-finding systems, the 'Piperack' and 'Mandrel' radar-jamming devices, and the H2S radar navigation screen which presented a complete map of the area beneath the plane. The Germans responded by developing their own radar defences with radar-guided night fighters. When the Americans came in they too joined in the bomber offensive, concentrating on day precision bombing with their heavily defended Flying Fortresses. Aerial warfare became a leapfrogging contest, one side gaining technological superiority in speed, manoeuvrability, armament or electronic aids, only to be surpassed by the other. The speed of bombers rose from 290 to 460 m.p.h., that of fighters from 360 to 540 m.p.h.; bombs from under 100 lb. to massive 'blockbusters' of 22,000 lb.; armament from machine-guns to quick firing canon and rockets.

Yet it is doubtful whether the British and American bomber offensive repaid the investment in it in terms of cost to the Allied side for damage inflicted on the German. Estimates of the cost on the British side range from 7% of the manpower of the fighting services to 25% of British war production (plus 15% of the American) while the damage to German war production was at most 9%. According to the official British historians of the campaign, Webster and Frankland, 'The area bombing was very far from inflicting any crippling or decisive loss on the enemy and had not prevented the great increase in armaments carried out in this period.' In 1941 Bomber Command was suffering more casualties than it was inflicting on the German population, and losing one plane and its crew for every ten tons dropped. Yet it could be argued that the campaign forced the Germans to put larger resources of production, trained aircrew and skilled engineers, fuel and scarce materials into fighter production than they would otherwise have done and, still more important, drew air cover and other fighting power away from the vital Russian front. Later, from the spring of 1944 when the Allies, with the aid of the one effective long-range fighter of the war, the American Mustang, established complete air superiority over Western Europe, the unopposed bomber played a vital role in the invasion of Europe and in disrupting German supplies and reinforcements.

But this is to anticipate. Until Hitler's attack on Russia in June 1941 and the Japanese attack on the American fleet in Pearl Harbour in December of that year, Britain carried on a lone war on two other fronts, a dangerous war of attrition against the U-boats in the Atlantic and a classic mechanized war against the Italians in North East Africa and then against them and the German Afrika Korps in the Libyan desert. The naval struggle went on throughout the War, a duel between the U-boats and the convoy escorts in which the stakes were the starvation of Britain and the crippling of the whole Allied war effort. The ghastly statistics of shipping sunk rose to a staggering total of 1,664 ships grossing nearly 8 million tons in 1942 before falling back in the later years of the War. Altogether, U-boats sank 2,828 ships totalling 14·7 million tons during the War (of which 11·5 million tons were British, more than half the 1939 total), for the loss of 785 U-boats destroyed out of a German total of 1,162. The Battle of the Atlantic was a near thing, but the side which could keep going longest and outbuild the other in shipping replacements and in submarine-destroying ships and aircraft won.

The campaigns in Africa were only marginally relevant to the main struggle, engaging Hitler's minor and unreliable ally Mussolini, and only a fraction of the German forces arrayed against Russia. Hitler had no grand design to join up with his (later) armies in the Caucasus, still less with the Japanese advancing through India. It is also difficult to see what the British had to gain by holding Egypt. From the entry of the powerful Italian Navy into the War the Mediterranean was no longer a British lake and the Suez Canal was no longer the gateway to the

Far East since it could only be used in the reverse direction (round the Cape) to supply the forces defending it. Egypt and Suez were defended for their own sake, or at most to deny Hitler and Mussolini one more easy victory at a time when the British were being defeated everywhere else. However, Africa was the training ground on which the British, and later the Americans, learned the new techniques of mechanized warfare and how to use them to beat the Germans. Without such a training ground there and in Sicily and Italy, the Allies could not have launched themselves from a cold start into Western Europe with any hope of success.

The campaigns by General Wavell's minute British and Commonwealth forces against the larger Italian armies in North and East Africa proved to be classics of mechanized warfare. The Italians, taking advantage of the turmoil following the fall of France, had invaded Greece, occupied British Somaliland, threatening the British supply line up the Red Sea, and advanced from Libya into Egypt. In December 1940 General O'Connor with 31,000 men advanced against Graziani's 80,000 Italians in the Western Desert. Brilliantly deploying his two divisions and 275 superior tanks, in two months O'Connor had captured the whole of Cyrenaica, destroyed ten enemy divisions, taken 30,000 prisoners, 380 tanks and 845 guns at a cost of under 2,000 British casualties. At the same time Generals Platt and Cunningham from Khartoum and Nairobi, with about 18,000 men between them, mostly motorized, advanced into Eritrea, Abyssinia and Italian Somaliland and in 'the most rapid pincer movement ever carried out' covered over 2,000 miles between them in less than six months, captured all the Italians in East Africa and liberated Addis Ababa. To add to these successes, on 11 November 1940 twenty-one bombers and torpedo-bombers from the aircraft carrier *Illustrious* sank three Italian battleships out of six in Taranto harbour, and on 28 March 1941 in a textbook naval battle between roughly equal forces off Cape Matapan Admiral Cunningham (the General's brother) sank three Italian eight-inch gun cruisers and two big destroyers and seriously damaged the battleship *Vittorio Veneto*.

These successes brought their retribution, however, in the shape of German intervention in Greece and Libya, the latter with the Panzer divisions of Rommel's Afrika Korps. The Greeks, with some British help, had fought the Italians to a standstill, but the German Panzer armies pounded Yugoslavia and Greece into defeat, forcing Wavell to send British reinforcements, including precious aircraft, to no purpose. The chief result was a lesser Dunkirk in April and May 1941 with 43,000 British troops evacuated from the Piraeus and the loss of Crete to the first wholly airborne invasion, by paratroops and gliders, in history. A further 15,000 British troops escaped from Crete but 13,000 were left prisoners, and three cruisers, six destroyers and twenty-nine smaller naval craft were lost. In Libya Rommel struck quickly on 31 March with 400 new and superior tanks – Panzer IVs with a more powerful 50-mm ($4\frac{1}{2}$-pounder) gun against the British 2-pounder – and pushed the British back to Egypt by mid-April. The Tobruk garrison held out, reinforced and supplied by sea, from March till it was finally relieved in December.

Before that, however, two world-shattering events had changed the course of the war and indeed of history. On 22 June 1941 Hitler invaded Russia. On 7 December a Japanese carrier force bombed Pearl Harbor and within half an hour put out of action most of the American Pacific fleet. These actions brought into the war on the British side the two largest industrial powers and, potentially, the two greatest military powers in the world, whose victory was to ensure the eclipse of the British Empire and their joint domination of the post-war world.

When Operation Barbarossa – the invasion of Russia – opened, the world held its breath, as Hitler forecast. It was not that the German armies were overwhelmingly superior in numbers. They put 145 divisions (about $3\frac{1}{2}$ million men) and 3,350 tanks into the field against a Russian army, when fully mobilized, of 12 million men, organized in 225 divisions, and 20,000 tanks. But the Russian army in 1941 was far from fully mobilized, and due to the purges of 1937 was officered by inexperienced generals. Its tanks and planes were inferior in quality and their crews inadequately trained. Above all, the Germans were better organized and by now extremely experienced. Although the Russians had no less than thirty-five motorized and armoured brigades they were no answer to the Panzer armies of nineteen armoured and twelve motorized divisions. The technique once more was that of the Blitzkrieg, based on air power and massed tanks, with which the German General Staff planned to win the war in eight to ten weeks. And they very nearly did. By the end of June their encircling tactics had won 150,000 prisoners, 1,200 tanks and 600 guns. By 10 July they were at the gates of Smolensk, 400 miles from the starting line. By 21 August they were before Kiev, when Hitler decided that the main objectives were not Moscow but Leningrad in the north and the Donetz industrial basin, the Crimea and the oilfields of the Caucasus in the south-east. By December they had captured the whole of the Ukraine as far as Kharkov and Rostov, the Crimea except for Sebastopol, were at the gates of Leningrad and within thirty miles of Moscow.

But they had outrun their timetable. The winter, earlier than usual, caught them without winter clothes and even without antifreeze for their tank engines. Instead of fighting for every yard of ground and every city the Russians had withdrawn hundreds of miles before them, 'scorching the earth' as they went. They were even prepared to give up Moscow if need be, and removed the government to Kuibyshev, 500 miles to the east. Behind the front partisans began to harass the German supply lines. The Germans had inflicted millions of casualties, but they had lost 750,000 men themselves, 200,000 of them killed, out of their much smaller army. The Blitzkrieg, faced with the vast spaces and the winter snows of Russia, had failed.

Just as the Germans ground to a halt in Russia, the Japanese attacked Pearl Harbor and brought the Americans into the war. Churchill, who had welcomed the Russians into the war but without certainty that they could avoid defeat, now saw salvation in the vast arsenal of America: 'So we had won after all!' But there was a long night of catastrophe and despair before the light of victory dawned. Admiral Yamamoto promised the Japanese Emperor and cabinet six months of victories if the Pearl Harbor attack succeeded. With almost the whole American battle fleet out of action – four battleships sunk and four damaged out of eight, besides three light cruisers and three destroyers sunk and others damaged and 188 planes destroyed, for the loss of twenty-nine Japanese planes and five midget submarines – he fulfilled his promise. The three American fleet carriers, out on exercises, escaped, but the Japanese had overwhelming superiority in the air, which in the Pacific War was to prove decisive: 2,625 planes against 593 American (many of which were soon to be destroyed in the Philippines and elsewhere) and 697 British, Dutch and Australian (many of the British obsolete and unfit for war). The only British battleship in the Far East, the *Prince of Wales*, they sank along with the battle-cruiser *Repulse* by bombing off Malaya on 10 December, thus further proving the superiority of the bomber to capital ships without air cover. The Japanese were already in China and had seized Indo-China from the French. They now conquered the American Pacific islands of Guam and Wake, invaded the Philippines, Malaya, Burma and the Dutch East Indies. Singapore, its great guns facing the wrong way, had surrendered to them on 15 February as did the remains of the American Philippine garrison on the Bataan peninsula on 9 April, and by 20 May they had conquered Burma and were at the gates of India. Within six months they had turned the South China Sea and South Pacific Ocean into Japanese lakes, surrounded by a ring of bases stretching from Burma and the Andaman Islands through Malaya, the Dutch East Indies, New Britain (Rabaul) and the Solomon Islands to the Gilbert, Marshall and Wake Islands.

186

Despite British fears they did not aim to conquer India or Australia but, with Britain and Russia with their backs to the wall and American air and naval power crippled, to hold on to and exploit their 'South-east Asia Co-prosperity Sphere' indefinitely.

Meanwhile, Hitler renewed his offensive in Russia in the spring of 1942, this time concentrating on the southern front and the drive to the Volga and the Caucasus. Although held at Leningrad and pushed back a hundred miles before Moscow, his Panzer armies succeeded by September in reaching Stalingrad on the Volga and the Maikop oilfield in the Caucasus, more than 1,000 miles from Poland. At the same time, after a seesaw of German and British offensives in the Western Desert, Rommel attacked once more on 26 May 1942, crossed the Egyptian frontier and by 1 July was at El Alamein, seventy miles from Alexandria. There he was halted by General Auchinleck until he was ready for his next assault in September and the final drive to the Nile Delta. But his next assault came up against a new commander, General Montgomery, who had studied Rommel's tactics and refused to play the old game of bringing out his tanks prematurely to be shot up by the more powerful German tanks and 88-mm anti-tank guns. Instead he dug in his tanks hull deep and made Rommel's tanks come to them, to be shot up by the artillery and dive bombers.

Stalingrad and El Alamein were the turning point of the war against Germany. The weight of American and Russian industrial power was beginning to tell. Russian factories deep beyond the Urals were beginning to pour out planes and tanks – especially the T-34, the most successful tank of the war – as good as any the Germans had and far more numerous. British and American factories also poured out tanks and planes, not always superior but in sufficient numbers eventually to overwhelm the Germans. What made the difference for Montgomery against Rommel were the 300 new American Sherman tanks, giving him a superiority of 1,351 tanks to 600. He also had 220,000 troops to Rommel's 108,000 and 900 planes against 345, which strafed Rommel's supply lines and kept him short of petrol. With a more than two to one superiority, Montgomery attacked on 23 October and after ten days of hard slogging 'knocked Rommel for six', capturing 30,000 prisoners and 1,000 guns, taking or destroying 520 of his 600 tanks and driving the rest out of Cyrenaica. As Churchill put it, over-simply, 'Before Alamein we never had a victory. After Alamein we never had a defeat.'

The battle of Stalingrad took place at almost the same time, but it was on a far greater scale. Once again, as in 1941, the Germans had failed to achieve victory before the winter set in and once more they paid for it. Although encircled and fighting in the streets and buildings, the Russians refused to yield. In the November snows they counter-attacked and encircled General von Paulus and his army. Hitler refused to let them retreat but failed to rescue them. In the ensuing débâcle the Germans lost 91,000 prisoners and as many more killed and wounded, 1,500 tanks, 6,000 guns and 60,000 vehicles. Although Hitler did not then know it, it was the beginning of the end.

1942 also saw the turning point in the Pacific. It came in two great naval battles, the first fought entirely from the air. In the Battle of the Coral Sea early in May 1942 the Americans caught Japanese fleets trying to extend their Pacific perimeter by the capture of Tulagi (which they took) in the Solomons and Port Moresby on the south coast of New Guinea in what appeared to be thrusts towards New Zealand and Australia. After initial skirmishing in which Admiral Fletcher's planes sank a light carrier, a light cruiser and some transports, the opposed carrier forces were evenly matched, the Americans with two carriers, five heavy cruisers, seven destroyers and 122 planes, the Japanese with two carriers, four heavy cruisers, six destroyers and 121 planes. In the mutual bombing and torpedo attacks, the Americans lost one carrier and had the other damaged while the Japanese had one of theirs seriously damaged; the Americans lost 66 planes, the Japanese considerably more. On the face of it it was a drawn battle, but the Japanese pulled back their Port Moresby invasion force, lost Tulagi and never again succeeded in extending their perimeter.

The other battle, of Midway in June 1942, was the greatest naval battle of the war. It involved on the Japanese side under Admiral Yamamoto himself no less than 162 ships, including seven battleships, four large and three light carriers, in an attempt to occupy Midway Island, next to Pearl Harbor the most important American base in the Pacific, and three small islands in the Aleutians. Against this armada Admiral Nimitz had only seventy-six ships, including three carriers, plus 115 planes on Midway itself. But Nimitz had the advantage, denied most commanders in war, of knowing the enemy's moves in advance since the Americans had cracked the Japanese radio-code. (This was later to cost Yamamoto his life, when on 16 April 1943 his movements were known and his plane intercepted in the Solomons.) The Japanese bombed Midway and expected attacks from there in return, but they were not prepared for the American carrier-based aircraft. In the bombing Yamamoto lost all four of his large carriers and, since the survivors could not land, all their 250 planes, besides other ships. The Americans lost one carrier, which sank without its crew while in tow, and 147 planes. It was a total American victory, and doomed Japan to defeat in the Pacific. The Japanese had only one large carrier and four light ones left (though six more building or under repair), the Americans three large ones in service plus thirteen building, and fifteen escort carriers. Air superiority, and therefore the initiative, passed to the Americans.

In North Africa El Alamein was immediately followed in November by Operation Torch, the Anglo-American landings in French Algeria and Tunisia. After a cease-fire with the Vichy French a great pincer movement was developed, with Generals Eisenhower from the west and Montgomery from the east converging on Tunis. Hitler retaliated by occupying Vichy

France – though he lost the French fleet, which scuttled itself at Toulon – and by reinforcing Rommel. The German and Italian armies held up the Allied conquest for six months and Tunis did not fall until May 1943, but they were totally lost: a quarter of a million men surrendered. Hitler considered that his decision to reinforce had kept Italy in the war and postponed the invasion of Europe by six months; but the British and Americans had enjoyed their first destruction of a German Panzer army and acquired invaluable experience for the invasion itself. Moreover, the Italians had lost all enthusiasm for the war and when the invasion of Sicily and Italy swiftly followed in July and September, Mussolini was bundled from power on 25 July and the new Italian government under Marshall Badoglio surrendered on 8 September. The Germans and some Italian fascists fought on and the Italian campaign became a hard slogging match as the Allies throughout 1944 fought their way up the spiny back of Italy. Partly because of the diversion of resources, especially landing craft, to Western Europe, northern Italy was not to be liberated until the last days of the war.

Germany was now threatened with the war on two fronts which she had always feared. Large German armies, sixty divisions, had to be kept behind the whole coastline from northern Norway to the Pyrenees and a huge horde of slave labourers from Eastern Europe were set to building the Atlantic Wall. The Anglo-American bombing campaign also diverted aircraft and production from the Eastern Front and helped the Russians gradually to build up a superiority in tanks and planes. The Russians had also learned the German Panzer technique and how to counter it. Typical of the war of attrition in 1943 was the battle of the Kursk salient, the largest tank battle ever fought. Against the wishes of Guderian, who was more concerned with the defence of the West, Hitler launched in July flank attacks with fifteen armoured and fifteen other divisions against the sides of the Russian bulge. The Russians let the German tanks come on, 'firming up' the sides of the pincers with their own tanks and guns, and swopping losses until the Germans could afford no more. Then they counter-attacked in turn, driving the Germans out of Orel, Kharkov, Smolensk and Kiev, and in January 1944 finally relieved Leningrad. 1944 was for the Russians 'the year of the ten victories', with almost the whole of Eastern Europe liberated and Hitler's allies, Romania, Finland, Bulgaria and Hungary, all driven out of the war. By the end of the year the Russian armies were in Warsaw and encircling Budapest, poised for the final onslaught on the German Reich itself.

On 6 June 1944 the British and Americans invaded Normandy. Operation Overlord under General Eisenhower was the biggest seaborne landing ever attempted. The forces involved in the first forty-eight hours included 2,800 ships and 4,000 landing craft, 150,000 men, 1,500 tanks and 13,000 planes, including gliders and paratroop transports. Moving such numbers in the correct order with all their supplies took months of elaborate planning and the development of new managerial techniques under the name of operational research. It also required custom-built devices such as the two prefabricated Mulberry harbours and Pluto, the oil 'pipeline under the ocean'. To cope with the elaborate beach defences of the Atlantic Wall the British developed specialized tanks, the 'funnies', including the amphibious DD (duplex drive), which sported a raisable canvas flotation screen, the Crab or flail-tank, with revolving chains to beat a path through the minefields, the Bobbin, which laid a thick canvas carpet over soft sand for following vehicles, a bridge-laying tank which could bridge a thirty-foot gap in thirty seconds, and the Crocodile, a flame-throwing tank for knocking out enemy pill-boxes and bunkers. Their success can be seen from the different experiences on the British and American beaches. The Americans, who accepted only the amphibious DD from the British and preferred infantry and bulldozers for clearing beach obstacles, lost far more men.

Once ashore, Montgomery's plan was for the British beachhead on the east before Caen to take the weight of the German armoured counter-attack, allowing the Americans to break out on the west side, seize the Cotentin peninsula and the port of Cherbourg, and then make a great sweep round western France to catch the Germans in a 'bag'. The Americans had difficulty with the *bocage*, the deep hedge banks of the small Norman fields. They overcame it by inventing on the spot their own 'funny', a tank fitted with tusks made from German steel beach defences, which bored a way through the banks. After that the plan nearly worked. In August most of the German armies in western France were caught in the Falaise pocket, and as they streamed out were strafed by the Allied fighter-bombers. They left behind 50,000 prisoners and 10,000 dead. At the same time in Operation Anvil on 15 August the Allies landed ten divisions on the French Mediterranean coast near Cannes. The Germans in southern France, fearing to be cut off by the advance from Normandy, withdrew up the Rhone valley. Paris rose in revolt and was occupied by de Gaulle and the Free French. The Germans, having lost half a million men including 210,000 prisoners and more than 2,000 tanks and self-propelled guns, retreated to the Rhine and the great rivers of Holland.

From Britain's, and especially London's, point of view the invasion and advance to the Rhine came only just in time. On 13 June the first of Hitler's secret weapons, with which he still hoped to win the war – long predicted by British Intelligence and bombed on the ground by Bomber Command – appeared in the form of the V-1 flying bomb. Though the fighter pilots and anti-aircraft guns soon learned to bring them down over the sea and open country so that by August 80% were being destroyed short of the target, 8,564 were launched and killed 6,184 people and seriously injured 17,981 others before their launching sites were overrun. On 8 September came the first of the V-2 rockets, faster than sound and carrying a one-ton warhead, against which there was no defence save destruction on the ground. Before the last one fell, on Orpington on 27 March 1945, 1,115 of them killed 2,724 people and seriously injured 6,476 more. More flying bombs and rockets were launched against Belgium, especially Antwerp and Liège, than against England. The flying bomb with its jet engine and the rocket, fuelled by alcohol and liquid oxygen, were essentially developments of the internal combustion engine. At the same time they were precursors of still more deadly weapons to come in the post-war era.

Meanwhile in the Far East the Americans were using their air and naval supremacy to perfect a new kind of warfare, combined operations involving aircraft, ships and marines, which came to be known as island-hopping. Though with far smaller numbers of men than in Africa and Europe, this campaign covered thousands of miles of ocean, from within bombing range of Australia and Honolulu to within bombing range of Japan itself. Once the Australians and Americans had got the better of the Japanese in New Guinea and the Solomons, which took all of 1943, the American commanders General MacArthur and Admiral Nimitz devised a strategy for approaching Japan in a series of hops from one strategic island to another, leaving the Japanese garrisons on the outlying and intervening islands, without supplies or reinforcements, to 'wither on the vine'. Two lines of advance were planned, one by a series of sea-borne landings along the northern coast of New Guinea and on through the Philippines, the other through the smaller islands of the central Pacific, from the Marshalls through the Marianas, both prongs converging on the Ryukyu chain south of Japan and its largest island, Okinawa. The Japanese tried to prevent both at once by the battle of the Philippine Sea in June 1944, in which Admiral Toyoda's fleet from the Philippines sailed out to destroy the American fleet in the Marianas. But it was outclassed: it had five fleet carriers and four light ones, five battleships and forty-one other war ships, and 473 planes, against Admiral Spruance's seven fleet and eight light carriers, seven battleships and ninety other war ships, and 956 planes. The Japanese lost three large carriers and 411 planes; the Americans 130 planes with one battleship damaged. This cleared the way for the American capture of the Marianas and the invasion of Leyte in the Philippines, the latter with a vast invasion fleet of 738 ships, including seventeen carriers.

As the Americans got nearer to Japan, Japanese resistance became fanatical, even suicidal. On Saipan in the Marianas in July 1944 the Americans suffered 14,000 casualties and all but a handful of the 24,000 Japanese defenders were killed or committed *hara-kiri*. Then in October, in the decisive Battle of Leyte Gulf, in which they lost three battleships, four carriers and twenty other ships for the loss of one American fleet carrier, two escort carriers and four other ships, the Japanese first unleashed in force their own secret weapon, the *Kamikaze* ('divine wind') raids on US ships. The *Kamikazes* were planes loaded with explosives flown by suicide pilots. Before the Americans got within invasion range of Japan they were to cost scores of ships and thousands of lives. In return, American planes began in November to bomb Tokyo and other Japanese cities.

There was a third line of advance, notable for two reasons: it was the only large-scale land campaign which was supplied almost entirely by air, and it was the only complete defeat of a large-scale Japanese army by land. This was the reconquest of Burma. The campaign was fought less for the sake of Burma itself than to keep Chiang Kai-shek and the Chinese in the war and open the road back to Malaya and the East Indies. It was fought in disease-ridden jungle and rain-soaked mountain. The three-pronged attack, by the American-led Chinese over the old Burma Road from Chungking, by the British XV Corps down the Arakan coast, and by the British and Indian Fourteenth Army in the Chindwin valley, had mainly to be supplied by the US Air Force and RAF, flying over the high mountains of the Arakan Yoma and, to supply the Chinese, the even higher mountains of the Himalayas. The Japanese objective was to cut the Burma Road and capture the supply airfields in Assam (India). In the spring of 1943 they nearly achieved it, but were

9a. Suburban Sprawl Council housing estate at Southall, Middlesex, 1931. Such semi-rural developments were only made possible by the motor bus. *Photo: Radio Times Hulton Picture Library*

9b. The Age of the By-pass Mickleham by-pass, 1939. Between the Wars some road-building reached motorway standard, or better: this one had cycle-paths for the self-propelled. *Photo: Radio Times Hulton Picture Library*

10a. Peace in Our Time   Neville Chamberlain returns with Hitler's piece of paper from Munich, September 1938. *Photo: Radio Times Hulton Picture Library*

10b. War in Our Time   German tanks in Poland, September 1939. *Photo: Radio Times Hulton Picture Library*

11a and b. Mechanized Warfare   1. Paratroops of the 82nd U.S. Airborne Division practising, 14 March 1944, for the invasion of Normandy. 2. A German 'Royal Tiger' Panzer squadron being briefed for the attack. The Tiger B was the largest and most powerful 'battle wagon' of the Second World War. *Photos: Imperial War Museum*

12a and b. The Automobile and Mass Production 1. A Morris assembly line in the 1930s: note the lack of mechanization. 2. A British Leyland assembly line in the 1970s: note the mechanization of the line itself and the power tools. *Photos: by kind permission of the British Leyland Motor Corporation*

thrown back in August and gradually forced back through Mandalay, captured in March 1945, to be trapped in Southern Burma by an amphibious assault on Rangoon in May. For the first time an entire Japanese army had been defeated in the field.

By December 1944 the Russians had pushed the Germans back to the German–Polish frontier and a line running west of Budapest and Belgrade. Astonishingly, with the Eastern Front little more than a hundred miles from Berlin, Hitler launched his final gamble in the west. He managed to get together a quarter of a million men, 1,100 tanks and 2,000 aircraft, partly by bleeding the Eastern Front, for a counter-thrust in the Ardennes, the hilly, wooded central wedge of Belgium. The ostensible objective was the newly opened Allied port of Antwerp but the real purpose was to delay the British and Americans for eight to ten weeks while the Germans took breath and re-organized. In bad weather, with snow and thick fog which temporarily suspended Allied air activity, the offensive, from 16 December to 28 January, succeeded in holding up the Allies for six weeks and cost them 77,000 casualties. But Hitler had lost his last throw: the cost was 70,000 casualties and 50,000 prisoners, besides over 500 tanks and 1,600 planes. He no longer had a mobile reserve to face the Russians, who launched their last great offensive towards Berlin on 12 January.

The end in Germany came swiftly. In Guderian's words, the Eastern Front was like a house of cards, and a breakthrough at one point meant collapse for the rest. In the west seven armies, American, British, Canadian and French, stood by 10 March on the west bank of the Rhine. British and American bombers, in Air Chief Marshall Tedder's 'transportation plan', hammered continuously at German communication and supply lines. The Americans found one Rhine bridge undamaged at Remagen and forced a bridgehead but the British on the wide lower Rhine had to mount an amphibious assault, 'an inland waterborne invasion', and British and American airborne divisions were dropped beyond the rivers, to be defeated at Arnhem. Once across, the American First and Ninth Armies encircled General Model's Army Group B in the Ruhr, capturing 400,000 prisoners; Model shot himself on 21 March. The British and Canadians liberated Holland and surged forward to Hanover, Hamburg and Lübeck. The Americans swept through southern Germany into Austria and Czechoslovakia where they met the Russians, and along the Elbe where, at Magdeburg on 12 April, they were only sixty miles from Berlin. On 16 April the Russians launched their final assault on Berlin. Hitler still refused to surrender and determined to take the German nation down with him. On 29 April in his Berlin bunker he married his mistress Eva Braun and then shot himself; she died of poison. Goebbels burned their bodies in the garden. On 4 May Montgomery accepted his successor Admiral Dönitz's unconditional surrender by emissary on Lüneberg Heath, formally ratified at Berlin by the Allies on 8 May. The war against Germany was over.

The war in the Far East was expected to last another eighteen months. The invasion of Japan would be bloody and prolonged. Japanese suicide tactics were displayed spectacularly at Iwo Jima in March 1945, where only 216 out of the garrison of 20,000 were taken prisoner, and at Okinawa between April and June, where only 7,000 out of 50,000 surrendered. The first cost the Americans about 10,000 casualties, the second nearly 40,000. At Okinawa more than 3,000 *Kamikaze* attacks were made, sinking twenty-one ships and damaging sixty-six more, killing nearly 5,000 sailors and wounding nearly 5,000 more. Although massive air raids were launched against Japan, killing 84,000 people in one night alone (9–10 March), the government showed no outward sign of surrendering (although they discussed it on 22 June).

Meanwhile, the Americans had perfected their secret weapon, with the aid of German Jewish and British know-how. On 16 July they exploded an atomic bomb in the New Mexico desert. To save American and Japanese lives in a prolonged invasion,

President Truman, who succeeded Roosevelt on his death on 12 April, ordered the first to be dropped on Hiroshima on 6 August and, when this failed to bring surrender, another on Nagasaki on 9 August. On 14 August 1945 the Japanese Government surrendered.

The Second World War was the most destructive war in history. More than 25 million people lost their lives, and countless others were maimed and injured. This was because the technological means of destruction, from the war plane to the tank and from the rocket to the atomic bomb, were infinitely more deadly than anything before. Since then of course they have become even more deadly and we have in the hydrogen bomb the means of destroying all sentient life on our planet. Amongst the weapons of destruction the most ubiquitous were those developments of the automobile, the tank and the aeroplane. It is one more effect of the automobile that the original pleasure vehicle of the rich and the later runabout of the masses should so quickly have become the enemy of mankind.

FURTHER READING

A. J. P. Taylor, *The Origins of the Second World War* (Hamish Hamilton, 1961, Penguin, 1964)

E. M. Robertson, ed., *The Origins of the Second World War* (Macmillan Papermac, 1971)

B. Liddell Hart, *History of the Second World War* (Cassell, 1970)

Peter Young, *World War, 1939 45: A Short History* (Barker, 1966)

J. F. C. Fuller, *The Second World War, 1939–45* (Eyre & Spottiswoode, 1949)

Cyril Falls, *The Second World War: a Short History* (Methuen, 1948)

Angus Calder, *The People's War* (Panther, 1971)

A. J. P. Taylor, *English History, 1914 45* (Oxford University Press, 1965), Chapters 12–16

Sir Winston Churchill, *The Second World War* (Cassell, 6 vols, 1948–54)

Alan Clark, *Barbarossa: The Russian-German Conflict, 1941–45* (Hutchinson, 1965)

Chester Wilmot, *The Struggle for Europe* (Collins, 1952)

Armin Halle and Carlo Demand, *Tanks: An Illustrated History of Fighting Vehicles* (Patrick Stephens, London, and Edita, Lausanne, 1971)

Kenneth Macksey, *Tank: A History of the Armoured Fighting Vehicle* (Macdonald, 1970)

R. M. Ogorkiewicz, *Design and Development of Fighting Vehicles* (Macdonald, 1968)

M. M. Postan, D. Hay and J. D. Scott, *The Design and Development of Weapons* (HMSO, 1964)

R. R. A. Wheatley, *Operation Sea Lion* (Clarendon Press, 1958)

Basil Collier, *The Battle of Britain* (Batsford, 1962)

Basil Collier, *The Defence of the United Kingdom* (HMSO, 1957)

C. Webster and N. Frankland, *The Strategic Air Offensive Against Germany* (HMSO, 4 vols, 1961)

S. W. Roskill, *The War at Sea* (HMSO, 3 vols, 1954–61)

I. S. O. Playfair, *The Mediterranean and the Middle East* (HMSO, 5 vols, 1954–73)

Eric Linklater, *The Campaign in Italy* (HMSO, 1951)

L. F. Ellis, *Victory in the West* (HMSO, 2 vols, 1962)

S. W. Kirby, *The War Against Japan* (HMSO, 5 vols, 1957–69)

M. M. Gowing, *Britain and Atomic Energy* (Macmillan, 1964)

9. THE CAR AND THE COMMUNITY: II. SINCE THE WAR

The period since the Second World War has seen the completion of that double helix which has characterized Britain in the twentieth century. In the downward spiral Britain has lost an empire and has ceased to be the leading industrial and trading power in the world. In the upward spiral, she has achieved unprecedented if precarious prosperity and completed the first truly comprehensive welfare state, which sets out to guarantee the social security, full employment, housing, education and health of every member of the community. In the downward spiral she had not fallen so far as some have feared, nor in the upward spiral has she risen so high as some have hoped. Britain nevertheless has suffered a double revolution, in her relations with the rest of the world and in her internal prosperity and social policy.

The War hastened Britain's decline as a world power. Britain put relatively more manpower and resources into the war effort than any other belligerent except Russia. For us it was indeed total war. Hitler failed to mobilize the German people, and especially the womenfolk, to the same extent as the British. With conscription and direction of labour, almost every able-bodied man and childless woman was drawn into the forces or war production. Though we suffered less damage than Germany or Russia, our capital equipment – machines, factories, roads and railways – were all run down and worn out. Most of our overseas investments, which had cushioned us against the inter-war depression, were sold off to pay for war supplies, and we incurred enormous debts with the United States and Canada and, in the form of 'sterling balances', with the countries from which our armies operated, notably India and Egypt. Thus, when American lease-lend ended abruptly in August 1945, Britain was in a desperate situation, unable to pay for the imports of food and raw materials she needed. Only another huge American and Canadian loan kept us going, until Marshall Aid came to the rescue in 1948. Balance of payments crises followed every second year into the 1950s and were solved by drastic measures such as the devaluation of the pound in 1949 and by policies of austerity – petrol rationing until 1950, food rationing until 1954, import quotas, and the allocation of scarce supplies such as steel to export industries.

Yet in spite of this we achieved a faster rate of economic growth than we had enjoyed since the mid-Victorian age. In the 1950s total output grew by 2·6% a year, in the 1960s by 2·7% a year – higher rates than in any decade since the 1870s. In the new, post-war climate of world economic expansion, however, it was a mediocre performance, less than any other Western European country or the United States, and much less than the average for them all, 4·2% a year in the 1950s, 4·8% a year in the 1960s. The causes of our poor economic performance have been endlessly debated but never resolved. They include a lower rate of increase in productivity (output per man) than other advanced countries, which in turn is related to a lower rate of capital investment and an even lower rate of return on it – British industry has the lowest ICOR (investment capital output ratio), which means the lowest increase in production for each unit of capital invested – and this can only be due to poor management skills and the restrictions on innovation and manning imposed by the trade unions.

Whatever the causes, the results are plain and painful enough. While over the two decades British output has risen by about 60%, that of the average Western country more than doubled. German output has risen $2\frac{1}{2}$ times, and Japanese more than trebled. At the same time, Britain's share of world trade in manufactured goods has declined from 22% in 1938 and 1953 to 14% in 1964, and since 1956 we have never been free of balance of payments difficulties. Economic growth may not be the most important thing in life compared with, say, a moral concern for the underprivileged or a civilized social life, but without it it is impossible to sustain a position as a world power or to expand provision for the underprivileged or for cultural enjoyment.

Nor surprisingly, therefore, Britain has gradually abandoned the stance of a leading military and imperial power. The military cost was not the only factor leading to the dissolution of the world's largest empire – the moral will to hold in subjection a quarter of the world's population had already gone, and in large part it was a magnanimous act of voluntary renunciation – but it is doubtful whether we could have afforded to hold on much longer. The turning point in our military role came with the Suez intervention in 1956, which finally proved that Britain could not act alone in confrontations with the Third World, and that such interventions were counter-productive. Almost all the larger colonies had been started on the road to self-government before the War, and the War hastened the process and intensified the demand for independence. India, Pakistan, Ceylon (Sri Lanka) and Burma were granted independence in 1947, all except Burma choosing to remain within the Commonwealth. Since then a regular procession of independence celebrations has marked the emancipation of all except a handful of the smallest colonies: Ghana and Malaya in 1957, Cyprus and Nigeria in 1960, Tanganyika and Sierra Leone in 1961, Uganda and the West Indies in 1962, Kenya and Zanzibar in 1963,

Nyasaland, Zambia and even tiny Malta in 1964, and so on. While the multiracial British Commonwealth of Nations which has replaced the empire still has moral force and influence as one of the few associations which bridges the Western and Third Worlds, it can no longer be considered a powerful political or economic entity. Its members increasingly go their own way in international affairs, often in opposition to each other, and in no sense follow Britain's lead. Meanwhile Britain herself has gone her own way, into the European Economic Community, which she joined on 1 January 1973 and confirmed by the Referendum of 5 June 1975. From the world's leading trading and imperial power to one member in nine, and not the strongest one, of the Common Market, in a single lifetime – that is a measure of the downward spiral of Britain in the twentieth century.

The upward spiral was also accelerated by the War. The Dunkirk spirit, the uniting of all classes behind the war effort, generated an enormous zest for post-war reconstruction and a determination never to return to the social injustice and inequities of the pre-war Depression. The symbol of this drive to build a better Britain was the Beveridge Report on Social Insurance and Allied Services of 1942, which rapidly came to be regarded as the blueprint of the welfare state. The term welfare state was invented, independently, by Archbishop Temple and Sir Alfred Zimmern in contrast to the 'warfare states' of the Axis powers, but it rapidly attached itself to the concept of a state which actively provided for the welfare of all its citizens in all the exigencies of life, including protection against what Beveridge called the five giants on the road to social reconstruction, want, squalor, disease, idleness and ignorance. This implied a comprehensive scheme of social security, with state benefits for unemployment, industrial injury, sickness, disability, maternity and death, family allowances, a subsidized housing programme, a free, comprehensive health service, a full employment policy and a state education system with equal opportunity for all children from the primary level to the university.

The welfare state thus conceived was completed, since much of it existed in partial form already, by the Labour Government of 1945–51. Apart from the Butler Education Act of 1944 and the Family Allowances Act in 1945, the founding legislation included the National Insurance and Industrial Injuries Acts, 1946, and the National Assistance and National Health Acts, 1948. On the 'vesting day', 5 July 1948, every man, woman and child in the United Kingdom was covered by a system of social insurance which in theory protected them in all the exigencies of life. There were, of course, drawbacks to the system. The insurance principle – one stamp, one card – and the flat-rate contributions and benefits meant that a safety net, the National Assistance Board, was needed for those who failed to pay their full contributions or those for whose needs the benefits were inadequate, and this meant a continuation of the means test which was so hated by the long-term unemployed in the 1930s. And neither the benefits nor the family allowances (for the second and subsequent children) were automatically proof against inflation and they tended to decline in real value. Later modifications, by the Conservatives in 1959 and the Labour scheme of 1974, would introduce the principle of income-relating into old age pensions, though not enough to make much difference to the general flat-rate insurance principle. Nevertheless, the welfare state, together with the maintenance of full employment and the general rise of living standards in the post-war period, made Britain a much more humane and civilized country for the poor and other victims of misfortune than it had been before the War.

This is not to say that the system was ideal, that poverty was totally extirpated, or even that much progress was made in the direction of social equality. It is true that very large sums were redistributed between individuals in taxes and benefits. In 1971, for example, a family of two adults and two children earning less than £381 would receive a net addition to their income of £840 while a similar family earning £3,750 or more would make a net contribution of £1,311. Yet on the whole there was less transfer of income from the rich to the poor than from the ordinary citizen in work and health to the ordinary citizen out of work, or sick, old, disabled or with many children. And the poorer workers often paid as large a share of their income in taxes, especially in indirect taxes on the goods they bought and in the regressive, flat-rate national insurance contribution, as did their 'betters'.

Moreover, the welfare state did not prevent the survival of poverty, at least by some definitions of the term. Although the harsh, grinding absolute poverty which Booth and Rowntree found around the beginning of the century had disappeared, a new concept emerged of relative poverty, which attached to those families who fell more than a certain distance below the average income of society (or the average manual worker's earnings), even though the average was rising. The usual level chosen as the poverty line is the quasi-objective supplementary benefit scale, formerly paid by the National Assistance Board and now by the Department of Health and Social Security, which measures the needs of applicants but which also tends to be adjusted upwards as average wages rise. Since this is a minimum standard which in the absence of any other resources can be increased by 40% in certain circumstances, some analysts also use a poverty line based on the supplementary benefit scale plus 40%. On the basis of the government's Family Expenditure Survey Professors Abel-Smith and Townsend calculated that in 1953–54 1·2% of the population fell below the first line and 7·8% below the second, and that in 1960 these figures had risen to 3·8% and 14·2%. On a similar basis Professor A. B. Atkinson showed that in 1966 and 1969 3·7% and 3·4% fell below the first. Gough and Stark, on the different basis of Inland Revenue surveys, estimated that in 1954 12·3% fell below the first and 21·0% below the second, in 1959 8·8% and 18·1% and in 1963 9·4% and 20·7%.

In an egalitarian welfare state these figures are startling, and raise the question whether in fact British society is becoming more equal. It has long been claimed, on the basis of Inland Revenue returns, that the distribution of income even before tax is becoming more equal, particularly since the War. In 1949, according to Atkinson, the top 1 % of income 'units' (individuals and married couples) received before tax 11·2% of the total income, the top 10% 33·2%, and these shares had fallen by 1967 to 7·4% and 28·0%. Such figures have been challenged on various grounds, chiefly because they take no account of tax avoidance, which conceals income such as capital gains and diminishes apparent income by dividing it between different family members. Capital gains, Atkinson estimates, would in 1959 have increased the share of the top 1 % of earners from 8·3 % to 14·1 % and of the top 10% from 29·2% to 35·6%. It cannot be claimed that the distribution of income is becoming substantially more equal before tax, but after tax it certainly can: the steep inflation of the 1970s has brought thousands into the higher taxation levels who never expected to reach them.

There is no denying that the average Briton has become more prosperous since the War, and that even the poor are better off, in absolute if not in relative terms, than they were before the War. Average annual income per head in real terms (at 1970 prices) has risen from £451 in 1951 (already higher than in the 1930s) to £824 in 1972, an increase of 83%. The average weekly earnings of adult male manual workers went up over the same period from £8·30 to £35·82 in current terms or, allowing for rising prices, by 81%. Since then the inflationary wage increases of 1973–75, averaging about 40%, have brought most wages ahead of other incomes. What this means in terms of higher living standards and access to consumer goods can be seen on all sides. In 1959 the prime minister, Harold Macmillan, remarked in a much misquoted phrase: 'Most of our people have never had it so good', and his deputy, R. A. Butler, had recently forecast a doubling of the standard of living within twenty-five years. In 1962 40% of households owned their own house, 45%

205

had a washing machine, 28% a refrigerator, 82% a television set and 19% a telephone. By 1973 52% owned their own house, 67% had a washing mahine, 78% a refrigerator, 93% a television set and 43% a telephone. In 1962 34% of households had the use of a car, most important symbol of the affluent society; by 1973 this had risen to 54% of whom 9% had two cars or more. The oil crisis may slow up but is unlikely to reverse this trend.

Increasing affluence accounts for the enormous expansion since the War in the numbers of cars and other motor vehicles. During the War, with petrol rationing and the cessation of car production for the private market, the total number of vehicles fell slightly, from 3,148,600 in 1939 to 3,106,800 in 1946, and the number of cars more steeply, from 2,034,400 to 1,770,000. With post-war austerity and petrol rationing and the diversion under government pressure of 60% of car production to the export market, the numbers rose only slowly until petrol rationing was abolished in 1950, motor vehicles to 4,409,200 and cars only to 2,257,900. Then in the early 1950s the end of rationing and supply restrictions, the expansion of production and the neglect of exhortations to export suddenly released a flood of cars onto the market. The number leapt to 3,525,800 by 1955, and motor vehicles to 6,464,400. Since then, after a slackening due to the 1956 Suez War and the reintroduction of petrol rationing in the first six months of 1957, numbers have forged ahead. In 1975 there were an estimated 18·1 million motor vehicles on the road, 14·7 million of them cars.

Of these, goods vehicles were a small minority, but a very important one, since they carried an increasing proportion of the consumer goods of the affluent society from the factories to the shops and from the shops to people's homes. They doubled from 560,000 to 1,173,100 between 1946 and 1956 and trebled to 1,645,300 by 1972. The really important part, long-distance heavy haulage, was even smaller. At the nationalization of road transport in 1947 the Road Haulage Executive of the British Transport Commission took over the bulk of the industry,

206

consisting of 41,000 trucks and vans in 3,700 concerns. (After partial denationalization in 1953, British Road Services still retained 16,000 vehicles.) Yet these, along with firms' own transport which became increasingly important, were enough to make great inroads into the railways' share of freight traffic, which in ton-miles steadily declined from 54% in 1952 to 32% in 1962 and 22% in 1972. The railways, nationalized in 1947 and brought under the same British Transport Commission (along with waterways, which now carried only a negligible percentage of freight traffic), also suffered from the competition of cars and buses for passenger traffic. Many of the buses were nationalized too, since the BTC automatically took over the railways' shareholdings in most of the territorial bus companies and between 1947 and 1953 acquired several more, including the huge Tilling Group and Scottish Motor Traction.

The Select Committee on Nationalized Industry in 1958 estimated the proportions of passenger miles provided by different forms of transport as follows: railways 21%, BTC buses 13%, other buses and coaches 25%, private transport 41%. Although the railways maintained roughly the same number of passengers (and passenger-miles) down to the early 1960s, they were gaining no share of the increased traffic of a more mobile society. Moreover, they stood still at increasing cost and with an increasing deficit. By 1960 they were 'in a grave financial plight', and the government decided to reorganize them. The Transport Act, 1962, broke up the British Transport Commission and replaced it by separate Boards for Railways (with six Regional Boards), London Transport, Docks, and Waterways, and a Transport Holding Company to take over the nationalized road haulage and bus holdings. The railways' debts were written off and they were put on a more commercial basis, to compete on level terms with road transport. To confirm this Dr (now Lord) Beeching was appointed first chairman of the Railways Board, with instructions to study the costs of every section of their operations with a view to cutting out those which were unprofitable. But this was a philosophy which, given the 'unfair' competition of the motor car (since no competitor, however cheap, could match its convenience, which owners were willing to pay handsomely for) and yet the absolute necessity of public transport for the survival of our towns, was not tenable in the conditions of modern society.

The affluent society also saw a great expansion in air travel. The War stimulated the demand for travel and the development of larger, faster aircraft. The introduction of the turbo-prop engine in the Viscount in 1950, of the first long-haul jet liner, the Comet I in 1952, the 'big jets', the Boeing 707 and Douglas DC8, in the late 1950s and the 'jumbo jets', the Boeing 747 and the Lockheed Tri-Star, in the early 1970s, brought standards of speed and comfort with immense passenger appeal, and the number of passengers travelling across the Atlantic by air overtook those by sea in 1957, and those across the Channel by 1961. The Anglo-French Concorde opened supersonic services from London to Bahrain and from Paris to Rio de Janeiro early in 1976. The 1950s saw a five-fold increase in air passengers in and from Britain, from 1,156,000 to 5,880,000, and the 1960s a further $2\frac{1}{2}$-fold increase, to 13,874,000. But only a minority of these were on domestic internal flights, which took only a fraction, under 1 %, of the total passenger-miles from land transport, public and private. With inter-city electrification the railways on all but the longest runs began to win back some of this traffic, and air transport, far from being a competitor for the motor car, merely added to the congestion between city centre and suburban airports.

The enormous expansion of motor cars represented more than a mere increase in private transport, convenience and congestion. It was nothing less than the democratization of the motor vehicle. Just as before the First World War the motor car was mainly a rich man's toy and between the Wars a middle-class privilege, so since the Second World War it has become the vehicle of the masses. Already by 1962 a third of the skilled working class and a sixth of the less skilled had cars, and in 1965 the AA estimated that 60% of those who had owned cars only since 1956 belonged to socio-economic groups C2, D and E, i.e. to the working class. By now, with more than half the households in the country having at least one car, car users have become a majority.

That does not mean that life will be more pleasant for the minority of non-owners, for whom the sense of under-privilege will grow even more acute, or that every member of a car-owning household will have equal access to its use. Where father regularly takes the car to work mother and children are, except at weekends, just as cut off and immobile as the carless family, and there remains a majority of non-drivers, children and teenagers, the disabled and others who have no regular or effective access to private transport. Even without the self-defeating congestion of the motor car these alone would make the case for the retention of adequate public transport, to which we shall return.

What effects has the democratization of the motor car had on society in Britain, on the way we live and where? First and most obviously, it has crowded our roads and streets with traffic, multiplying the congestion, noise, pollution and danger to life and limb we saw before the War. Between 1938 (and a similar level after the War) and 1970 the amount of traffic in vehicle-miles on the roads more than quadrupled, and by 1980 it is expected to increase by nearly another 50%.

This rate of expansion was neither expected nor prepared for by governments of either party. In 1945 the Ministry of Transport estimated a 75% increase in vehicles by 1965 over pre-War figures, but the number had doubled by 1950. In 1954 it planned for a 75% increase in traffic by 1974, but that figure was reached by 1962. In 1959 it forecast $12\frac{1}{2}$ million vehicles by 1969, but that number was passed in 1964. The Ministry for years after the War still thought of the car as a minority luxury: it calculated that in new towns only one garage space would be needed for every four houses. Consequently, government policy on the traffic problem took the form of palliatives which did not touch the fundamental system: a road safety campaign ('Keep death off the roads'), chiefly educative and exhortatory, except for the compulsory testing of vehicles more than ten years old from 1956; a very modest programme of road building and improvement – between 1948 and 1953 annual expenditure on road maintenance and minor improvements ran in real terms at only two thirds of the level of 1936–38, and on construction and major improvements at only about one fifth; and in towns, schemes of traffic management to speed the flow of traffic, including traffic lights, zebra crossings, one-way streets, parking restrictions and, from 1956, parking meters. Motorways were envisaged by the Special Roads Act of 1949, but the first eight miles of motorway, the Preston by-pass, were not opened until December 1958.

It gradually became obvious that this casual approach, which assumed that the existing road network with minor modifications could cope with the expansion of traffic and that a 'saturation point' would ultimately be reached at which congestion and the self-frustration of the motor vehicle would choke off the demand for cars, was inadequate. The rising tide of traffic overwhelmed the complacency of the planners. Road casualties, which had fallen below the pre-war level despite the larger traffic, mainly because of minor road improvements and better driving habits, rose again and passed the 1938 figures of injured by 1955 and of killed by 1960. The Royal Society for the Prevention of Accidents showed the cost of road accidents to the community (in damage to property, medical treatment, loss of output and administrative cost, but not apparently in the loss of earnings to the victims' families) as steadily rising from £136 million in 1950 to £267 million in 1966.

Why do people buy cars and what do they do with them when they have bought them? One of the few surveys of car ownership and use, *People and the Motor Car* by the Department of Transportation and Environmental Planning of Birmingham University in 1964, showed that most owners bought for a combination of reasons, for business use, travel to work and social purposes, but that most non-owners, only a small percentage of whom were not interested in buying a car, placed social reasons firmly in front. Few purchasers were put off by congestion on the roads or the expense and difficulties of garaging and parking. The average driver in a one-car family drove 9,470 miles a year, compared with 9,230 miles in a two- or more-car family and 8,850 in a family without a car (presumably driving a firm's vehicle). Commuters strongly preferred to go to work by car where possible, and the proportion doing so varied from about a third in local authority estates to over half in high-income residential areas. Of those doing so, about two thirds managed to park off-street, and most off-street places were provided by the employer. Travel to and from school was also increasingly by car, and rose considerably, even for short distances of under one mile in the higher-income areas. Shopping was the next favoured use, and a majority of drivers in all income areas reported that they had the use of the car for shopping whenever they wanted it. The car was used more frequently in higher-income areas for shopping in the city centre than it was in low-income areas, where the local shops and shopping centres, accessible on foot, were more favoured. Lack of parking facilities was a constraint, and half or more gave it as a reason for not using the car for shopping. Visiting friends and relations was the most popular social use, and from 48% to 55% of drivers, according to residential area, used the car at least once a week for social visiting. Only about a third used the car for visiting pubs or restaurants once a month or more, and only 9–10% more than once a week. Most drivers, 72–80%, never went to the cinema or went less than once a month, only 8–12% went by car to a dance once or more a month, and only 6% to a theatre as frequently. Sport was more popular, 17–24% driving to a sporting function at least once a week, but still a minority activity. Church-going by car varied from 17–23% at least once a week in private estates to 10–14% in local authority estates. From 23% to 42% of drivers used their cars for driving to other indoor activities, presumably clubs, societies, libraries, museums and the like, and 51% to 67% for driving to outdoor activities, such as picnics and walks. And the overwhelming majority, 78% to 94%, rising with income, generally or occasionally used them for holidays.

These figures, showing the steady rise in car use with income and migration to better-quality residential areas, underlined the vast potential for the growth of car ownership. They suggested that the saturation level in car ownership would be higher, at 0·6 cars per head, than the 0·45 predicted by the Road Research Laboratory. And that meant that the problem of the motor car was still larger than the authorities responsible for planning for it had expected.

The first harbinger of a new awareness of the problem and its complexity was the publication in 1958 of Colin Buchanan's *Mixed Blessing: The Motor in Britain*. A planner at the Ministry of Housing and Town Planning, Buchanan claimed it as the first general survey of the impact of the motor vehicle on our society. He was certainly amongst the first to recognize that the traditional divorce between town planning, concerned with the buildings which generated traffic, and transport planning, concerned exclusively with the roads and other systems of communication, perpetuated by the 1947 Town and Country Planning Act, must be ended and a determined effort made to treat towns and their traffic as a whole. It was not sufficient to plan building zones and skylines without considering the traffic which towns and buildings generated and at what levels of movement and by what modes traffic could be accommodated in them; or to plan schemes of traffic management to speed the flow without considering what the traffic was doing there in the first place. It was easy to assume, for example, that a large part of it was through traffic, which could be decanted by building a by-pass, but Buchanan showed that only in small towns (under 50,000 population) could a majority of the traffic be by-passed,

212

while large towns generated most of their own traffic. The problem of through traffic was a relatively easy one, therefore, and could best be solved not by individual town and village by-passes but by the 'universal by-pass' created by the motorway network, the first 700 miles of which were announced by the government in 1956. But the problem of traffic in towns was a much more difficult one, and did not admit of any single easy solution. The most urgent task was to resolve the pedestrian–vehicle conflict between soft, vulnerable human bodies and hard, lethal metal boxes of great speed and power: 'The pedestrian–vehicle mix-up is the horrible, all-pervading entanglement which prevents anything being sorted out.' Buchanan's preferred solution was vertical segregation, cars, vans and buses underneath the buildings for access, pedestrians on a new street level or shopping deck above. He also endorsed the idea of traffic precincts, self-contained areas between the ring and radial arteries, entry to which by through traffic would be discouraged.

These ideas and others were developed by the Buchanan Report on *Traffic in Towns* of 1963, by a working group within the Ministry of Transport under his chairmanship, 'to study the long-term development of roads and traffic in urban areas and their influence on the urban environment'. The report described

a problem which must surely be one of the most extraordinary facing modern society. It arises directly out of man's own ingenuity and growing affluence – his invention of a go-anywhere, self-powered machine for transport and personal locomotion, and his growing ability and inclination to invest in it. It is an extraordinary problem because nothing less is involved than a threat to the whole familiar physical form of towns.

It was not just a question of building more roads and parking spaces, since American experience had shown that even with eight-lane freeways and most of the downtown areas given over to parking lots the city centres still could not cope with all the traffic which tried to use them. It is, of course, possible to site factories, shopping centres and even office blocks outside the towns, with large car parks for motorized access. The new 'hypermarkets', just beginning to reach Britain from the Continent and the United States, show the trend. But, despite the telephone and telex, most business and administration still prefer regular face-to-face communication, and city centre commuting will probably remain with us for the foreseeable future.

The report showed, by case studies of Newbury, Leeds, Norwich and the West End of London, that there was a limit to the number of cars which could be tolerated in any given urban area, even with the most traffic-conscious town planning, without permanent deterioration of the environment. It showed that this limit could be calculated in terms of the numbers of vehicles able to enter the town daily and during the peak periods and planned for in terms of the number of parking places provided, chiefly for short-stay parkers, the assumption being that only a small minority of daily commuters, larger in small towns, smaller in large, could be permitted to travel by car. The solution offered was an expensive one, but less expensive than allowing the towns to grind to a halt altogether. It was first of all to divide each town into 'rooms' or environmental areas in which the chief activities, shopping, business and administration, industry, residence, and so on, took place, and 'corridors' or distributor and access roads, which brought the traffic to the environmental areas but did not allow it to pass through them. Secondly, the environmental areas were to be re-developed where necessary on the vertical segregation principle, with vehicles below and pedestrians on a deck or artificial ground level giving the main access to shops, offices and other buildings. This redevelopment entailed a new technology, 'traffic architecture', which conceived the construction of roads and buildings as a unified whole, to be planned and built together. The result would be a sort of 'layer-cake' urban environment, a three-dimensional world in which strolling shoppers

13a and b. Planning for the Automobile   1. Pedestrian shopping centre at Coventry, 1956, one of the first in Britain. *Photo: Radio Times Hulton Picture Library.* 2. Pedestrian university campus, University of Lancaster. *Photo: by kind permission of P. W. Joslin, 18 Dalton Square, Lancaster*

14a and b. Planning for the Automobile 3. Marriage of pedestrian way and motor road at Cumbernauld New Town: note the pedestrian overpass snaking across the roads to reach the high-rise flats. *Photo: by kind permission of Cumbernauld Development Corporation.* 4. A 'spaghetti junction' on the M4 motorway: such engineering works are among the monuments of twentieth-century archaeology. *Photo: by kind permission of the Transport and Road Research Laboratory, Crowthorne, Berks.*

15a. The Road to the Sun The first turbojet service by British European Airways Viscount, 1950. Jet flights have revolutionized international travel and the package holiday. *Photo: Radio Times Hulton Picture Library*

15b. Beyond the Automobile? A photo-montage impression of the 'Cabtrack' system of urban transport, with individual self-operated passenger cabs passing on elevated tracks between overhead stations. *Photo: by kind permission of the Transport and Road Research Laboratory, Crowthorne, Berks.*

16. The End of an Age?　　The self-congestive monster chokes itself to death: traffic jam near the Elephant and Castle, London, 1966. *Photo: by kind permission of London Transport*

and commuters looked down from bridges and terraces onto the urban motorways and public transport routes below.

The only existing approaches to this motorized Utopia could be found in a few garden cities, new towns and bombed cities which had been rebuilt. Some of the first generation of new towns built under the New Towns Act of 1946 were provided with pedestrian town centres and environmental areas free from through traffic, of which Stevenage is a good example. Only with the second generation, however, beginning with Cumbernauld in Scotland, do we get a new town expressly designed for one car per family, with a 'layer-cake' town centre with vertical segregation of pedestrians and vehicles and a footpath network from all parts of the town. Coventry is the best example of a bombed city redeveloped with a pedestrian shopping centre with some vertical segregation. Birmingham's Bull Ring centre has shown what a large city centre redevelopment can do to segregate shoppers from traffic and make the central area a civilized place to stroll.

These examples are the exception, however, and most towns aiming at salvation of their shopping centres from the motor car have had to be content with horizontal segregation, by closing particular streets to vehicles and creating pedestrian malls, like London Street, Norwich or Market Street, Lancaster. The main reason is the high cost of vertical segregation, and since the Buchanan Report there has been a reaction against spending such enormous sums of money simply to accommodate an inevitably inadequate number of cars. The problem here, as Buchanan realized, is that no town could depend solely on private transport, and the bigger the town the less of its passenger traffic can be carried by car. The journey to work is the critical test. In 1966 the percentage of workers in the central areas of the six largest conurbations outside London travelling by car varied from 14% in Glasgow to 27% in Birmingham; in London it was only 12%. Even so, it was private cars rather than buses, taxis and goods vehicles which formed the bulk of the traffic, particu-

215

larly in peak periods. In no conceivable redevelopment of our cities, however expensive, could everybody travel by car: a three-lane motorway can carry about 4,500 cars per hour or, say, 6,000 commuters (and only if there is sufficient parking provision for them); if buses are substituted for them, the capacity can rise to 30,000 an hour, while a suburban railway can carry up to 40,000 passengers an hour. Only the smallest towns could rely entirely on the private car for the journey to work. It is obvious that without adequate alternatives to the motor car in the form of public transport the cities would grind to a halt.

And not only the cities. One effect of the motor vehicle, the bus as well as the car, has been to spread most residential development in low-density housing further and further from the traditional town and city centres. Everywhere central urban areas are losing population as people move out to the suburbs and beyond to all the villages within driving distance of a commuter station. In fact the motor vehicle is transforming the old distinction between town and country into a new continuum of urban/rural settlement, differing only in density from one area to another. The whole country is undergoing what Professor David Donnison calls 'cultural urbanization', as dwellers in town and country alike gain access to the same urban services, shops, offices, museums, libraries, hospitals, football matches, theatres and cinemas, watch the same city-produced television shows, listen to the same city-based local radio stations, and so on.

The lower the density of population, the more vital the motor car is. Low density gives more freedom to drive and the motor car comes into its own, to drive to work or to a commuter station, to visit friends, to go for drives and picnics, and so on. But it also makes adequate public transport impossible to provide economically. Rail transport, even with electrification, requires concentrations of population around comparatively small numbers of stations. Even bus transport requires modest concentrations, in suburban estates and the like, and cannot economically provide regular services to small villages and scattered houses. The dispersal encouraged by the motor car has produced at the margin a pattern of settlement in which no form of public transport could be economically viable – a fact of which some non-driving members of car-owning households are becoming acutely aware.

Even within the more densely settled areas the spread of the private car has produced a vicious circle for the passenger transport industry. Because of their comfort and convenience rather than their competitive cost, the cars take passengers from train and bus. Receipts for the latter diminish, the service deteriorates and still more passengers prefer, or are forced by the lack of service at the times they want to travel, to go by car. The result is a downward spiral of public transport services which ends in closure of stations, branch lines and bus routes. This process was dramatically highlighted in the case of railways by the Beeching Report of 1963, which showed that the greater part of the railway system was uneconomic. One half of the stations produced only 2% of the passenger receipts, and the most unprofitable services were stopping trains, whose direct costs alone were nearly twice the revenues received from them. Apart from coal and coaching freight (parcels and mail), the only profitable services were some suburban commuter lines and the fast inter-city routes. The Report naturally recommended that the potentially profitable services, chiefly mineral and liner freight, inter-city passenger transport and the heavy suburban services, should be developed, that 400 passenger services should be withdrawn or modified, and over 2,000 stations and 5,000 track miles closed to passengers. Allowing for the closure of duplicate track by the electrification of the inter-city routes, this would mean that only about 8,000 route miles out of 17,000 would survive. But this would leave large areas without public transport or with only infrequent bus services, and pleas were soon heard for the retention of many branch lines on social grounds, even at the cost of public subsidies.

Similarly with bus transport. Both in town and country irregular and overcrowded buses, almost never co-ordinated with rail and other bus timetables, drove people to private transport. Between 1955 and 1965, for example, the buses entering Central London in the morning rush hour declined by 1,900; their place was taken by 29,000 private cars carrying 39,000 people but occupying five times the road space. In the country at large between 1956 and 1960, while car traffic increased by 22% bus traffic declined by 13%. The problem was worst in the rural areas where scores of services were taken off. The Jack Committee on Rural Bus Services and the Highland Transport Enquiry both reported in 1961 that, despite various suggestions for alleviation such as the carrying of passengers by postal vehicles, there was no alternative to direct subsidy.

The growing awareness that the private car could not provide a complete service for the whole community and that at the same time public transport could not compete economically on equal terms has led to schizophrenia in government policy. In general, Conservative governments have tried to make public transport self-supporting and the nationalized parts of it compete with each other, while Labour governments have emphasized social need and have been more prepared to subsidize unremunerative but socially necessary services. The Conservatives in 1953 denationalized road transport and left a diminished British Road Services to compete with private haulage, but the powers given to the Transport Commission to sell off the old railway companies' buses were never exercised. In 1962 the Transport Commission was broken up into its constituent parts which were then forced to compete with each other. By contrast, the Labour government's White Paper on *Transport Policy*, 1966, started from the position that the problem of the automobile was insoluble without an integrated policy for transport as a whole:

The rapid development and mass production of the motor vehicle over the past twenty years has brought immense benefits to millions of people: increased mobility, a fuller social life, family enjoyment, new experiences. It has also produced new, quick and convenient means of moving goods. But at the same time it has brought severe discomforts: congestion in the streets of our towns; the misery of the journey to work for commuters; noise, fumes and danger as the setting of our lives; a rising trend of casualties on our roads and a threat to our environment in both town and countryside which, if it continues unchecked, will ensure the pleasure and benefit for which we use the car will increasingly elude us. The aim of a rational transport policy must be to solve this paradox.

Transport must be planned in relation to the needs of industry and society. 'Our towns and cities will never be able to cope with their traffic, or the transport needs of millions of people, without strengthening, improving and expanding their public transport services.' If some of those services were uneconomic but 'socially necessary', in that without them the towns would not work or residential communities would be cut off, then the community as a whole must pay part of the cost, just as it pays for roads, schools, libraries, sewers and other non-profit-making services.

The railways were to be judged by the extent to which they met the country's overall transport needs. 'Commercial viability is important, but secondary.' Having determined the size and shape of the necessary system, including the main trunk network and its feeders, important commuter routes in and around the main cities and conurbations and certain lines essential to the life of remote areas (which might still entail further closures, but 3,000 track miles less than Beeching, leaving a network of 11,000 miles), the government would guarantee its operation by meeting the deficits of 'socially necessary' services, but the main services, bulk freight and the liner service, inter-city passenger services and commuter services in the conurbations would continue to pay their way.

The road building and improvement programme would be considerably expanded and speeded up, 700 miles of motorway completed by 1970, and more emphasis placed on the relief of urban congestion. Urban land use and transport would be planned together, so as to bring the generation of traffic and the provision for it both in urban roads and parking places into balance. A start would be made in providing a modern network of 'high-capacity traffic routes' (urban motorways) in the towns, but the roads would have to be coordinated with an efficient public transport system under the control in the conurbations of local passenger authorities. The Regional Economic Planning Council had agreed to set up machinery for the integration and coordination of public passenger services, including connections and interchange facilities, timetables, etc., and legislation was planned to enable local authorities and the government to subsidize rural bus services. Freight haulage would be intregrated by a national freight organization which would take over the responsibilities of the Railways Board and the Transport Holding Company and offer the customer an integrated door-to-door service by road and rail. (The White Paper also dealt with the development, reorganization and ultimate nationalization of the ports, and with the development of two networks of waterways, a small commercial network and an 'amenity' network for pleasure craft.)

This ambitious plan for an integrated national transport system was implemented by the 1968 Transport Act, which reorganized the nationalized transport undertakings, created conurbation passenger transport authorities, set up a new system for regulating and licensing road goods transport, and gave local authorities new powers to regulate traffic in towns. In particular, it set up the National Freight Corporation to take over the Transport Holding Company's and part of British Rail's freight interests, and the National Bus Company to take over the Transport Holding Company's buses (except in Scotland where they came under a separate Scottish Bus Group, part of the Scottish Transport Group responsible to the Secretary of State for Scotland). This policy was confirmed by the all-party Commons Select Committee on Expenditure in its report

220

on Urban Transport Planning in 1973, which recommended a major shift of resources from urban road building to subsidized public transport. But since then it has been abandoned by the Labour Government of 1974, which has resurrected the requirement that all nationalized industries should be self-supporting. Whether such a policy can survive the pressure of the trade unions in the public sector for wage increases on a scale which only the taxpayer can support is a moot question.

Meanwhile, by 1972 the first 1,000 miles of motorway had been completed, plus over 2,000 miles of dual carriageway. Very little was urban motorway, and in 1973 the Greater London Council, under pressure from the environmentalist lobby, reversed its plans for a 'motorway box' around London. British Rail has completed its mainline electrification from London to Glasgow and is running inter-city trains at speeds up to 100 m.p.h., but the London commuter lines and the Underground are still grossly overloaded in the rush hours. The National Bus Company is making a profit, but there has been little sign of a revival in rural bus services or the co-ordination of timetables, especially with rail. The private car continues to make inroads into the profitability of much public transport while still providing no answer to the problems of how to offer mobility to the majority of non-drivers (including those in car-owners' families) and how to get the majority of commuters to work.

Recently, the rise of the environmentalist lobby, bringing a new awareness of the need for a civilized environment free from noise, poisonous fumes, and danger to life and limb, has reinforced the demand for control of the motor vehicle and safety on the roads. The testing of ten-year-old cars, motor cycles and other vehicles under 30 cwt from 1956 was gradually extended to three-year-old ones by 1967. Mrs Barbara Castle, a non-driving Minister of Transport, won notoriety by introducing the breathalyser test for offenders suspected of driving under the influence of alcohol in 1967. The fitting of safety belts in cars has been made compulsory. The provision of public walkways within buildings such as shops and office blocks was encouraged by regulation in 1973, a further step towards the segregation of pedestrians, vertically or horizontally, in our towns, and a Land Compensation Act in the same year made it possible to compensate owners of property not just for the land taken for roads and motorways but for the blight they caused on either side, thus allowing the building of roads and the redevelopment of adjacent areas to be planned as a single task.

Sir Geoffrey (now Lord) Crowther, introducing the Buchanan Report in 1963, remarked:

> We are nourishing a monster of great potential destructiveness. And yet we love him dearly. Regarded as 'the traffic problem' the motor car is clearly a menace that can spoil our civilization. But translated into terms of the particular vehicle that stands outside the door, we regard it as one of our most treasured possessions or dearest ambitions, an immense convenience, an expander of the dimensions of life, an instrument of emancipation, a symbol of the modern age. To refuse to accept the challenge it presents would be an act of defeatism.

Can the monster be tamed, or replaced by something more convenient and less dangerous? What are the prospects for the automobile, if any, and for transport and society beyond the automobile? In the last chapter we shall take a look into the future.

FURTHER READING

Ministry of Transport, *Traffic in Towns* (the Buchanan Report) (HMSO, 1963, Penguin, 1964)

Ministry of Transport, *Transport Policy* (HMSO, 1966)

C. K. Atkins, *People and the Motor Car* (Department of Transportation and Environmental Planning, University of Birmingham, 1964)

Paul Ritter, *Planning for Man and Motor* (Pergamon, 1964)

J. Tetlow and A. Goss, *Homes, Towns and Traffic* (Faber, 1968)

Stephen Plowden, *Towns Against Traffic* (Deutsch, 1972)

F. D. Sando and V. Batty, 'Road Traffic and the Environment', *Social Trends*, No. 5, 1974 (HMSO, 1974)

William Plowden, *The Motor Car and Politics, 1896–1970* (Bodley Head, 1971)

P. M. Townroe, ed., *Social and Political Consequences of the Motor Car* (David & Charles, 1974), especially D. V. Donnison, 'Urban Policies and the Motor Car'

D. H. Aldcroft, *British Railways in Transition: The Economic Problems of Britain's Railways since 1914* (Macmillan, 1968)

John Hibbs, *The History of British Bus Services* (David & Charles, 1968)

R. E. G. Davies, *A History of the World's Airlines* (Oxford University Press, 1964)

B. Abel-Smith and P. Townsend, *The Poor and the Poorest* (Bell, 1965)

I. Gough and T. Stark, 'Low Incomes in the United Kingdom', *Manchester School*, 1968

J. C. Kincaid, *Poverty and Equality in Britain* (Penguin, 1973)

Dorothy Wedderburn, ed., *Poverty, Inequality and Class Structure* (Cambridge University Press, 1974), especially A. B. Atkinson, 'Poverty and Income Inequality in Britain' and J. L. Nicholson, 'The Distribution and Redistribution of Income in the United Kingdom'

A. B. Atkinson, *The Economics of Inequality* (Clarendon Press, 1975)

R. Brech, *Britain in 1984* (Darton, Longman, Todd, 1963)

223

10. THE END OF THE
AUTOMOBILE AGE?

In October 1973 the Arab states, incensed by the war with Israel, placed an embargo on oil and increased its price. In the next twelve months the Organization of Petroleum Exporting Countries quadrupled the price, and discovered that the 'oil weapon' was more than a means of military and diplomatic pressure. It was a means of becoming fabulously rich and/ or redressing the economic balance between a large part of the Third World and the industrial countries. Since then they have been emulated, less successfully, by other commodity-producing countries and the prices of all raw materials have rocketed, contributing to the current world-wide inflation. Although prices by 1975 were settling down at a higher level, the world economy will never be the same again, with cheap food and raw materials exchanged for expensive manufactured goods and sophisticated services. The advanced industrial countries will have to pay a larger share of their production to obtain their essential resources and therefore suffer a slowing down of their headlong rush towards even higher living standards at the expense of the rest of the world.

The oil crisis was perhaps the first symptom not merely of the

225

demand of the Third World for a fairer share of the world's wealth, which many people will welcome: the United States with 6% of the world's population takes 30% of the world's resources, and Western Europe and Japan nearly as much again. The oil crisis was also a harbinger of the pressure of population on the world's finite supply of raw materials. World population will increase from 3·8 billion to 6·3 billion by the end of the century, and even without an increase in living standards will put pressure on food and other supplies which can only lead, whatever the short-term fluctuations, to a long-term rise in prices. Not that the rise in prices will benefit the Third World in general. On the contrary, it merely transfers the oil-producing countries to the camp of rich exploiters. The high price of oil, needed by the poorer countries for cooking as well as transport and power supply, makes them poorer still, and through their diminished purchasing power for other goods may well contribute to a deepening world slump. It is one of the contradictions of the world economy that, in order to save employment in the industrial countries, we may have to devote a large part of our production not to raising the living standards of the poor nations but to making the rich oil producers still richer.

What effect is the oil crisis likely to have on the use of the automobile and the future of the car industry in this country? To judge by the number of cars on the road and the speeds they still travel at, very little. Despite a doubling of the price of petrol (including tax), consumption has only been reduced by about 10%. The Automobile Association reports that most motorists would be willing to pay £1 a gallon before considering using other means of transport. Nevertheless, an absolute shortage of oil – which might result from a renewed war in the Middle East – or a world slump deeper than the present recession which reduced incomes here, not to say an independent collapse of the British economy due to hyperinflation driving us out of our export markets, could easily put the motor car out of the reach of a majority of car drivers. North Sea oil might delay the evil day, but the current proved reserves would last only about thirty years. The end of the automobile age is not a theoretical impossibility.

There are other reasons why the automobile in its present form may be at the end of its tether. The lovable monster is its own worst enemy. It pollutes the atmosphere with carbon monoxide and lead compounds which poison our lungs and cause brain damage and lung cancer. It directly kills thousands and maims hundreds of thousands of innocent victims every year: in 1973 7,407 were killed and 346,325 injured in road accidents. Above all, it is self-frustrating in that the more vehicles there are congesting the roads the more difficult it is to use them. As we have seen, only a small minority of commuters – from 12% in London to 27% in Birmingham – use their cars for getting to work, and already the streets are choked with traffic. The American remedy of eight-lane urban highways and city-centres largely given over to parking lots has not solved the problem there and is unlikely to work here. Meanwhile, the low marginal cost of travelling by car once it is acquired – little more than the cost of petrol, oil and parking – makes any conceivable form of public transport uncompetitive. Buses and suburban trains become uneconomic, fares have to be raised and become more uncompetitive, and public transport declines in a vicious spiral, forcing still more use of the motor car and still more congestion. We are being driven towards the classic paradox that we cannot live with the motor car and yet cannot live without it. Has the automobile a future?

Given the present dispersal of the population in huge sprawling conurbations and outlying commuter villages around the great cities, the automobile or something very like it is vital to our way of life. In theory of course we could change our way of life. We could go back to the Victorian distribution of population in tightly packed city-centres and in suburbs within walking distance of the railway stations, Or we could go forward to the electronic society, with work performed at home controlled

227

by telecommunication links from central headquarters staffed by a handful of managers – though some form of transport would still be needed to convey the raw materials, component parts and finished products. But neither of these solutions is likely within the near future: people are too attached to spacious living and repelled by multi-storey dwellings for the first and business capital is too concentrated in central offices and factories for the second. Social capital, too, is heavily invested in dispersed housing and amenities and despite the price of petrol the net movement of population is still outwards rather than inwards. With a few exceptions like the West End of London, the social prestige gradient still rises from the centre outwards and, indeed, the cost of petrol reinforces this: the high petrol-consuming car has become one more ostentation of the rich.

Thus, in the present state of society we are stuck – oil sheiks permitting, and we may not need their permission when North Sea oil comes on full-stream in the 1980s – with the motor car or something very like it. A substitute would have to offer the same instant personal mobility, the same all-weather door-to-door service, the same capacity to go almost anywhere at a moment's notice. It might take the form of a small personal hovercraft or helicopter, but these would still require petrol or a similar fuel, would still produce noise and pollution, would still require parking space, and might produce even more congestion and problems of traffic management – in the latter case of three-dimensional traffic lanes in the sky. It is conceivable that some smaller device attached to the person, a powered trolley or a flying pack, could provide the same instant mobility without the problem of parking – just leave it in the cloakroom or left-luggage office. The US Air Force already has an experimental man-lifting jet-propelled back-pack. But all such devices offer little or no protection from the weather or from collisions, require special clothing and are inherently unstable. Small, easily parked personal machines already exist in the form of mopeds, scooters and motor bicycles, and because of their lack of weather protection and greater accident risks their popularity has declined since about 1960. (With the oil crisis, however, bicycles have increased in popularity and in 1975 sales exceeded a million for the first time.)

There is thus no immediate alternative to the motor car which does not bring with it much the same problems or worse. Although the oil crisis may slow it down, the government expects that the number of cars on the road will rise from the present 14.7 million (and a total of 18.1 million motor vehicles) to 18 million (and 22 million) in 1980, 26 million (and 30 million) in 1990, and 30 million (and over 40 million) by 2011. By then car ownership will reach saturation, at 0.45 cars per head. The noise, pollution, accidents and congestion will also reach saturation. We must therefore turn our minds not to abolishing the automobile but to improving it so as to reduce or get rid of the problems and to supplementing it with other forms of transport.

One solution is to tailor the motor vehicle to the town rather than, as in the Buchanan Report of 1963, the town to the motor vehicle. In 1967 a Ministry of Transport working group published a report on *Cars for Cities*. The best hope, it decided, lay in designing a small car for city use which would enable more vehicles to use the same space. Since the average journey to work was no more than $5\frac{1}{2}$ miles and the average car carried no more than two people, it could be a two-seater of limited range and a maximum speed of 40 m.p.h. These 'citycars' would be 3 feet to 4 feet 4 inches wide and would need only 7-foot lanes instead of the standard 12-foot. The benefits would be small if mixed with other traffic, enabling only 10–15% more people to commute to work by car, but if they were segregated in special lanes, with some exclusive streets and fly-overs, up to twice as many commuters could be carried. Twice as many cars could also be parked at the kerbside or in parking garages, or four to five times as many in mechanical garages where they could be 'posted' in 'slots'.

Yet twice as many car commuters would still be only about a quarter of those coming daily into London, and little more than half in Birmingham. The streets would still have to carry the buses for other commuters and the delivery vans to the shops, factories and offices. The 7-foot lanes would have to be additional to the bus and van lanes, perhaps in a special elevated network which would be very costly to install. Private investment in a second car unsuitable for non-urban travel would also be heavy, and considerable incentives would have to be offered such as favourable tax rates and concessionary parking to induce commuters to buy. The working group considered alternatives to private ownership, including hiring citycars as self-drive taxis from the edge of town and a system of pooling or club ownership by which drivers could leave the citycar anywhere for some other pool-member to pick up, but rejected them as impracticable. Most travellers would need them at the same time in the same direction, inwards in the morning and outwards at night, and there would be great difficulty in arranging interchange at the peripheral car parks and in protecting them from vandalism. The citycars would therefore be private, second or third family vehicles, additions rather than replacements, and would simply release normal cars to congest the suburban and rural roads. Less car means more road, but only if it is a substitute for a larger one, not a supplement. A more likely trend, already encouraged by the need to economize petrol, is towards the smaller conventional car.

The working group also considered alternative power units to the traditional petrol engine. The diesel engine was more economical, but only in larger sizes for commercial vehicles. The gas turbine with its low vibration, comparatively small size and high power-to-weight ratio was particularly suitable for large goods vehicles and long-distance coaches, but it was noisy and unsuitable for stop-and-start urban travel. The compact rotary engine, the Wankel, already in use in some cars, was smoky and uneconomical in town usage. All these used oil and created pollution like the petrol engine. The air-cycle engine, which alternatively heats and cools a working fluid such as helium in a closed circuit, would be silent and pollution-free but, requiring very high temperatures and expensive materials, would be uncompetitive for a long time to come. The obvious solution for urban vehicles was the electric battery motor, but existing batteries were too heavy, too expensive, too short in range and low in performance to be competitive: the batteries would cost as much as the car and the range between charges would be no more than perhaps fifty miles. Some kind of fuel cell, producing electric power chemically from a continuous input, of zinc and air or hydrogen and oxygen, offered the best hope for a practicable electric car, but so far the fuels were expensive and often dangerous and an efficient electric car still lay in the future. The working group therefore assumed that the citycar would still be powered by the conventional petrol-driven piston engine, modified if possible to reduce its noise, smell, pollution and danger in accidents.

Automatic vehicle control was the most futuristic device the group considered. Electro-magnetic guidance from wires beneath the road and electronic control of proximity to the car in front either from the roadside or within the car itself were technically feasible, but still in the experimental stage. It would have particular value on motorways and in town use, reducing driver fatigue, keeping vehicles in lane, maintaining a steady flow and allowing them to run more closely together. But the difficulties, of guidance at junctions, of overtaking, of dealing with breakdowns and above all of avoiding pedestrians who might be difficult for the proximity sensors to scan, were enormous. If these could be solved, the investment in road-guidance systems and vehicle-borne electronic devices would be still more enormous, and automatic control would take decades to introduce, during which time the mixture of controlled and uncontrolled roads and vehicles would be a particular problem.

The working group also recommended a number of other

improvements: a wider variety of taxis with two-person ones for most town purposes and larger ones like minibuses or American twelve-seater limousines for airport and similar work; more comfortable and manoeuvrable goods vehicles with automatic transmission and better load-handling to reduce driver fatigue and improve turn-round; more and smaller city-centre pay-as-you-enter buses; and a new financial framework – a hint at higher taxes or subsidies? – to enable the bus to compete more effectively with the private car, 'which although cheaper to them [the users] personally is often more expensive to the community as a whole'.

Such improvements would be welcome, but they would in no way revolutionize urban transport or more than palliate the problem of living with the motor car. For the foreseeable future we shall still have to live with the motor car or something so like it as to bring the same problems of noise, pollution, congestion and danger to life and limb. Unless economic collapse or military catastrophe intervenes the age of the automobile will outlast most Britons alive today. We may improve it in various ways but we cannot escape it, and as its numbers increase the problems will get worse. The numbers of people needing transport of all kinds will rise, too. The population of Britain is projected to grow from 54 million in 1971 to 61 million by 2011. This is equivalent to adding a city of 175,000, larger than Bolton or Brighton, to our population every year. We already have one of the highest population densities in the world, 845 per square mile in England and Wales, though most of it is concentrated in the 10% of the land area which is built up; by 2011 there will be over 1,000 per square mile. All these new people will need somewhere to live, and where they live will depend above all on the transport available.

A more fundamental approach is needed if we are to retain even the restricted mobility we now possess in the increasingly congested conditions of the next forty years. The best way is to begin at the beginning and ask ourselves what kinds of movement we require and what kinds of transport are available to supply them. As Professor C. A. O'Flaherty of Leeds University has pointed out, we need four main types of movement, in and between areas of differential densities of population:

1. transport between urban concentrations, chiefly inter-city travel but also including airport links and the like;
2. transport within urban concentrations, intra-city movement between shops, offices, bus and rail stations, and so on;
3. transport between urban concentrations and the suburbs, satellite towns and villages from which the commuters, shoppers and other city visitors come;
4. transport within the rural areas, between villages, isolated homesteads, local amenities, etc.

These types of movement can be provided for on the basis that the distribution of population and land use remains much the same as today, i.e. that we keep the same fundamental framework of city, town, suburb and village; or that they can be transformed by designing, or allowing market forces to generate, new patterns of population distribution and land use which 'blow open' our towns and cities and scatter their activities to places where they will be more accessible to the forms of transport available, and above all to the motor car.

Let us begin by assuming that we shall keep our traditional and familiar hierarchy of city, town, suburb and village, increasingly joined together in conurbations. The first category of transport demand, for travel between major cities, is the easiest to meet. It is already met in three ways, each of them capable of considerable improvement. The fastest and most efficient in theory is the jet aeroplane, which can link any pair of major airports in the country in about thirty to sixty minutes. But it may take an hour or more at each end to reach, usually by coach or taxi, destinations in the city centre, thus nullifying the time saved by flying. Add to this the well-known delays and uncertainties of air travel due to weather, mechanical breakdown, queuing for boarding cards and luggage, and the like, and the advantage

233

of flying disappears over all but the longest and oversea routes, which on domestic flights means mainly to and from Scotland and Northern Ireland. Large helicopters or vertical take-off aircraft would enable flights to originate and end nearer city centres, but until they can be made much quieter their introduction will depend on public tolerance of their noise and disturbance.

The least efficient but spuriously most seductive way is by motor car via the inter-city motorways which are scheduled to double to about 2,000 miles by the early 1980s. The motor car, though convenient and instantly available, cannot compete for speed with the train over distances above 100 miles, and there are good road safety reasons why drivers should avoid the fatigue of double journeys of 200 miles or more. Apart from fatigue, the inconvenience of the car for inter-city travel is the problem of what to do with it when you get there. In most city centres the commuter is discouraged by parking restrictions and the shopper and short-stay business visitor is encouraged by parking meters or other short-stay parking facilities. But the inter-city business man (or administrator or academic) who needs more than one or two hours for his meeting, is a neglected client for whom better arrangements could be made in the form of more medium-term parks or garages. The difficulty is how to prevent his facility being pre-empted by shoppers and even commuters. Perhaps it can best be solved by some of the schemes of traffic management for city-centre traffic discussed below, combining peripheral car parks with public transport.

The best solution for most inter-city travel of less than 300 or 400 miles is some form of express train. Electrification, the segregated track and central control enable average speeds of 100 m.p.h. to be maintained with great comfort, no fatigue and the convenience of direct access to the city centre. This performance will be stepped up to 130 m.p.h. in the later 1970s with the introduction of British Rail's high speed train with its lightweight aerodynamic self-balancing coaches, and to 155 m.p.h. by the

234

gas-turbine-driven advanced passenger train during the 1980s. Still higher speeds up to 300 m.p.h. may be attained by 'levitating' a wheel-less train, either by air cushions of the hovercraft type or by electromagnetic repulsion. British Tracked Hovercraft are, despite cuts in their government grant, still working on the first, in conjunction with Professor Eric Laithwaite's revolutionary linear induction motor, while Professor Bhalchandra V. Jayawant of Sussex University has built a working model of the second. Both would be almost silent and pollution-free and would provide the fastest conceivable land transport between cities, but, since the conventional duorail track even as realigned for the advanced passenger train would be inadequate, at very large cost in capital investment.

The high-speed train would also be appropriate for linking city centres to their airports, but the difficulties here are that few railway links already exist and the traffic, even in the day of the jumbo jet, is too light and intermittent to warrant a large investment in permanent construction. Monorails are ideal for this purpose, and certainly some form of lightly constructed overhead monorail track built along existing roads would be cheaper than building a conventional railway from scratch. But this would probably become feasible only if built as an integral part of a more general city monorail system, and is best dealt with under the heading of intra-city transport.

Travel within the city centre, as distinct from travel to it from other centres or suburbs, is a problem all on its own. In such high density areas mass travel is at its best, and the resources and imagination of the transport engineer and planner are stretched to the limit. It is not just a matter of advanced technology applied to vehicles and track or roadway. It is a question of handling large masses of people and their fares and luggage, at rates up to 30,000 and more an hour, through interchanges between street and conveyor and between conveyor and other transport termini. Up to now the chief forms of intracity transport have been pedestrian – walking is still a vital part

235

of the interchange systems – the bus and the taxi, and the underground (or occasionally overhead) railway. The private car has played only a small part because of the difficulty of parking, though the goods vehicle continually circulates with its deliveries to shops, offices, warehouses and industrial premises. Some of these traditional forms of transport can be further improved. Pedestrian travel can be made far more efficient and comfortable by constructing continuous footways, preferably elevated, along the front of or inside shops and office buildings – the present pedestrian subways under main intersections, with their exhausting changes of level and possible harbouring of criminals, are a poor substitute for these. 'Travelators' or moving pavements for specially busy sections are useful, and highly sophisticated ones which can accelerate and decelerate at the start and finish are becoming available, but these are perhaps best reserved for changes of grade (escalators and moving ramps) and busy interchanges (underground and other stations). Buses and taxis can be speeded up by the provision of exclusive lanes, particularly in rush hours, already in existence in some towns and capable of great extension. New underground railways, preferably with automatic train control, like the new Victoria Line would enormously benefit other cities than London, but are expensive, and both London's Fleet Line and the £72 million Manchester underground project have been postponed on grounds of cost. Minor changes, like the use of pneumatic tyres for trains experimented with on the Paris and Montreal Metros, can offer big improvements in comfort and operation.

Despite the potential for improvement, however, our intra-city transport systems are grossly overloaded and are likely to become more so. New forms are needed, and the demand for high-density mass transport in city centres makes it an attractive field for innovation. The one most advocated is the monorail, of which there are many forms and designs. It is essentially any kind of tracked vehicle which can be supported or suspended from an overhead framework built over or alongside existing

236

streets and roads, attached to buildings, or slung across open spaces, rivers and other obstacles. Its virtue is its grade separation, or segregation from all other traffic, so that it can speed its passengers unhindered from station to station. It can be steel- or rubber-tyred, or be levitated by air cushions or magnetic repulsion. It need not even be strictly monorail since, like the American Westinghouse Skybus or the Swiss Habegger Minirail, it can be a lightweight dual-rail system or 'minitrain' on exactly similar supports. The essential thing is that it should be a continuous, unimpeded, overhead transport system capable of carrying up to 30,000 passengers per hour per track. Such a capability would enormously increase the mobility of passengers in and around our city centres. But its effectiveness would depend on how extensive the scheme was, how it was linked to the traditional suburban transport system and to peripheral car parks, and on public tolerance of the visual and aural intrusion of swift and possibly noisy vehicles flashing overhead or past their windows. Over all lies the question of cost: if it took fifty-five years after the electrification of the London Tube to build the next section of underground, the Victoria Line, how long would it take to build a complete monorail system?

Even more sophisticated intra-city mass transport systems than the monorail are being designed. The American carveyor uses a special track like a continuous conveyor belt, underground or overhead, to despatch individual vehicles carrying eight to ten passengers from station to station. More revolutionary is the continuous integrated transporter which is an endless train of coaches moving at a steady 20-25 m.p.h.; the passenger would enter from a loading compartment on the station platform which would accelerate until it reached the same speed as the train and he could step across. Most revolutionary of all is the concept of the network cab or tracked, guided individual taxi, which uses an overhead track similar to but lighter than the monorail to carry individual four-seat cabs to any station on a network, directed by dialling the destination number into the central

237

computer. There are several different systems being studied in Britain, the United States and Sweden. The British study, Cabtrack, envisaged a close network in central London and a much wider one in the Birmingham area. The London study suggested it would be so successful that it would have to charge higher fares than the bus and underground to prevent saturation of the system, while the Birmingham one claimed that it was capable of replacing much of the existing bus system. An individual vehicle carrying the passenger to a chosen point within a few minutes' walk of his destination, the network cab combines most of the advantages of the private car and an efficient public transport system. If its intrusion into familiar streets is acceptable, and if its economies are as favourable as is claimed, it might well be the answer to the problem of intra-city transport.

Suburban transport to and from city centres by commuters, shoppers and other visitors is probably the most difficult problem of all. As suburbs and residential villages spread further out into the countryside under the influence of the motor car, the problem of collecting travellers from a wider area of low-density residence and depositing them daily in a dense central business district becomes more and more difficult. We have seen that the motor car itself cannot solve the problem, since it can never carry more than a fraction of those wishing to travel, and even in the miniaturized form of the citycar would still be inadequate to the task. One negative solution is to make driving more expensive by charging still more heavily for parking and/or by 'road pricing', i.e. charging a fee for the use of urban roads which would be higher nearer the centre and at peak periods. Road pricing is already technically feasible by equipping all vehicles either with meters or with electronic identity plates which would reflect the number of the vehicle back to roadside meters, the charge being collected regularly like a telephone or electricity bill. The difficulty with the scheme is that it would unduly favour the rich and press hard upon poorer city dwellers who live near the centre and would find their chance of owning a car still more restricted. It might also encourage the well-to-do to leave the central areas in still greater numbers, thus hastening the social decay and formation of ghettos which the motor car has already begun to cause in the United States.

A more positive approach is to make public transport, or a combination of public and private transport, more attractive than commuting all the way by car. More comfortable express buses, in reserved lanes or on special tracks, could offer faster journeys than traffic-jammed cars, and make it worth the commuter's while to walk to and wait at a bus stop. Better facilities for parking and waiting (e.g., for wives picking up husbands) at commuter rail stations, already in widespread use around London, would attract more commuters onto the railway. Better interchange facilities, especially by co-ordinating feeder buses with rail timetables, would encourage more transfer to public transport. If all else fails, the subsidies to public transport recommended by the 1966 White Paper and the 1973 all-party Commons Committee might be cheaper, and certainly less destructive, than pulling down most of our city centres to make room for roads and car parks.

A more revolutionary solution might be a guided car, a small battery/mains electric vehicle capable of operating on ordinary roads and on an elevated track, such as the American StaRRcar, which would carry the commuter under its own battery power to a pick-up station, where it would transfer to the track and mains drive. It need not be individually owned but left on the track to proceed under automatic control to the next customer, an exactly similar car being picked up for the journey home. In effect this would be an extension to the residential areas of the network cab principle, and might offer the ultimate solution to the commuter problem, though at a very high price.

The last type of movement required is that in the outer suburbs and rural areas, between home and work (for increasing numbers of jobs are located there), and local shops, golf clubs, riding schools, boating marinas, picnic spots and other leisure facilities. Here the motor car comes into its own and still has the largest role to play, and there is no point in looking for expensive substitutes which the traffic would not bear. The problem here is of a different order, how to offer the non-drivers, including those in car-owners' families, at least some of the mobility of the car driver. The isolation of the carless country-dweller is probably greater now than at any time since the coming of the motor bus, if not the local railway train. The present dispersal of population makes it impossible to provide public transport economically in all directions, and massive public subsidies to a small and, on average, better-off minority would be out of the question. All that could be hoped for would be a subsidized minibus service to larger villages or small towns once a day or perhaps twice a week. This problem is insuperable with present technology and economics. In the rural areas the motor car is king but, alas, a merciless tyrant to non-users.

Yet this last type of movement suggests a solution to the problem of living with the motor car which, at the cost of reversing the whole trend of social development since the beginning of civilization and turning our urban way of life inside out, might well be forced upon us. It is frankly to accept that the cities cannot accommodate the automobile, even with the most advanced, expensive, Buchanan-type traffic architecture, and therefore to 'blow open' our towns and disperse all the activities we associate with them to places which the motor car can reach. This is already happening. There are already rural factories (Wedgwoods at Barlaston, Staffordshire) and office blocks (the Renold Chain Company at Styal near Manchester Airport), rural shopping centres and hypermarkets (Caerphilly and Chandlers Ford near Southampton), rural hospitals (at Cheddleton, Staffordshire, Cheadle, Cheshire and many more), rural universities (York, Lancaster, Kent, Warwick and the Open University at Milton Keynes), even a rural opera house (Glyndebourne), all served by the motor car and bus. It is easy to imagine rural museums, art galleries and funfairs – many country houses open to the public are just that – rural libraries, cinemas, theatres, even rural town halls and government departments. Modern telecommunications, the telephone, telex, 'picturephone' and closed-circuit television, facilitate such dispersal. No doubt certain business activities such as the Stock Exchange and the commodity markets would still require face-to-face contact by large numbers of people, but there is no reason why they should meet in central London. It would make sense to locate most of the large traffic-generating activities where they could cope with and provide parking space for their own traffic. It would certainly be cheaper and better than tearing down our ancient cities and rebuilding them on the Buchanan layer-cake principle.

Yet the cost, social and environmental rather than economic, would be traumatic: the decay of our historic cities which might become like the ghost towns inherited by the Anglo-Saxons from the Romans, the destruction of the green belts around our conurbations and the erosion of the remaining countryside. More deeply disturbing would be the reversal of the whole trend of social history since civilization began, away from creative proximity in closer, more densely settled communities and towards a uniform dispersal of population over the whole landscape. No doubt there would be compensations. The meaning of community would change, is already changing, from a fortuitous group of near neighbours to a more self-chosen group of friends scattered among a much larger area of strangers. People with like minds and interests would congregate at centres of activity many miles from their homes, as they already do for such pastimes as horse-racing, motor rallies, Open University summer schools, and the like. But the course of all civilization, as its name implies, towards ever closer concentration in larger communities, in a word the process of urbanization, would be reversed. The ultimate end of the automobile age might not be the huge vertical cities envisaged by some planners and forecasters like Doxiadis or the Hudson Institute but a society spread thinly across the

241

landscape in a continuous *rus in urbe* or *urbs in rure*. And whether that would be Utopia or purgatory, to be planned for or planned against, is for each one of us, motorized or pedestrian, to decide.

FURTHER READING

C. A. O'Flaherty, *Passenger Transport Present and Future* (Leeds University Press, 1969)

Institution of Mechanical Engineers, *Transport in the Year 2000* (IME, 1965)

Institution of Mechanical Engineers, *Proceedings of the Convention on Guided Land Transport*, 181, 1966–67, Part 3G

Bill Gunston, *Transport: Problems and Prospects* (Thames & Hudson, 1972)

C. G. B. Mitchell, 'New Technology in Urban Transport', *Proceedings of the Institution of Civil Engineers*, 52, 1972

Ministry of Transport, *Cars for Cities* (HMSO, 1967)

Ministry of Transport, *Road Pricing: The Economic and Technical Possibilities* (HMSO, 1964)

US Department of Housing and Urban Development, *Tomorrow's Transportation: New Systems for the Urban Future* (Washington, DC, 1968)

Terence Bendixson, *Instead of Cars* (Maurice Temple Smith, 1974)

Richard Marsh, 'British Rail of the Future', *Modern Railways*, May 1972

Brian Richards, *New Movement in Cities* (Studio Vista, 1966)

Emma Rothschild, *Paradise Lost – the Decline of the Auto-Industrial Age* (Allen Lane, 1974)

Percy Johnson-Marshall, *Rebuilding Cities* (Edinburgh University Press, 1966)

Peter Hall, *London 2000* (Faber, 1963)

Constantine Doxiadis, *Ekistics: An Introduction to the Study of Human Settlements* (Oxford University Press, 1968)

INDEX

Abel-Smith, Professor, 204
Addison, Christopher, 95
Affluence of car workers, 125–6
Air warfare, 63–6, 173–4, 175, 178–81, 196
Amalgamations and mergers in the motor industry, 115–18
Anglo-Persian Oil Company, 48
Anti-Corn Law League, 18
Areas of Great Landscape, Historic or Scientific Value, 166
Areas of Outstanding Natural Beauty, 165–6
Aristocracy, the, 17–19
Assembly line, 109–10, 112, 120–1, 124
Ashfield, Lord, 144
Associated Commercial Vehicles, 116
Atkinson, Professor A. B., 204, 205
Austin, Herbert, 11, 41
Automobile Association, 53–4, 138
Automation, 113, 123–4
Aveling, Thomas, 34
Aviation, development of, 49–52, 134–5; expansion since Second World War, 208; inter-city travel, 233–4; *see also* Air warfare

Babbage, Charles, 106
Beeching Report 1963, 217
'Belisha beacon', 140
Bentham, Samuel, 106
Benz, first motor car to appear in Britain, 7, 39
Benz, Karl, 38
Beveridge, William, 23; Beveridge Report, 94, 202
Bicycle, the, 36, 40, 156
Birth rate, post-First World War, 92
Blatchford, Robert, 36
Boer War, 14, 21, 47
Bollée, Amédéé, 35
Boom of 1925–29, 100
Booth, Charles, social survey of, 19–21, 204
Booth, General William, 21
Bosanquet, Helen, 23
Boydell, J., 34

243

Breathalyser, 221
British Electric Traction, 130
British imperialism, 12–14
British Motor Corporation, 116, 117–18; merger with Leyland, 117–18
British motor industry, early years, 111–13; problems of, 114–15; post-Second World War, 114–15; mergers, 116–18; production capacity, 118–19; poor performance of, 119; models, number of, 120; quality control, 120, 122–3
British Motor Syndicate, 39
British Motoring League, 136
British Transport Commission, 206, 207
Brown, Samuel, 37
Brunel, Marc, 106
Buchanan, Colin, 149
Buchanan Report 1963, 213–14, 222, 229
Bus and coach transport, 46–7, 142–5, 217, 218
Butler, Edward, 39
Butler Act 1944, 96
Butlin, Billy, 158, 159

Caithness, Earl of, 34, 35
Cameron, Lord, 121
Camping Club of Great Britain, 157
Canstatt-Daimlers, 40
Caravanning, 157, 162
Cars for Cities, 229–32
Carson, Sir Edward, 27
Cartwright, Edmund, 36
Carveyor transport system, 237
Cayley, Sir George, 49–50
Charity Organization Society, 23
Chevrolet, 42
Children Act 1908, 25
Coal Industry, 88, 100
Cody, S. F., 50

Colonies, British, self-government, 201–2
Conservation of the countryside, 165–8
Continuous integrated transporter, 237
'conurbations', development of, 147, 150
Cook's Tours, 159
Cooperative Holidays Association, 157
Council for the Preservation of Rural England, 165
Countryside, conservation of the, 165–8
Crosville Motor Services, 134, 143
Crowther, Sir (later Lord) Geoffrey, 222
Cugnot, Nicholas, 31
'cultural urbanization', 216
Cycling clubs, 36, 156–7

Daimler, Gottlieb, 37–8, 39, 40
Dance, Sir Charles, 32
Day trippers, 163–5
de Havilland, Geoffrey, 51
Depression of the 1920s, 83–4
Diesel, Rudolf, 48
Dion, Count de, 35, 38
Dominions, the, 85–6
Donnison, Professor David, 216
Drake, Alfred, 37
Dreadnought, the, 48
Dunlop, J. B., 40
Duryea, Charles, 39

Early motoring, 45–8
Economy, the: post-First World War, 81–6; post-Second World War, 199–201
Edge, S. F., 41
Edmunds, Henry, 43
Education: 95–6; industry and, in 19th century, 9–11; Edwardian era, 25

Edwards, J. R., 117, 118
Electric-battery bus, 46
Electric cars, 39
Electric tram, 46
Elliott, F. L. D., 54
Ellis, Hon. Evelyn, 40
Emigration, 92–3
Empire, the British, 85–6
Environmentalist lobby, 221
European Economic Community, 125, 202
Evans, Oliver, 106
Exports, British, 114

Farman, Henri, 50
Fessenden, Reginald, 52
First World War: 58–78; submarines, 61–3; convoy system, 63; air power, 63–6; armoured cars, 67, 73–4; railways, use of, 67–8; poison gas, 73; tank, advent of the, 74–7
Fisher, H. A. L., 95
Fleming, Sir Ambrose, 52
Flow-line production, 108–9
Foden, Edwin, 34, 47
Ford, Henry, 39, 108–11, 120–1
Ford Model-T, 42, 43, 44, 109, 110, 111
Forest, Lee de, 52
Forest Parks, 166
Fowler, John, 34
Free trade, 84, 85
Fuller, Major-General J. F. C., 175
Future of the motor car, 227–42

Garden cities and suburbs, 147, 149–50
Gas engines, 37
Geddes, Sir Eric, 99–100
Geddes, Patrick, 147
General Motors of America, 115
General Strike, 100
Gibb, Sir George, 55

Gold standard, 100
Goods, transport of, 145, 206–7
Government of India Act 1935, 86
Government traffic policy, 99–100, 209–10, 218–22
Green belts, 166
Grey, Sir Edward, 59
Guided cars, 239
Gurney, Sir Goldsworthy, 32

Hadow Committee 1926, 95
Hancock, Walter, 33
Handley Page, Frederick, 51
Hand-made motor vehicles, 107–8
Harmsworth, Alfred (later Lord Northcliffe), 17
Harriman, Sir George, 117, 118
Hart, Captain Liddell, 175
Hawker, Harry, 51
Henderson, Arthur, 88–9
Hewetson, Henry, 7, 39
Highland Transport Enquiry, 218
Hiking, 157
Hill, Octavia, 23
Hispano-Suiza, 41
Hobart, Major-General P. C. S., 175
Holiday camps, 157–9
Holiday Fellowship, 157
Holiday resorts, impact of the motor car, 155–6
Holidays abroad, 159–61
Holidays, the motor vehicle and, 153–69
Holidays with Pay Act 1938, 154
Home Rule Act 1914, 27
Hooley, Terence, 39
Horse-drawn transport, 28, 35, 130
Housing: council estate development, 147–8; private estates, 148
Hovercraft, 235
Howard, Ebenezer, 150
Hudson, J. M., 143
Huygens, Christian, 36

Industrial disputes, 121–3; *see also* Strikes
Industrial Relations Bill, 125
Industrial Revolution, 8, 9, 13, 18, 32
Industry: education for, in 19th century, 9–11; structure and management, post-First World War, 87–8
Inter-city travel, 233–5
Internal combustion engine: development of, 36–8; vast range of peaceful uses, 134
Intra-city transport, 235–8
Irish Home Rule, 27, 86

Jack Committee on Rural Bus Services, 218
Jacquard loom, 106
Jayawant, Professor Bhalchandra V., 235
Jenatzy, Camille, 39
Johnson, Claude, 43, 53

Kearton, Sir (later Lord) Frank, 117

Labour movement, post-First World War, 88–9
Lake District National Park, 167–8
Lancashire Steam Company, 47
Lanchester, Frederick, 11, 40, 41, 50, 108
Land Compensation Act 1973, 222
Langen, Eugen, 37
Lansbury, George, 23
Law, Bonar, 27
Lawson, Harry J., 36, 39, 40
Leisure, motor car and, 137, 153–69
Lenoir, Etienne, 37
Lever, W. H. (later Lord Leverhulme), 17
Leyland, 48, 116–17; merger with BMC, 117–18

Licensing of goods vehicles, 145
Licensing system for public transport, 144
Lipton, Sir Thomas, 17, 18
Liquid fuel, breakthrough to, 37–8
Loch, Charles, 23
Locomotive Act 1861, 35
London to Brighton run inaugurated, 40
London Passenger Transport Board, 144
London Traffic Act 1924, 144
Lorries, advent of, 47–8
Lucas Company, 40
Lyons, Sir William, 117

Maceroni, Colonel, 33
McKenna Duties, 111
Macmillan Committee on Finance and Industry, 99
Manchester Technical School, 12
Marconi, G., 52
Markus, Siegfried, 37
Mass production, 105–27
Masterman, C. F. G., 21, 52
Maurice, General Sir Frederick, 22
May, Sir George, 100
Maybach, Wilhelm, 37, 41
Mearns, Andrew, 21
Mechanics' Institute, 12
Medhurst, G., 32
Mercedes, 41
Mergers in the motor industry, 115–16
Middle-class amenity, motor car as, 137–8
'militants' and 'agitators', 121–2
Minis, 120
Murdock, William, 31
Models, number of, 120
Money, Sir Leo Chiozza, 18
Monorail system, 235, 236–7
Moore-Brabazon, J. T. C. (later Lord Brabazon), 50, 138
Morals, post-First World War 'revolution' in, 90–1

Morris, William, 11, 42, 43–4, 101, 111, 113
Morris Mechanizations and Aero Limited, 113
Morrison, Herbert, 144
Motor bus, 46–7
Motor Union, 53–4
Motor vehicles: numbers between two World Wars, 129–30, 135–6; numbers since Second World War, 206, 208–12; MOT tests, 221; possible substitutes for, 228–9; small cars for city use, 229–30; working group's suggested improvements, 229–32; alternatives to private ownership, 230; alternatives to petrol engine, 230–1; automatic vehicle control, 231; *see also* British motor industry
Motoring lobby, 138, 140
Motorways, 210, 219–20, 221
Mowat, C. L., 96

Napier, Montagu, 41
National Bus Company, 220, 221
National Freight Corporation, 220
National Insurance Act 1911, 24–5
National Parks, 165, 167–8
National Recreation Survey 1967, 163
National Trust, The, 164–5
National Unemployed Workers' Movement, 102
Nationalization of road transport, 206–7
Naval warfare, 61–3, 177–8, 182, 183–4, 186, 194
Network cab system, 237–8
New Deal, 101
New Towns Act 1946, 215
1930s, economic recovery in, 101
Nuffield Trust, 101

O'Flaherty, Professor C. A., 233
Oil industry: beginnings of, 49; crisis in, 225
Oldsmobile, 41, 108
Ottawa Conference 1932, 85–6
Otto, Nicholas, 37

Package tour holidays, 159–60
Panhard-Levassor, 38, 41
Papin, Denis, 31
Parking facilities in city centres, 234
Parliament Act 1913, 27
Parsons, Sir Charles, 48
Partridge, Arthur, 144
Peak District National Park, 168
Pearl Harbor, 182, 184, 186
Pedestrians' Association, 138, 141
Pedestrians: segregation of, 221–2; travel in cities, 235–6
People and the Motor Car, 210–12
'People's Budget' 1909, Lloyd George's, 25
Perkins, Jacob, 333
Peugeot, 38
Physical Deterioration, Select Committee on, 22
Plowden, William, 138
PLUTO, 191
Political issue, the motor car as, 52–5, 140–1
Pollution, 227
Poor Law, 19, 21, 23–4, 94–5
Population: 92; drift of, 99, 146–9, 216–17, 227; growth in, 232
Potter, Richard, 18
Poverty, 19–24, 102–3, 204
Powered machinery, advent of, 106
Prehistory of the motor car, 31–7
Prices, 112–13, 136, 226
Provincial Omnibus Owners' Association, 143
Public Assistance Committees, 24

Public transport: 142–5;
integrated national system, 220;
suggestions for improving and
enhancing, 239

Railways: 87, 88, 130–4; steam, 8,
15; motor vehicle as an
auxiliary, 15; strikes and
disputes, 15–17; Acts of 1888
and 1894, 15; competition from,
33, 130–1; operating companies,
132; operating expenses, 132;
improvements, 132, 221; speeds,
132; electrification, 133; venture
into road transport, 133–4;
holdings in bus companies,
134, 143; railway museums,
visitors to, 164; since Second
World War, 207–8; decline of
passenger use of, 217; passenger
overloading in rush hour, 221;
inter-city travel, 234–5;
underground, 236
Ravel, Joseph, 35
Recreation, see Leisure
'Red Flag' Act 1865, 7, 8, 35
Reform Act, 89
Regent Street Polytechnic, 12
Remnant, J. F. R., 54
Renault, Louis, 38
Representation of employees on
boards, 124–5
Restriction of Ribbon
Development Act 1935, 140, 149
Reuther, Walter, 123–4
Rickett, Thomas, 34–5
Road and Rail Traffic Act 1933,
131, 145
Road Board of 1909, 139
Road casualties, 138, 210
Road classification, 146
Road Fund, 54–5
Road improvements, 139–40,
146, 219–20
Road pricing system, 238–9

Road safety, 138–9, 141–2, 210,
221–2
Road Traffic Act 1930, 131, 144
Rochas, Beau de, 37
Roe, A. V., 50, 51
Rolls, Hon. Charles, 12, 43, 50, 53
Rolls-Royce, 43, 51, 108, 116
Rowntree, B. Seebohm, social
survey of, 19, 204
Royal Automobile Club, 53, 138
Royal Commission on Technical
Instruction 1881, 9
Royal Commission on Transport
1929, 131, 144, 145
Royal Society for the Prevention
of Accidents, 210
Royce, F. H., 11, 42–3
Rucker, Martin, 39
Rural areas and outer suburbs:
transport in, 239–40; dispersal
of town activities to, 240–1
Russell, John Scott, 33

Salomons, Sir David, 40
Salter Conference 1932, 145
Scottish Bus Group, 220
Sea cruises, 160
Second World War: 171–97;
British motor industry and, 113;
tanks, 171, 172, 175–6, 187–8,
191, 192; bomber aircraft, 171,
173, 174, 180–2; Czechoslovakia,
172–3, 174; fighter aircraft,
173–4, 180; Blitzkrieg, 174–5;
Poland, 174–5; German
Panzers, 175, 176–7, 178, 184,
190; 'Phoney War', 176;
submarines, 177, 178, 182; naval
warfare, 177–8, 182, 183–4, 186,
194; air warfare, 178–81, 196;
Battle of Britain, 178–9; Battle of
the Atlantic, 182; African
campaigns, 182–3, 184, 187,
189–90; Italians in, 183; United
States and, 184, 186, 188–9, 191,

193–4, 195–7; Greece, 184; Russia and, 184–5, 187, 188, 190–1, 195; Japanese and, 185–6, 188–9, 193–5, 196–7; Battle of Stalingrad, 187, 188; Battle of El Alamein, 187–8; Battle of the Coral Sea, 188–9; Operation Torch, 189; Battle of Midway, 189; Operation Overlord, 191; beach defences of the Atlantic Wall, 191; Normandy invasion, 191–2; Operation Anvil, 192; V-1 flying bomb, 192; V-2 rockets, 192–3; Battle of the Philippine Sea, 193–4; Burma, 194–5; atomic bomb, 196–7

Selandia, the, 48

Selden, G. B., 38

Select Committee on Nationalized Industries 1958, 207

Self-Propelled Traffic Association, 40

Serpollet, Léon, 33, 35

Sex Disqualification Removal Act 1919, 89–90

Ships, motorized, advent of, 48

Short Bros, 50, 51

Shrewsbury, Earl of, 12

Smith, Adam, 105, 106

Snowden, Philip, 84

Social impact of the motor vehicle, 129–50, 209, 210–12

Social reforms of the Edwardian era, 24–5

Social services, 96

Society of Motor Manufacturers and Traders, 136, 138

Sopwith, T. O. M., 51

Special Areas Reconstruction Associations, 101

Special Roads Act 1949, 210

Speed limits, 141

Spens Report 1938, 96

Squire, John, 33

Stafford, Marquess of, 34

Standard Motor Company, 108

Standard of living, improvement since Second World War, 205–6

Stately homes, visitors to, 163–4

Statute of Westminster 1931, 85

Steam bus, 46

Steam carriages, 32–3, 34–5, 39

Steam lorries, 47

Steam turbines, 48

'stockbroker belts', 149

Stokes, Donald (later Lord Stokes), 116, 117–18

Stopes, Dr Marie, 92

Straker Squire motor bus, 47

Strikes, 15–17, 26, 88; *see also* Industrial Disputes

Suburban development, 148–9

Suburban transport to and from city centres, 238

Suffragette movement, 26–7

Sumner, James, 47

Sweden, Volvo, 124

'système Panhard, Le', 38

Taff Vale strike, 15–16

Tangye, Richard, 34

Tawney, R. H., 95

Taxation, 96–7

Temple, Archbishop, 202

Thompson, F. M. L., 28

Thomson, R. W., 34

Thornycroft, 47

Tilling and British Automobile Traction Ltd, 134, 143

Tourist industry, 159–62, 163

Town and country planning, 146, 149–50; Act of 1932, 165; Act of 1947, 165, 212

Townsend, Professor, 204

Traction engines, 34

Tractors, 113

Trade and commerce, post-First World War, 82–6

Trade Disputes Act 1906, 16

Trade unions, 88; Act of 1927, 100

Traffic congestion, 146, 227
Traffic laws, 39, 40
Traffic signals, advent of, 140
Traffic in Towns, 213–15
Tramcars, 130
Transfer machines, 113
Transport: four main types of movement needed, 233; integrated national system, 218–21; *see also* Government traffic policy
Transport Act 1962, 207
Transport Act 1968, 220
Transport Policy (White Paper 1966), 218–19
'Travelators', 236
Trevithick, Richard, 31, 32
Tripp, Sir Alker, 139
Turbinia, the, 48

Unemployment, 23, 93–4, 97–8, 100–2
Unemployed Assistance Board, 94
United States, numbers of motor vehicles, 135
Universities, 12
Urban Transport Planning Report 1973, 221

Vauxhall, 41, 121
Verbiest, Ferdinand, 31
Victorian and Edwardian class society, 17–19

Violence in the early 20th century, 26–8
Volkswagen, 117, 120
Volvo, 124

Wages and salaries, 102
Washington Naval Treaty 1922, 85
Watkin, Sir Edwin, 18
Watt, James, 31
Webb, Beatrice, 18, 23
Weir Committee, 133
Welfare state, advent of, 93, 202–5
Wells, H. G., 51
Wheatley, John, 95
Whitley, J. H., 88
Whitney, Eli, 106
Wireless telegraphy, 52
Wolseley, 41
Women's fashions, post-First World War, 91–2
Worker participation in management, 124–5
Workers' Educational Association, 12
Workers' Travel Association, 157, 158
Worsby, W., 34
Wright Bros, 50

Young, James, 49
Youth Hostels Association, 157

Zeppelins, 51, 52
Zimmern, Sir Alfred, 202